Milton's Puritan Masque

Barbara K. Lewalski

For Barbara —

With gratitude and
respect.

Maya

Milton's Puritan
MASQUE

Maryann Cale McGuire

ATHENS
The University of Georgia Press
MCMLXXXIII

Copyright © 1983 by the University of Georgia Press
Athens, Georgia 30602
All rights reserved

Set in 11 on 12 point Garamond
Printed in the United States of America
Designed by Francisca Vassy

The paper in this book meets the guidelines for
permanence and durability of the Committee on
Production Guidelines for Book Longevity of the Council
on Library Resources.

Library of Congress Cataloging in Publication Data

McGuire, Maryann Cale.
Milton's Puritan masque.
Includes bibliographical references and index.
1. Milton, John, 1608–1674. Comus. 2. Milton, John,
1608–1674—Religion and ethics. 3. Masques.
4. Puritans—Great Britain—History—17th century.
5. Recreation—Great Britain—History—17th century.
I. Title.
PR3557.M38 1983   821′.4   82-3457
ISBN 0-8203-0674-6

For Daniel

CONTENTS

Contents

Acknowledgments

No Milton study stands alone. Each owes a debt to the insights, historical scholarship, and critical queries raised by other essays. Likewise, no Milton critic can ignore the debt to other Miltonists who have influenced her own perspective and approach.

Andrew Sabol introduced me to the masque as a complex of music, stagecraft, and literary art. This study evolved from discussions with Barbara Lewalski and grew into a doctoral dissertation, which she directed. Rosalie Colie asked the questions which refined my thesis; some years later, Irene Samuel asked the hard questions which forced me to defend it. Joseph A. Wittreich and Raymond B. Waddington read the entire text; their suggestions and comments have made it a better book. My husband did those thousand things which must be done when one's spouse is writing. Any errors or omissions remain my responsibility.

A generous grant from the Newberry Library allowed the completion of chapter 1. A grant-in-aid from the Emory University Faculty Research Fund assisted in the completion of chapter 4.

My debt to my own "fair branch," who was born during the early stages of this study and who soon provided a study of innocence and virtuous achievement, is expressed in the dedication.

M.C.M.

A Note on Texts

REFERENCES TO *COMUS* AND TO MILTON'S EARLY ENGLISH
poetry are drawn from *Poems of Mr. John Milton* (1645; reprint,
Menston, Eng.: Scolar Press, 1970). References to Milton's
Latin poems and to his later poetry are drawn from *John Milton: Complete Poems and Major Prose*, ed. Merritt Y. Hughes
(New York: Odyssey, 1957). Quotations from Hughes's volume are cited in the text and in the notes by the abbreviation
CPP. References to Milton's prose works are drawn from *Complete Prose Works of John Milton*, ed. Don M. Wolfe, 4 vols.
(New Haven: Yale University Press, 1966). Quotations from
Wolfe's volumes are cited in the text and in the notes by the
abbreviation *CP*.

Milton's Puritan Masque

Milton's Masque:
Meaning, Form, and Context

COMUS IS A PURITAN MASQUE. THERE IS AN INSISTENT paradox in the term *Puritan masque*; indeed the paradox is my subject. Because of the problems involved in attributing to anyone or anything that slippery label *Puritan*,[1] this study will consider what kind of Puritanism the young author brought to the masque. Its focus will be on the odd spectacle of a Puritan, or perhaps more properly a Puritan in the making, tampering with artistic materials belonging to what was, from a contemporary perspective, the opposition. It will consider the poem resulting from Milton's appropriation of the masque, which was a royalist form, the revisions that made the form a fit vehicle for his insights, and the theoretical underpinnings and complex of circumstances that make sense of his achievement.

Milton himself seems to have realized that his masque was an anomaly, although it was apparently well received in performance. Henry Lawes reported that he had it published because he was tired of writing out longhand copies for admirers. Further, the gracious dedication that prefaced the first edition—to Lord Brackley, a performer in the Ludlow production and son and heir to the Earl of Bridgewater, in whose honor it was presented—suggests something of the patrons' delight in Milton's work. Despite the Egertons' favorable response, the poet had reservations about the masque's reception in published form. The first edition in 1637 appeared anonymously. Milton signaled in his Virgilian epigraph a sense of foreboding that goes beyond the conventional modesty of a youthful poet: "Eheu quid volui misero mihi! floribus austrum / Perditus" (Alas! what wish, poor wretch, has been mine? / I have let the south wind in to my flowers).[2]

The epigraph seems an uncanny prognostication, in view of the masque's fate at the hands of critics from Samuel Johnson to the present. The wind of critical inquiry has indeed blown persistently—though not always harshly—over this poetic garden of Milton's; for, as generations of readers have recognized, the masque presents manifold problems, both formal and thematic. Critics have repeatedly pointed out the ways in which Milton's work differs from other masques: it is too long, too literary, too dramatic; it does not observe accepted decorums regarding aristocratic participants; it includes a conflict between the forces of order that is at once too direct and too inconclusive in its outcome; it celebrates personal restraint rather than festive release; and it is not devoted to the adulation of royal power.[3] The philosophic or religious message of the Ludlow masque is also the subject of extended commentary. It has been read in terms of various systems of thought—Platonic, Patristic, Thomistic, Neoplatonic, and Anglican. Although it is most frequently understood as a pagan-Christian synthesis in the great Renaissance-humanist tradition, there is still no general agreement on its meaning.[4]

A contextual reading of the masque—one that takes into account its general historical milieu and the individual mind that produced the work—illuminates its problematic form and meaning. Contextual approaches to *Comus* are nothing new, but they have tended to focus on its immediate occasion. Presented on September 19, 1634, *A Masque Presented at Ludlow Castle* was probably commissioned to celebrate the earl's recent installation as Lord President of Wales and the Marches. Because of the recent Castlehaven affair, a lurid scandal involving close relatives, the Egertons may have requested that personal virtue be its theme. The earl's three youngest children took major roles: Alice, fifteen years old, played the Lady; her brothers John, aged eleven, and Thomas, nine, took the parts of the Elder and Younger Brothers. Henry Lawes, the children's music tutor and a friend of Milton's, provided the music, rehearsed and directed the piece, played the role of the Attendant Spirit, and no doubt suggested John Milton as his collaborator. Contextual critics have examined the effect on the masque of these circumstances of its performance—the youth of the performers, the family history of the Egertons, the liturgical rites and traditional festivities associated with the original production on Michaelmas, the availability of rehearsal time and performing space, and Milton's inexperience in such affairs.[5]

Although its occasion offers useful insights, *Comus* has yet to profit from an examination of its historical and authorial context comparable to those which have increased our understanding of Milton's later poetry.[6] By exploring the historical context, we may determine the range of literary and intellectual choices available to Milton as he wrote his masque. The authorial context can point to the choices he in fact made.

Repeatedly revised during the 1630s and perhaps even into the next decade,[7] *Comus* had for its historical background the religious and political wranglings between Puritans and Royalists which divided England into mutually hostile camps. A series of dramatic and widely controversial events—William Laud's program for liturgical and doctrinal conformity, Charles I's refusal to convene Parliament and his efforts to raise money without legislative approval, and the creation of martyrs on both sides—hardened the positions of both factions, leading almost inexorably to civil war.

A masque-writer could not simply ignore contemporary controversies for, as we shall see in chapter 1, varieties of entertainment became in themselves a subject of major controversy. Perhaps because the diverging opinions on sports and entertainments were less abstract and could be more immediately felt in the daily lives of average individuals than weightier differences on religious doctrine or political theory, the recreation debate engaged the popular imagination with particular intensity. In effect, recreation became an omnibus issue, a battleground where the central differences between the two parties on moral, economic, political, religious, and aesthetic points stood out in stark and simple relief. By writing a masque, a quasi-dramatic entertainment, Milton stepped into a controversy in which he could not and indeed did not remain neutral.

Even more than other varieties of entertainment, the masque demanded ideological commitment. Almost by definition a royalist form, its conventions of thought and structure were bound up with the interests of the political and religious establishment. Masques commonly served as vehicles for royalist propaganda, directly purveying official positions on such matters as the projected marriage of Charles to the Spanish Infanta, the ship money case, the divine right of kings, and the debate on sports. In addition, the formal characteristics of the masque, its action, persons, and rhetoric, were shaped by royalist perspectives.[8] Its deliberate segregation of common actors, who played roles in the disorderly scenes of the antimasque, from the aristocrats, who dominated the idealized, ever-triumphant world of the main masque, reflected the assumptions of the upper class. The conspicuous consumption that went into producing a masque—the enormous expenditures on scenery, costumes, machinery, and the best artists of the day for theatrical extravaganzas performed at most two or three times—exemplified "the princely virtue of magnificence."[9] The masque also asserted the principle of natural prerogative, the ruling class's belief in its inherent right to the goods of the earth. Furthermore, the transformation scene, which very early became a standard element in most masques, supported the doctrine of sole prerogative by casting the monarch as the absolute ordering principle. Similarly, the vertical movements of the masquing figures, which became common in Caroline masques, expressed the royalist belief in divine support of their policies. In short, the masque served as a dynamic symbol of the royalist world view.

How Milton responded to the tensions of his time and, more particularly, to the royalist positions upheld by conventional masques is clear. His early life suggests a predisposition to Puritanism—a middle-class, London background, a home life that encouraged Bible study and psalm singing, a Puritan minister in the parish pulpit, Puritan masters at St. Paul's, and residence at that Puritan hotbed, Cambridge. When he left the university in 1632 without taking orders, Milton had apparently given up all thought of ordination, at least for the time. He was later to assert that directives aimed at excluding from the pulpit all but the impeccably orthodox left him "church-outed by the Prelates." In retirement at his father's home—first at Hammersmith, then Horton—Milton devoted himself to further study of the classics. Since he occasionally traveled to London to buy books or learn "something new in Mathematics or in Music," he was not cut off from political developments in the nation's capital. No doubt moved by the growing religious and civil controversies, he embarked on the extensive readings in history, theology, and political theory that he would in the coming decades put to use in his pamphlets for Puritan causes.[10]

Milton's writings during the 1630s reflect his religious and political leanings. Critics have long recognized the Puritan concerns that inform "The Nativity Ode" and "Lycidas."[11] In addition, Milton's first poetic effort following the performance of *Comus*, the Greek paraphrase of Psalm 114, indicates his growing Puritan sympathies. He had already paraphrased this psalm in English some years earlier. That he turned to it again underlines its relevance to him in the 1630s. Psalm 114, which celebrates God's delivery of the Israelites from Egypt, was habitually applied by Protestants to the adversities and looked-for triumphs of the latter-day saints.[12]

Suggestive as such circumstantial evidence is, *Comus* best indicates Milton's developing Puritan sympathies during the 1630s. Milton entitled his work *A Maske*, intending that it be understood in relation to the form, yet he deviated in important ways from received conventions. As Rosalie Colie has taught us, genre in the Renaissance was not a set of rules for composition, but "a set of interpretations, of 'frames' or 'fixes' on the world."[13] Milton's "fix" did not coincide with the one that shaped other masques. His violation of masque convention resulted from neither ignorance nor carelessness, but from his rejection of the form's traditional royalism. As Angus Fletcher has cautiously observed, Milton's masque does not make the usual royalist assumptions: "There is much less sense of regal or princely power in *Comus* than any masque of comparable stature and this is the result of nascent Miltonic libertarianism."[14]

Not many critics, however, have recognized the extent to which *Comus* was actively shaped by Milton's developing Puritan sympathies. William Haller, Christopher Hill, and Mary Ann Radzinowicz comment in passing on the work's relation to Puritan positions; but the only extended examination of *Comus* as a Puritan work of art is Georgia Christopher's study, which examines the masque's debt to such Reformation thinkers as Luther and Calvin. Although her approach is suggestive, Christopher argues for too rigid a conformity on Milton's part to Protestant orthodoxy and does not consider the inevitable interplay between the work's Puritan message and its received generic convention.[15]

Milton's is a Puritan masque, but it is informed by the poet's distinctive brand of Puritanism. To understand his Puritan views we must examine Milton's writings before and after *Comus*, not assuming that his thought or art remained static, that the author of the *Vacation Exercise*, the *Reason of Church Government*, or *Paradise Lost* is identical with the poet who produced *Comus*, but rather recognizing that the masque represents a stage in the continuum of his development. It is in fact a crucial turning point, standing as it does between the apolitical or even conformist attitudes of his early writing and the Puritan partisanship evident in "Lycidas" and his prose works.

My concern, thus, is with literary history, as well as with the religious and political history of seventeenth-century England. If *Comus* reflects historical events as the poet saw them, it also sheds light on the evolution of his way of seeing. Chapter 1 considers the interplay between the times and the poet: it examines the recreation controversy, specific events that made entertainment a matter of debate, the major arguments of Puritans and Royalists, and Milton's developing position on recreation, the masque, and related issues touched by the controversy. In subsequent chapters, I explore the way that Milton's views on recreation, interacting with his other strongly held beliefs, inspired and directed his radical revision of masque convention.

Chapter 2 discusses what is probably Milton's most crucial change: his rejection of the notions of stasis and achieved perfection that naturally pervaded conventional masques since they were committed to the religious and political establishment. He introduced instead a principle of dynamism, probably rooted in the Puritan conviction that individual and collective life ought to involve a process of continuing reformation. Milton's sense of dynamism infuses *Comus* as its central theme, informs his treatment of person and action, and affects how audience or reader experiences the work. Stanley Fish has commented on the questioning and uncertainty provoked in readers by the intentional fluidity of thought and image in Milton's masque. He proposes that Milton, by allowing us multiple perspectives on objects and events, presents us with a morally complex world where judgments do not come easily. Fish asserts, "No one of the questions raised by the masque is to be answered unequivocally." [16] In my view, however, Milton leads us from questions to answers. Although the masque's conclusion points to additional questions to be resolved and further discoveries to be made, *Comus* leaves us also with a fully articulated moral vision.

The subject of chapter 3 is the rhetoric of Milton's masque. Milton repudiated the lavish, multimedia rhetoric of conventional masques and, taking into account Puritan objections to the form, adjusted the way the masque communicates with and persuades its audience. Chapter 4 explores the love cult that informed Caroline masques, Milton's view of it, and his attempt to propound a morally preferable mode of loving.

I hope to suggest throughout my discussion of the masque the pivotal place that *Comus* occupies in the corpus of Milton's works and its importance as a milestone in the poet's development as a thinker and an artist. In the guest book of an Italian Protestant refugee he visited in Geneva in 1639, Milton inscribed:

—if Vertue feeble were
Heaven itselfe would stoope to her.
Coelum, non animum, muto dum trans mare curro.
[My skies I change, not my spirit, as I race across the sea.][17]

His choice of the concluding lines of *Comus* as an autograph— they are used here almost as a personal motto—suggests that he considered the work an accurate expression of his convictions at the time. Something further of the significance Milton attached to the masque is indicated by his placing it in the 1645 edition of his works as the last of the English poems, that is, even after "Lycidas." He allowed it to stand as his crowning achievement, his most complex and polished effort thus far in his career, and the final product of his poetic apprenticeship. As the last of the early poems, *Comus* looks forward to later works. It reveals the commitments that would shape Milton's controversial prose. It also points to the major achievements of his later years, foreshadowing the literary revisionism that was to revitalize epic and dramatic forms and the convictions that would mark him as a writer engagé.

CHAPTER ONE

Reforming the Masque: Milton and the Recreation Controversy

AMONG MILTON'S CONTEMPORARIES, SPORTS AROUSED acrimonious and intense debate, essentially because his contemporaries defined the term far more broadly than we do. For them, sports included not only athletic endeavors, spectator activities, and sportsmen's hobbies, such as hunting, fishing, and billiards, but also holiday celebrations, parades, games of all kinds, love play, banquets, drinking, literature, drama, and the other arts.[1] Virtually every activity not linked directly to religious, domestic, or occupational duties could fall within the province of sports, which thus claimed a substantial portion of every individual's time and energy. Moralists of all persuasions agreed that man's natural tendency toward unruly, frivolous, and immoral recreations needed to be curbed; still they argued bitterly over precisely how to regulate the tendency and what specific activities to allow.

For Milton as for other men of the time recreation was a momentous issue, inextricably bound up in the basic moral questions all men must face in their public and private lives. He had considered sports earlier, but it was in his works of the mid-1630s—"L'Allegro" and "Il Penseroso," "Ad Patrem," sections of the *Commonplace Book*, "Arcades," and most importantly *Comus*—that he enunciated the views that remained fairly constant throughout the rest of his career.

Although concern over recreation had periodically sparked debate almost from the beginning of the Reformation in England, it flared into heated controversy in the 1630s with the increasing tension between Puritans and Royalists. As we shall see, Milton chose to ally himself with the Puritan position, and his writings from the 1630s on reflect a sympathy with many of the basic principles, though not necessarily with the specific programs or pronouncements, of contemporary Puritans.

On sports, as on most other issues, there were substantial variations among members of the Puritan and the royalist factions. But in the decades immediately preceding the civil war, two chief positions emerged based on different but characteristic ways of regarding human nature. Puritans considered recreation within the context of the larger issue of Christian calling. The pious man's duty in this life is to serve God in his allotted work and in worship and to contemplate his salvation. Diversions by their very nature turn men away from their spiritual responsibilities, even if only temporarily. Puritans sensed a competition between Christian duty and the recreations popular among their contemporaries, a competition that became particularly acute on the Sabbath. The *Book of Sports*, which officially approved rural pastimes on Sunday, and the Caroline practice of Sunday theatricals at court angered Puritans, who felt that the civil and religious establishment favored worldly pleasures over dedication to God.[2]

In contrast to the Puritan insistence on religious calling, the Established church took a more tolerant view of human nature and the desire for diversion. Although they sympathized with the need for temporary escape from responsibility, Anglicans recognized the need to control festive energies by channeling them into approved activities. The church prescribed as safety valves such public sports as church ales, Christmas festivities, and springtime and harvest celebrations. Its assumption was that people, if provided with supervised opportunities for play, would not turn to vicious pastimes. Opponents argued, in contrast, that approved sports released the festive spirit and then could not keep it properly under control; repeated accounts of immorality associated with rural sports and court revelry suggest that there was some truth to these charges.[3]

Sports had social and political as well as moral implications. James I was quick to recognize that if the people were kept duly amused, they would be unlikely to rebel. In *Basilikon Doron*, he comments approvingly on "publicke spectacles of all honest games" and "honest feasting and merrinesse" as a "forme of contenting the peoples mindes, [that] hath beene used in

all well governed Republickes."[4] James's cynicism was succeeded by his son's high-minded faith in the governing power
of play: for Charles I recreation was a pillar of political order.

The same impulse that leads modern politicians to label their
administrations the Great Society or the New Frontier led
Charles to present his reign as a reformation. Appropriating a
code word from his Puritan adversaries who were agitating for
the elimination of "Catholic" elements from the Established
church, Charles gave the term *reformation* a startling new definition. In part, the Caroline reform was an effort to justify
Stuart rule on the grounds that the Stuart monarchs had renewed the glories of ancient Britain.[5] Charles—like his father
before him—pointed to his descent from the mythical Trojan
Brutus, first king of Britain, styled himself the emperor of a
united Great Britain, and thus professed to have restored to
the island its rightful rulers and its original integrity as a nation. But, in addition, this reformation was a process of increasing centralization of power under an autocratic monarch.
Charles claimed to have renewed the vitality of the country by
an amending of manners, which involved the control of lower
faculties by the higher in each individual and an analogous
political reorganization that subjected the unruly lower orders
of society to the higher. Recreation had a crucial part in the
Caroline reformation. Not only did the official policy on sports
serve as a means for effecting reform, but in the very process
of participating in approved recreations, the English people
enacted Charles's vision of the well-governed realm.

The 1633 masque *Coelum Britannicum*, which Stephen Orgel
has called "the greatest theatrical expression of the Caroline
autocracy," an "allegory . . . about the radical reformation of
society,"[6] reveals the dependence of the king's reorganization
on modes of entertainment. According to the central device of
the masque, Jove, impressed by the virtuous order of Charles's
court, resolves to reform his own by cleansing the heavens of
unruly passions and licentiousness. He banishes as morally unfit for their celestial positions the beasts of the zodiac and his
former mistresses, previously transformed into stars. Questions then arise about what beings are to be stellified in their
place and given the power to guide human actions. Various

candidates offer themselves but are rejected as unworthy, until Charles, Henrietta Maria, and their court are chosen to serve as the new lights of the universe. Only their images, however, are taken to heaven; their persons, for the benefit of mortals, are left on earth to reign in brilliance.

Coelum Britannicum overtly presents and defends the sovereign's policies. Momus, a presenter figure who as Theo-Mastix (satirist of the gods) has the liberty to criticize even the most powerful, enumerates the changes Jove has made in his heavenly court in terms that humorously recall Charles's efforts at reform:

> Edicts are made for the restoring of decayed housekeeping. . . . Bacchus hath commanded all taverns to be shut, and no liquor drawn after ten at night. Cupid must go no more so scandalously naked, but is enjoined to make him breeches. . . . The gods must keep no pages nor grooms of their chamber under the age of 25, and those provided of a competent stock of beard. Pan may not pipe, not Proteus juggle, but by especial permission. Vulcan was . . . fined for driving in a plate of iron into one of the sun's chariot wheels and frost-nailing his horses upon the fifth of November last, for breach of a penal statute prohibiting work upon holidays, that being the annual celebration of the Gigantomachy. In brief, the whole state of the hierarchy suffers a total reformation, especially in the point of reciprocation of conjugal affection. Venus hath confessed all her adulteries, and is received to grace by her husband. . . . Jupiter too begins to learn to lead his own wife . . . and there is no doubt of an universal obedience where the lawgiver himself in his own person observes his decrees so punctually.[7]

Jove's reformation of manners and governments, based primarily on regulation of the ways people amuse themselves, echoes specific acts Charles instituted to encourage the practice of keeping open house, promoting the customary rural festivities, regulating taverns, upholding the traditional holidays when servants could not be required to work, prohibiting dancing and piping during the hours of divine service, and so on. It also points to the unofficial reforms Charles made at court: his effort to eliminate gross instances of sodomy and adultery of the sort that had been notorious during his father's reign and correspondingly to glorify married love through the example of the royal couple and through the introduction of a Neoplatonic cult.

While providing a vehicle for publishing Charles's vision of reformed recreation, *Coelum Britannicum* also reflects something of the king's efforts to employ the masque and indeed all officially sanctioned sports as the very means of accomplishing reform. In a series of antimasques, unruly spirits appear and are banished and with them are exorcised all excesses that can disturb the peace and stability of the court and the nation. Among those eliminated are the forces of Hedone, who represent the upper class's overindulgence in pleasures "that drew this reformation on the gods." Also banished are a group of vices—cowardice, ambition, and calumny—which are said, like Puritans, to infect Britain and are best sent to New England.[8] Through the process of dismissing groups of antimasquers, order is sustained and disruptive forces are ritually exorcised, leaving Royalists—purged of their failings—in control.

Coelum Britannicum then concludes with a direct lesson on sports and kingship from a royal perspective. The king and queen, surrounded by courtiers who encircle them like "wreaths of stars," are invited to revel forever as embodiments of enduring and absolute ideals. They and their court present to the "panting rout" of common humanity an example of virtue. Their moral significance and their roles in the political scheme of things are shown to be one and the same, for the entire mythology of the masque grows out of the assumption that self-government and political government can be effected by the single act of submission to the monarch. Recreation is important to this process of rule. While the royal couple and their court are engaged in the revelry of *Coelum Britannicum*, they stand forth as exemplars of all virtue. Further, the refined recreation of masquing involves the participants in a process of ordering that affects the moral nature of individuals and the political organization of the entire nation. The complementary acts of casting out excesses and selecting a model of virtuous conduct—which constitute the plot of *Coelum Britannicum*—

purge those who participate in or observe the masque. The political and moral ordering is achieved through aesthetic response. To prefer the gorgeous spectacle associated with the monarch to the rowdy and grotesque antimasques implies the moral choice of virtue over vice and the political choice of obedience to the monarch over anarchy.

As might be expected, Puritans objected to the political functions of sports. They attacked the enormous cost of court productions like *Coelum Britannicum* as a needless waste of human and material resources. They also saw in such theatrical spectacles a perversion of aristocratic privilege. When aristocrats turned to their costly diversions, they asserted in an unmistakable manner their right to dissipate the nation's goods in whatever frivolous way they pleased, while ignoring their traditional duties as responsible governors. In addition, the official program of popular sports drew criticism because of the means by which it was executed. The crown's use of the religious establishment to publish and enforce the policy suggested the complicity of church and sovereign in a plot to corrupt the people. Lucy Hutchinson offers a typical Puritan comment on sports in pre-revolutionary England: "The generality of the gentry of the land soone learnt the Court fashion, and every greate house in the country became a sty of uncleannesse. To keepe the people in their deplorable security till vengeance overtooke them, they were entertain'd with masks, stage playes, and other sorts of ruder sports. Then began fornication and all sorts of ribaldry to be no conceal'd but countenanced vices, favour'd wherever they were privately practis'd because they held such conformity with the Court example."[9] Official sports were for many Puritans the means of spreading moral infection from a godless court to the rest of the kingdom. They also distracted people from that pursuit of true religion necessary for Christian reformation, and they drew attention away from an encroaching political tyranny by encouraging enslavement to the passions.

The promotion of sports by the Caroline church and by the monarchy and the increasingly vocal discontent among Puritans provided the background for Milton's musings on the subject. Three events of the early 1630s would have brought the recreation debate to Milton's attention with particular force just before and during the period when he was writing and revising *Comus*: the royal couple's visit to Cambridge, the Prynne— affair, and the reissuance of the *Book of Sports*.

The first of these events, the visit of Charles and Henrietta Maria to Cambridge in March 1631/32, demonstrated the great significance attached to theatrical diversions. Royal visits to universities had always been treated with elaborate concern. Sovereigns expected from such occasions lavish testimonies of loyalty, and aristocratic audiences expected to have the validity of their assumptions about the world confirmed. These visits represented possible benefits for the institutions involved and for their members. Young playwrights competed for the honor of having their compositions produced, and university admin- istrators struggled to select plays that hit precisely the right note. Careers could be made or broken by a miscalculation of a noble audience's tastes; and, as the 1631/32 visit revealed, Charles, his consort, and his court could be extremely sensitive to any failure to meet their exacting expectations.

Two plays were chosen to entertain the king and queen dur- ing their stay at Cambridge, the *Rival Friends* by Peter Hausted of Queen's College and the *Jealous Lovers* by Thomas Randolph, a Trinity man. An argument developed over which play was to be presented first. Dr. Butts, vice-chancellor of the university, finally decided in favor of Hausted's, with Randolph's per- formed three days afterward. However, although Randolph's comedy was well received, Hausted's met with strong disap- proval. Shortly after the performance, Hausted printed his play with a preface in which he attempted to discourage "black- mouthed Calumny" by insisting that most members of his au- dience (by implication, the court) liked his play, that only Trinity students hissed it, and that the poor reception was merely a matter of intercollegiate rivalry.[10] Other evidence suggests that neither the courtiers nor the king was pleased with the *Rival Friends*. Dr. Butts committed suicide shortly after the king's visit, apparently because of despondence over the royal displeasure.[11]

There is good reason for the failure of Hausted's play. One could damn it on aesthetic grounds alone. But from the charges

Hausted felt called on to answer in his preface, it appears that the comedy failed by not sufficiently playing to its audience's expectations. Hausted defended himself by saying that "to have shown them [i.e., his audience] nothing but what they see daily had been but coarse entertainment."[12]

Hausted did make some effort to respond to his audience's prejudices. He held up for ridicule a corrupt and hypocritical lay patron, whose speech patterns and avowed religious beliefs branded him as the stereotypical stage Puritan, and he lampooned a series of unscrupulous young ministers, also Puritans, whose primary interest was in personal advancement, not in the spiritual health of their flocks.[13] This bit of topical satire, however, did not satisfy those gathered to watch the *Rival Friends*, because the play grossly violated other expectations.

To begin with, Caroline courtiers were willing to accept a fair amount of didacticism, but they expected morals to be conveyed by delightful means, by varied modes of expression which included visual and verbal arts. In his preface, Hausted notes that his play did not employ elaborate scenery and defends his choice on rhetorical grounds: "I do confess we did not go such quaint ways as we might have done; we had none of those sea arts, knew not how or else scorned to plant our canvas so advantageously to the wayward breath of the spectators, but freely and ingenuously labored rather to merit than ravish an applause from the theater."[14] Lavish sets may not have been possible because of expense or other practical considerations. However, Hausted argued that he preferred to appeal directly to reason through literary means of expression, rather than to lower faculties, the senses, through visual arts. This argument could not have endeared him to courtiers accustomed to the elaborate productions staged by Inigo Jones at court.

Hausted refused to accede to the Neoplatonic doctrines of love which had become popular at court and attacked this type of love as false love. A major character in the comedy is Anteros, whom he understood, not as the embodiment of reciprocal love (like Jonson's more traditional Anteros in *Loves Welcome at Bolsover*),[15] but as a moralistic critic of Cupid's excesses. Impatient with the niceties of Platonic courtship, Hausted's

Anteros serves in the play as a castigator of humors. In particular, he deflates the posturings of refined lovers, offering, for
example, early in the play a line calculated to discourage adoration of the feminine: "I knew there was a woman in the
wind; / I smelt her." In his explanatory preface, Hausted remained intentionally ambiguous as to whether his woman-hater
expressed the normative values of the play or was the satiric
embodiment of a foolishly extreme position. Hausted was anything but ambiguous in his attitude regarding the Neoplatonic idealization of the beloved, which he explicitly condemned
in his preface as sinful idolatry.[16]

That Hausted's treatment of love proved objectionable is
doubly clear from a comparison of his play with Randolph's
Jealous Lovers, the well-received comedy presented three days
after Hausted's. Randolph's play records the trials and triumphs
of several contrasting pairs of virtuous and unvirtuous lovers,
exalts the heroic powers of feminine beauty and chastity, and
ends with the tidy marriage of chaste lovers.

While Hausted's comedy failed to please its aristocratic
spectators, it was greeted with no more favor by the Puritans
in the audience. Hausted suggests as much in his preface when
he derisively rejects Puritan censure of his play as anti-
intellectual bigotry, as "false and abominable imputations laid
upon it by my tribe with the short hair and long ears" because
Puritans are "at open defiance with this, but with all kinds of
learning."[17] Certainly the *Rival Friends* deserved the charges of
anti-Puritan bias that Puritans habitually directed toward academic theatricals.[18] The caricatures of Puritans as venial hypo-
crites, which Hausted incorporated into the play, proclaimed
his anti-Puritan perspective and justified the objections raised
by many Puritans of the day to university theatricals.

Early writings reflect the young Milton's position on university performances. In "A Vacation Exercise," though it was
not written for the visit of important dignitaries, he made his
contribution to academic entertainment. "Elegia Prima" appears to be an academic play. In *An Apology for Smectymnuus*,
Milton attacked the indecorum of soon-to-be-ministers appearing in academic plays of questionable moral value, the
generally low literary quality of such dramas, and the equally

low aesthetic sensitivities of their audience (*CP*, 1:887). These references do not in themselves necessarily identify him as a supporter of the Puritan position in the sports controversy. They do, however, reflect his acquaintance with the usual run of university theatricals and his contempt for many of them.

The visit of the king and queen to Cambridge in 1631/32 may have had an effect on Milton's thinking about entertainments designed for the privileged classes. Milton was in residence at Cambridge during this royal stay. He had also been present during the king's earlier visit in 1628,[19] but the controversy over Hausted's play, the intense intercollegiate rivalry, and the sensational publicity provoked by the vice-chancellor's suicide must have made the latter occasion memorable. During his residence at Cambridge, Milton probably began to formulate the opinions on academic entertainments that he recorded in the *Apology for Smectymnuus*. The *Rival Friends*, as a particularly sophomoric example of academic drama, may have proved a formative influence. He may also have learned more broadly applicable lessons about recreation from the episode. The response to Hausted's play from its courtly visitors and the university community demonstrated what royalty expected from theatrical entertainments and what Puritans and others objected to in official attitudes. Dr. Butt's suicide and the harsh rebuke that so unnerved the unfortunate man illustrated the importance sports had assumed; recreation had become a life-or-death matter.

Whatever else, the reception of Hausted's and Randolph's plays gave Milton a firsthand look at the problem of designing occasional entertainments for an aristocratic audience. Hausted and Randolph presented Milton with two contrasting models of writers balancing the claims of their art against the expectations of their audiences. Neither example was entirely satisfactory: Randolph acceded to convention, producing a bland and hackneyed play, while Hausted assaulted convention head-on, losing his audience. In his masque, Milton followed neither method. Without either violating or acquiescing in convention, he offered appeals to the senses and made chastity his central theme but did both in ways that led his audience beyond clichés to new insights.

If the entertainments prepared for the royal couple at Cambridge created a furor among visitors from the court and members of the university community, the publication of William Prynne's *Histrio-mastix* and the reissuing of the *Declaration of Sports*, two events closely related in the public mind, drew the attention of virtually the entire nation to the controversy over recreation.

A self-proclaimed conservative, not a revolutionary, Prynne nonetheless angered the political and religious establishment by his early pamphlets attacking the custom of drinking healths, the aristocratic fashion of dressing hair in lovelocks, and the Laudian innovations in church ceremony.[20] With the publication of *Histrio-mastix*, Prynne's opponents found an opportunity to bring him to trial. An index entry in Prynne's book, reading "Women actors, notorious whores," was construed as a deliberate insult to Queen Henrietta Maria, who was at the time rehearsing her ladies for a presentation of Walter Montagu's *Shepheard's Paradise*. Critics were also quick to see a treasonable attack on the crown in Prynne's approving narration of tales demonstrating that kings and magistrates who either participated in or encouraged theatrical productions met unfortunate and untimely ends. The prosecution charged Prynne with endeavoring "to infuse an opinnyon into the people that ytt is lawful to laye violent handes uppon Princes that are either actors, favoureres, or spectatores of stage playes."[21] Although the title page of *Histrio-mastix* bears the date 1633, the work actually appeared late in 1632; by January 1632/33 Prynne was brought before the Star Chamber. Found guilty of crimes described as libel and sedition against the church and state, Prynne was stripped of his academic degrees, ejected from the legal profession, pilloried with his ears cut off, and sentenced to life imprisonment in the Tower.

The severity of his punishment is surprising, since the charges Prynne marshaled against plays, masques, and other forms of entertainment were hardly exceptional. He repeated the usual Puritan criticisms that such activities on Sunday profaned the Sabbath, that they encouraged idleness, required a frivolous immersion in things of the world, wasted money and human energy which could be better invested in other pursuits, and

led to immoral behavior. What is striking about *Histrio-mastix*
is its style. Extending to over one thousand pages and flawed
by extreme prolixity, repetitiveness, humorless vituperation,
and a wearisome piling up of appeals to authority, the book
has been viewed by many modern commentators as the ravings
of a monomaniacal lunatic.[22] But to dismiss Prynne thus is to
underestimate his stature in the eyes of his contemporaries.
His personal courage in suffering made him in the public mind
a Protestant martyr on the model of Foxe's heroes. Parliament
was later to acknowledge his importance by commissioning
him to write a defense of its sovereignty and by making him
chief prosecutor of William Laud. Most important for our pur-
poses, Prynne was regarded as a skilled controversialist.

Despite the drawbacks of Prynne's style, *Histrio-mastix* has
an emotional force that stems from the sincere, though admittedly extreme, sense of moral outrage it conveys. This outrage reveals itself in the coherent patterns of images he develops,
perhaps the most pervasive of which involves disease, infection, or decay—all associated with unworthy sports. Plays,
Prynne claims, are "the most pestilent corruptions of all mens
(especially young mens) minds & manners; . . . the most mis-
chievous plagues that can be harboured in any Church or State."
Widely accepted, they have become "an infectious leprosie,"
"inveterate gangrend ulcers" that "need sharpe emplaisters,
biting corrosives, else they will not be cured."[23] *Histrio-mastix*
depicts a morally sick society, corrupted from within; the plays,
masques, and other forms of entertainment enjoyed by its
members are symptoms of its malaise and the means by which
the moral infection spreads throughout the population to consume the entire political body. The linguistic excesses of Prynne's
book result from his horror-stricken perception of the imme-
diacy and power of the disease threatening his society. He intended his book to serve as bitter medicine, to puncture the
pustule of infection, to provide needed moral correction.

Prynne's opponents took his charges in *Histrio-mastix* seriously as an attack not only on recreation itself but on the essential principles on which social order depended. In the court
proceedings against him, the judges spoke not of specific charges
of criminal behavior but of the general menace the man pre-

sented to society: "This booke [i.e., *Histrio-mastix*] is to effecte disobedyence to the state, and a generall dislyke unto all governments. . . . The truthe is, Mr. Pryn would have a newe churche, newe government, a newe kinge, for hee would make the people altogether offended with all thinges att the present."[24] For his political and religious opponents, Prynne embodied the danger that Protestantism in its most extreme form poses. Understood as an absolute, the premise that every man is his own priest places the rule of conscience above rule through established institutions. Hence his prosecutors saw in Prynne a portent of the anarchy that occurs when the inner light is let loose on the world without any guidance from authority.

From condemning Prynne as an irresponsible iconoclast, it was only a short step to casting him in the cosmic struggle between good and evil as a minion of the anti-Christ: "This man, forsakeinge Christes rule, as one of the devilles faithfull agentes, followes his instructiones."[25] In view of the mythic dimensions Prynne assumed, it is no wonder that when he was tried in 1636, along with John Bastwick and Henry Burton, for conspiracy and seditious activities, Laud's ire fell with particular harshness on him, although the other two had been equally outspoken and were more effective, popular leaders.[26]

Others were willing to take Prynne seriously, not as an infernal agent, but as a spokesman for their concerns. For them, his works did not threaten anarchy but challenged readers to make the basic Christian choice between God and the world. Following the line of thought that we have seen was well established among Puritans, Prynne treated plays and other forms of entertainment as symbolic of worldly vanity, thus linking the matter of recreation with Christian calling. The dedicatory epistle that prefaces *Histrio-mastix* concludes with a prayer urging readers to choose between two mutually exclusive spectacles: "Let other men therefore who love their Stage-playes better than their God, their soules, resort to Theatres whiles they please . . . but let Christ Jesus be your all in all, your onely Spectacle, and joy on earth, whose soule-ravishing heart-pleasing presence, shall be your eternall solace, your everlasting visible all-glorious most triumphant Spectacle in the highest heavens. . . . Amen."[27] One must choose between worldly sport here and now and the joys of heaven hereafter. Though Prynne is not explicit on this point, one must also choose between obedience to God and obedience to ungodly secular rulers.[28]

Although Prynne did not openly advocate civil disobedience as a response to the official policy on sports, his royalist opponents understood that his scrutiny of plays led logically to moral criticism of the monarch himself. *Histrio-mastix* was a timely book, for it served to focus the debate between Puritans and Royalists about recreation. The extreme language of his book and the extremity of the Star Chamber's reaction to it reflected not only the intensity of the nation's feeling about sports but also the degree to which opinions about the matter laid bare the most crucial differences between the two camps. Loyalists recognized the book as more than just a condemnation of plays and other sorts of theatrical productions. One of Prynne's prosecutors commented on the comprehensiveness of his attack: "Bayes in windowes, new yere guifts, May games, danceing, pictures in churchs, &c. all he comprehendes under the title of stage playes, which he dothe to withdraw the people's affection from the kinge and the Government."[29] For those on the opposite side, Prynne's book came to represent Puritan determination to achieve an inclusive reformation of society and the willingness of the pre-revolutionary Puritan to pit the integrity of his individual conscience against institutional authority.

Milton was no Prynne. While Prynne condemned female actors as whores and kings or civil officials who engaged in theatrical entertainments as unfit governors, Milton by contrast created in *Comus* for his young aristocratic performers— one of them female—roles that required dramatic speech, song, and dance. Yet even so glaring a disparity between the two men on recreation is a matter of the application of moral principle and of degree rather than of disagreement over the principles themselves. On the basic assumptions that informed their positions, Prynne, the Puritan zealot, and Milton, the late Renaissance man of letters, were not so far apart. Unquestionably Milton's statements of his view bear no resemblance to Prynne's rambling and vituperative diatribes. But, as we shall see, Milton, like Prynne, gradually became convinced that sports must be compatible with the rigorous demands of Christian living and that many of the common recreations of his day were morally corrupting.

There is no evidence that the Prynne affair had any bearing on the reissuing of the *Declaration of Sports*. However, Prynne's satire does reflect the mounting Puritan hostility to the government's promotion of traditional rural festivities, which led to the republication. The *Declaration* presents the official position of the early Stuarts on popular recreations designed for the common man. As Winston Solberg observes, this document did not deviate markedly from policies set during the reigns of Edward and Elizabeth but simply attempted to resolve the controversy about the lawfulness of certain recreations and about the consistent enforcement of existing statutes throughout the country.[30]

Originally issued in 1617 as a royal rebuke of "some puritans and precise people" in Lancaster who had prohibited Sunday sports, the *Declaration* was published in 1618 by James I as a statement of national policy. James pronounced as legitimate on Sundays such specific recreational activities "as dauncing, either men or women, Archerie for men, leaping, vaulting, or any other such harmless Recreation, . . . May-games, Whitson Ales, and Morris-dances, and the setting up of Maypoles and other sports therewith used." However, the *Declaration* forbade the participation in allowed recreations by those "that will not first come to the Church and serve GOD."[31]

Though intended as a compromise, the *Declaration* pleased neither Sabbatarians nor those who opposed compulsory church attendance.[32] Nevertheless, in October 1633 Charles reissued the *Declaration* in exactly its original form, except for additional comments explaining his reasons for the republication. Alarmed by several murders of bastards conceived at church ales and wakes, judges in Somerset had forbidden traditional festivities and had had announcements to that effect published from local pulpits. Laud was outraged by the intrusion into ecclesiastical jurisdiction, the king by the violation of royal prerogative. Charles reacted by reissuing the *Declaration*.[33]

Puritan response to republication of the hated document was

immediate and intense. Solberg has noted that Puritans did
not contribute much to the substantial body of controversial
literature on the *Declaration* until the 1640s. Prynne was a
grisly example of what happened to those who openly opposed
the royal policy. Opposition took other forms: emigration to
New England increased and many clergymen were suspended
for refusing to read the *Declaration* from their pulpits. One
minister was reported to have read the *Declaration* and then the
Ten Commandments and to have concluded by directing his
congregation, "Dearly beloved, ye have heard the commandments of God and man, obey which you please."[34] What objections Puritans did voice were the familiar ones. Strict
Sabbatarians argued that the measure was an infraction of the
Fourth Commandment. Others with less rigid notions about
Sunday observances insisted, in more general terms, that the
Declaration violated the spirit of divine law. Noting the origin
of many of the traditional festivities in pre-Christian rites and
their preservation in the calendar of the English church as a
leftover from the days of allegiance to Rome, opponents de-
nounced them as pagan and papist.[35] Derived as they were
from false religions, Puritans argued, it was hardly surprising
that they drew people from pious pursuits to idolatrous and
immoral acts.

In response to such charges, supporters of the king and the
Established church began to churn out defenses. They justified
the *Declaration*, first of all, on humanitarian grounds. Men
needed time out from their grueling labor of earning a liveli-
hood, and Sunday was the logical day for leisure activities since
it was the only day of the week not devoted to work. Christopher Dow advocated "such honest recreations, as might serve
for their [the people's] refreshments, and better enabling them
to goe through with their hard labours on other dayes." Another commentator insisted, "It is morally impossible for them
[Christian people] with comfort and ordinary diligence to continue 24 houres together, in spiritual and religious exercises
and meditations."[36] Bishop Robert Sanderson, in his reasonable and moderate tract of 1636, claimed that the rowdiness
that often occurred in conjunction with licensed sports did not
affect their legitimacy. Recreation must be accommodated "to

the condition of the Person: Walking and Discoursing which
to men of liberall education, is a pleasant Recreation, is in no
way delightsome to the ruder sort, who scarse account any
thing a sport which is not loud and boisterous." There is no
reason why those who, because "of their meane education and
parts, hardly aspire to know the pleasure of other delights,
should not use such, as they are capable of." [37]

A second argument was that lawful recreations served as a
useful tool of government. They were the carrot on the stick,
Dow suggested, in that one must go to church to be eligible
to participate in the sports. Many who otherwise would not
attend services thus "may bee allured and compelled to present
themselves in the Churche at the publicke worship of God."
The claim was substantiated by the Bishop of Bath and Wells,
who on polling his clergy reported "that upon Feast days (which
are for the most part everywhere upon Sundays) the service of
the Church hath been more solemnly performed, and the Church
hath been better frequented both in the Forenoon and in the
afternoon, than upon any Sunday in the year." Proponents also
claimed that the liberal policy regarding recreation prevented
religious factionalism. If convinced that Protestantism required strict observance of the Sabbath, people would be
tempted to "fall off to Popery, as a Religion more agreeable to
human Society." King James suggested a political interpretation for the Horatian literary dictum, "Omne tulit punctum,
qui miscuit utile dulci" (He bears off every vote, who blends
profit with pleasure). [38]

The third major argument used to defend the *Declaration*
took as its central premise the doctrine of Christian liberty.
Supporters claimed that in the absence of prohibitions by the
law of the land or the law of God, the officially approved recreations could be practiced freely by Christians if they so desired. Sunday sports, defenders were quick to point out, were
not compulsory, since the *Declaration* allowed but did not require Sunday festivities for those with religious scruples. They
thus aligned themselves with religious tolerance and freedom
of conscience, noting that Sabbatarians, in contrast, wished to
make their strict beliefs regarding Sunday observances binding
on all. [39]

As might be expected, Puritan opponents proved unwilling to accept royalist positions. They rejected the humanitarian argument that men need time off from their serious responsibilities. Being born again as a Christian, the Puritan Thomas Taylor insisted, means "we must ayme at an absolute conformity betweene the *whole* word and our *whole* man." The rule of God governs both the outer man—"Our speeches, and actions, . . . our lookes and behaviours, our callings and conditions"—and the inner man—"the soul and the conscience, the heart and the will, yea, the affection and thoughts." Recreation could not be countenanced as time-out from serving God, because the dedicated Christian never takes time off from God, but worships Him in all activities. The regenerate, Taylor claimed, do not need sports as relief from their daily labors and religious duties, since a Sunday spent in worship is itself recreational, in the fullest sense of the word. Indeed, the inability to find delight in the spiritual exercises of the Sabbath is a sign "that the spirit is quenched in thee."[40] Puritans did not condemn recreation in itself. Rather they argued for a consistency of life that did not allow for any activity, including the recreational, which did not comport with or further the individual's religious commitments.

The royalist view of official sports as a means of governing also elicited Puritan objections. To them it seemed apparent that the king and his advisers encouraged immorality to enervate the nation and reduce subjects to greater docility that they might be more easily ruled. Popular complacency, the "deplorable security" that Lucy Hutchinson isolated as the aim of approved sports, had thus political and religious implications.

The Anglican argument on Christian liberty was the basis for perhaps the most extended commentary by Puritan opponents. Essentially, the two sides differed on what constitutes Christian liberty. Did the approved sports violate divine precept, or were they innocent pleasures that the Christian was free to enjoy? The conflict arose from a basic disagreement over what modes of behavior and what commitments demonstrate the regenerate state, a disagreement that Sears McGee has aptly explained in terms of the two groups' interpretations of the

Decalogue. Puritans generally emphasized the duties of the First Table (Commandments 1–4), which have to do with man's responsibilities to God. Anglicans, on the other hand, laid greater emphasis on the duties of the Second Table (Commandments 5–10), which involve man's behavior toward his neighbor. Puritans were likely to insist on a scrupulous obedience to the injunction in the Fourth Commandment to keep the Sabbath day holy, while Anglicans allowed greater latitude in Sunday activities and regarded recreation on the Sabbath as a morally indifferent matter, as long as the recreations themselves were not immoral and did not interfere with church attendance.[41]

A second difference between the two sides had to do with the relation between individual freedom and the need for collective order that the approved sports represented. From the Anglican perspective, the established policy provided for freedom of conscience, allowing individuals to choose whether they wanted to participate in sports, but at the same time kept liberty from breaking down into licentiousness or anarchy by placing sports under the purview of the church.[42]

Dissenting response to this view was colored by what has been called the central dilemma of the Puritan experiment: the problem of balancing freedom against discipline.[43] Initially, Puritans were united by their common opposition to licensed sports, which they claimed abused Christian liberty and religious discipline. They insisted that the festivities licensed by the *Declaration* wreaked havoc on social order. So frequently were these sports the occasions for sinful behavior that sinful conduct came to be seen as an integral part of the sports themselves. In fact, it became conventional for Puritan biographers and autobiographers to list participation in traditional rural pastimes, along with gaming, drinking, sins of the flesh, and attending the theater, as an error of an unregenerate youth.[44]

In addition, Puritans claimed the *Declaration* interfered with individual worshipers' freedom to spend Sundays in devotion. Baxter, for example, was to remember from the pre–civil war days of his childhood that approved recreations were so boisterous that they disrupted his family's reading of the Scriptures. Admittedly, interference of this sort was incidental, but

Prynne argued further that the prelates intentionally hindered the pious in their worship and encouraged the worldliness of the unregenerate by the unpopular act of banning "all after-noone Sermons on the Lords day: that so the profane vulgar might have more time to *dance, play, revell, drinke, and pro-phane* God."[45]

Puritans agreed during the prewar period on their abhorrence of the Caroline policy on sports; but by the mid-1640s when they held the reins of government, a basic disagreement, which before had surfaced only occasionally, became a strongly divisive issue. The question they faced was: granted that the previous regime had not struck a proper balance between liberty and discipline, how was the balance to be righted? Or, as the matter applied to recreation, what new policy on sports could preserve individual liberty and social order, while avoiding the abuses evident under the Stuarts? Quite early, Parliament chose to close the theaters and to prohibit traditional sports. Some Puritan thinkers (including Milton himself) were to claim that discipline was overemphasized at the expense of individual freedom, but for the majority of Puritans in power the need for discipline was of primary importance.

This does not mean that freedom was ignored. Rather, Puritans defined it in a way that incorporated the demand for social order. For most Puritans, Christian liberty was not discussed in terms of a series of prescribed, proscribed, indifferent, and thus allowable activities. It was a dynamic of collective life and not a release from arbitrary restraints as Anglicans conceived of it, but a freedom to work for the continuing edification of the Christian community. Treating the spiritual community in metaphoric terms as a living organism, John S. Coolidge explains the Puritan concept of Christian liberty as the vital principle by which the community lives and grows: "It is an active engagement in a struggle like that of an organic life to resist dissolution. The exercise of Christian liberty is subject to constraints analogous to those by which life is conditioned on pain of ceasing to be."[46]

The activities allowed by the *Declaration* needed to be controlled because they were frequently detrimental to the Christian community, distracting the unregenerate from worship, interfering with the devotions of the pious. Yet, in addition, as McGee points out, it was the duty of the spiritually rich— and not an unwarranted intrusion into the moral decisions of others—to supervise the activities of the spiritually poor. Baxter commented on the need for enforcing Sunday observances among the ungodly masses: "If all men were left to themselves, what time they should bestow in the worshipping of God, the greatest part would cast off all, and grow into atheism or utter prophaneness, and the rest would grow into confusion."[47] Charity, in this view, demanded that every regenerate Christian serve as his brother's keeper. Banning sports that distracted other men from their calling did not abrogate Christian liberty but enhanced it.

Milton's response to the controversy surrounding the *Declaration* placed him on the Puritan side of the issue, though not without qualification. He did not from the 1630s onward give credence to the royalist arguments that sports provide a necessary relaxation from the responsibilities of Christian life, and he never argued that a program of sports be used as a governing device. While he sided with the Puritans on these two points, his stand on the libertarian argument revealed his essential independence of thought, his readiness to depart from the Puritan mainstream and assert his own principles. As he repeatedly considered the relation of freedom and sports over a period of years, he came to oppose the dominant Puritan position, arguing against inflexible restrictions on the kinds of recreation allowable and on the times and places they could be performed. Despite this difference, Milton conceived of Christian liberty in essentially Puritan terms as a freedom to grow spiritually. But he recognized that freedom to grow necessarily demands freedom from the restraints that hinder growth. Thus, Milton was finally to place the individual's right to develop morally and intellectually by making his own choices above the need for communal discipline which had led to the Puritan restrictions on sports.

Milton's continuing interest in recreation is evident from the many comments on sports and related issues scattered throughout his writings before and after the masque. Events of the 1630s—the uproar provoked by Hausted's play, Prynne's

Histrio-mastix, and the republication of the *Declaration*—apparently influenced Milton strongly; for it is in the immediate aftermath of these events when the controversy was at its peak, roughly between late 1632 and 1634, that Milton formulated his mature position on recreation. Although he previously had written about sports and their proper nature and function, his earliest writings deliberately shy away from firm assertions. "Prolusion VI," "L'Allegro," and "Il Penseroso" consider a major point of contention, the relation between pleasure and moral and spiritual responsibility, but offer only inconclusive suggestions on how the two are to be reconciled.

"Prolusion VI," delivered in 1628 as a vacation exercise, argues the proposition that "Sportive Exercises on occasion are not inconsistent with philosophical studies." Modern readers, almost universally appalled by the vulgarity and coarse humor of the oration, have been unable to find any justification for it, except as an experiment in scurrility of the sort Milton later used in a few of his polemical tracts. Milton himself was apparently disturbed by the levity of the piece, since several times he tries to justify his tone and subject. Claiming at one point that the occasion demands time out from the usual decorums, he asks for "comic license." And he sets forth the Anglican position that sport provides a necessary release from work, relieving "the boredom brought about by satiety and . . . making us the more eager to resume our interrupted tasks." But Milton also suggests, somewhat inconsistently, that comedy does not require a release from work and responsibility, that the playful and the serious are not mutually exclusive. Recreation is not simply a permitted diversion; rather devotion to duty and sport are interrelated, each a prerequisite for the other:

> For my part, I consider that a man who can be so given up to foolish jests as altogether to neglect for them his serious and really useful work, is incapable of distinguishing himself in either of these spheres: not in that of serious work, for if he were by nature adapted and suited to dealing with serious matters he would not, I am sure, allow himself to be so easily led away from them; nor yet in that of frivolity, because no one can be master of a fine and clever wit who has not first learned to behave seriously. [*CP*, 1:276–77]

Milton here concludes with a paradox without further explanation. A similar tension between diversion and duty emerges in "L'Allegro" and "Il Penseroso," where it is not left unresolved, but rather is incorporated into the poet's progress from common to visionary experience.

When Milton composed the paired poems has not been definitely established. Scholars have argued for various dates between 1629 and 1634, though 1631 or 1632 is most frequently accepted.[48] What does appear certain, however, is the preference expressed in the two poems for sports that are *serio ludus*, and not merely diversion—a preference that characterizes Milton's masque and subsequent writings.

"L'Allegro" and "Il Penseroso" depict a process of intellectual, imaginative, and spiritual growth. Don Cameron Allen has summarized the essential element in the process:

> The structure of "L'Allegro" and "Il Penseroso" is based on a
> daily but continued ascent. . . . The poet rises towards a
> comprehension of his created end, towards "the everlasting
> companionship" with "holy minds and intelligences." "L'Alle-
> gro" describes the lower level of each degree; "Il Penseroso"
> the higher. By a continued mounting of the slopes of the in-
> tellect from common experience, to intellectual experience, to
> religious inspiration, the poet trusts to arrive at the supreme
> poetic gratification.[49]

As Michael Fixler suggests, the appearance of Orpheus in the two poems underlines the differing quality of experience and of poetic vision in each. "L'Allegro" concludes with the description of a passive, inert Orpheus, who hears rather than produces death-conquering strains. "Il Penseroso" offers a vital and active Orpheus, who as vivifier and mystical artist produces music that "Drew iron tears down Pluto's cheek, / And made Hell grant what Love did seek."[50] While "L'Allegro" is characterized by candor and a spontaneous delight in immediate, sensory stimuli, "Il Penseroso" continually directs our attention to what is hidden, pushing us to look into the essential nature of things, to transcend the immediate and attain visionary insight.

In the course of tracing the poet's growth toward "some-

thing like Prophetic strain," the poems also reflect something
of the peculiar tensions felt by men of Milton's day in the
conflict provoked by the recreation debate. Milton sets the
joyous, unreflective life of "L'Allegro," which can include among
other pleasures the traditional sports encouraged by Cavaliers,
against the serious, contemplative vision of "Il Penseroso," in
which such sports find no place amid philosophical musings,
cloistered devotions, and cosmic reflections.

The mirthful life of "L'Allegro" specifically includes the rural celebrations encouraged by the *Declaration*:

> Som times with secure delight
> The up-land Hamlets will invite,
> When the merry Bells ring round,
> And the jocund rebecks sound
> To many a youth, and many a maid
> ·
> And young and old com forth to play
> On a Sunshine Holyday.
> [ll. 91–95, 97–98]

It also comprehends such courtly entertainments as tourna-
ments, "Where throngs of Knights and Barons bold, / In weeds
of Peace high triumphs hold" (ll. 119–20), and wedding
masques, where Hymen presides "In Saffron robe, with Taper
clear," as well as "pomp, and feast, and revelry, / With mask,
and antique Pageantry" (ll. 126–28). These diversions are essential to the mirthful life, for the goddess who presides over
"L'Allegro" has among her attendants Sport himself.

Through his emphasis on youth, health, and vitality, Milton creates in "L'Allegro" a world in which the morally tolerant and optimistic perspectives of his Anglican contemporaries
are perfectly reasonable. The mirthful life is not immoral. The
persona asks specifically to abide with Mirth and "The Mountain Nymph, sweet Liberty":

> Mirth, admit me of thy crue
> To live with her, and live with thee,
> In unreproved pleasures free.
> [ll. 37–39]

Liberty is not to be read here as license or freedom from normal moral restraints. Rather her summoning represents a belief that man should be free to enjoy the innocent pleasures the world has to offer.[51] The nymph Liberty is important to the vision of "L'Allegro" because she offers freedom from, as well as freedom to. The presiding goddess is called "heart-easing Mirth," apparently in recognition that men need at least temporary release from their burdensome occupations. The poem does include agricultural chores—plowing, milking, mowing, cooking country meals, and binding up the harvested grain—but all described in delightful pastoral terms that make them seem more play than work. There are no references to religious responsibilities. "L'Allegro" offers a playtime world in which men need not confront the implications of their mortality, in which they are free to take time from their serious pursuits, including their spiritual callings, to enjoy mirthful sport.

The reference to Orpheus and "his half-regain'd *Eurydice*," with which "L'Allegro" concludes, indirectly acknowledges the incompleteness of the mirthful life and eases the reader into the more advanced thought of "Il Penseroso." Rejecting the "heart-easing Mirth" of "L'Allegro" as "vain deluding joys," "Il Penseroso" offers no recreations, either rural or courtly, comparable to those of mirthful life. Instead the pastimes of the melancholy life are those of the reader who, alone in his tower, peruses Plato, tragic literature, the visionary poetry of Musaeus, Orpheus, or Chaucer, and chivalric romances—like Spenser's *Faerie Queene* perhaps—in which the literal narrative is overlaid by higher levels of significance and "more is meant than meets the ear" ("L'Allegro," l. 120).

Although the poem does not use terms that specifically recall Puritan formulations, "Il Penseroso" illustrates in an extreme form a perspective similar to that of prewar Puritans involved in the recreation debate. The pensive man does not indulge in diversionary sports. None of his activities interrupt his contemplations, but rather serve to enhance his understanding of the universe and its maker. The poem concludes with what is presumably the greatest delight of the contemplative life, the joy of religious and prophetic vision.

In "Elegy VI" Milton had assured his friend Charles Diodati that the sports of the Christmas season are no enemy to poetry. But he expressed his own preference for visionary poetry, which requires the poet-seer to live sparingly, to limit his participation in seasonal festivities. The dichotomy between the two kinds of poets that Milton marks in "Elegy VI" is incorporated into the progression of his paired poems. The reader shares in "L'Allegro" experiences that are pleasant but limited. "Il Penseroso" allows entry into more fully satisfying experiences, including recreations with more than diversionary import. Although Milton does not condemn sports of the kind advocated by the *Declaration* he allows them to be superseded by the superior delights of "Il Penseroso."

The paired poems reflect Milton's changed position in the recreation controversy. When he considered the matter in his writings following "L'Allegro" and "Il Penseroso," he no longer left the central issues unresolved or offered vague and ambiguous answers. Instead he articulated a position that reflects his sympathy with the Puritan disapproval of the officially sanctioned sports and his own interest in promoting acceptable kinds of entertainment. Probably he was moved to formulate his new stand not only by the intensity of debate on the subject during the 1630s but also by his contributions in "Arcades" and *Comus*.

In "Ad Patrem," Milton defended poetry and, more specifically, literary entertainments. If, as some scholars have claimed, he wrote the poem either immediately before or after the performance of *Comus*, he may have been attempting to answer his father's objections to his masque-writing.[52] Certainly the poem seems to speak to criticism of poetry as frivolous or otherwise unworthy.

He reasserted the same faith in the vatic poet's divine insights that had infused the "Nativity Ode," Elegy VI," and "Prolusion VI": "Nec tu vatis opus divinum despice carmen . . . / Sancta Prometheae retineus vestigia flammae." ("You should not despise the poet's task, divine song, which preserves some spark of Promethean fire.") The poet's Orphic powers necessarily involve a social responsibility. Perhaps bearing in mind the much discussed immorality and vanity of sports at the Caroline court, Milton looked back to an idealized past when a poet used temperate celebrations as occasions for teaching the public:

> Carmina regales epulas ornare solebant,
> Cum nondum luxus, vastaeque immensa vorago
> Nota gulae, et modico spumabat coena Lyaeo.
> Tum de more sedens festa ad convivia vates,
> Aesculea intonsos redimitus ab arbore crines,
> Heroumque actus imitandaque gesta canebat,
> Et chaos, et positi late fundamina mundi,
> Reptantesque Deos, et alentes numina glandes,
> Et nondum Aetnaeo quaesitum fulmen ab antro.

Songs were the usual ornaments of royal tables in the times before luxury and the bottomless appetite of gluttony were known, when Lyaeus sparkled at the banquet in temperate cups. Then the custom was that the bard should sit at the festal banquet, wearing a garland of oak leaves on his unshorn locks, and should sing of the deeds and emulable achievements of heroes, and of chaos and of the broad foundations on which the earth rests, of the deities who once went creeping about in search of their acorn-food, and of the thunder-bolt not yet sought out of the depths of Aetna. [*CPP*, pp. 83–84]

Two aspects are essential to his portrait of the poet here: first, his sense that there is no conflict between divine insights and participation in festive gatherings and, second, the implication that the ideal poet must involve himself in the lives of men, reaching them through the social forums available to him. In addition to his vatic function, the poet serves, in Douglas Bush's words, as "the scholar artist of the elite."[53] Clearly Milton's view of the poet allows for sociopolitical *engagement* and thus for the writing of a masque.

In sections of the *Commonplace Book*, written between 1637 and 1638, Milton offered specific comments on theatrical entertainments that record his thinking during the period when he was revising *Comus*. Refuting Tertullian's assertion in "De Spectaculis" that public shows should be forbidden for Christians, Milton argued that all dramatic representations should not be banned because some are immoral. Instead he commended Tertullian for suggesting the production of "better plays, that is, divine and heavenly plays, which, in great number and of great value, the Christian can anticipate concerning the coming of Christ and the Last Judgement."[54]

Although his reflections on drama in the *Commonplace Book* are illuminating, Milton's earliest and fullest expression of his interest in reforming sports is embodied in his masque and to a lesser extent in "Arcades." In view of the well-known hostility of seventeenth-century Puritans to the theater and to the quasi-theatrical recreations of the upper classes, Milton's involvement with an entertainment first and then a masque would seem to mark him as an anomaly among Puritans. There was, in fact, some interest among Puritans in nurturing "reformed drama." Even William Prynne, whose name has become synonymous with Puritan bigotry against the stage, was willing to tolerate plays under special conditions, although he admittedly left so small a crack that drama could scarcely get a foot in the door. Similarly, Richard Baxter avoided wholly condemning drama. He conceived of a moral drama that uses theatrical representations much in the way that parables are used in the Bible, that is, to make doctrinal teachings immediate and direct.[55] Such interest in reformed drama inspired only a handful of compositions, such as Richard Flecknoe's *Love's Dominion* (1654) and James Shirley's *Cupid and Death* (1653), both occasional theatrical pieces designed to fit the needs of Interregnum audiences.[56] Milton's distinction is that he realized in artistic form what Prynne and Baxter admitted only as a theoretical possibility, and he realized it far earlier than Flecknoe or Shirley.

His first experiment in revising modes of aristocratic entertainment was "Arcades," the opening segment of an estate entertainment. It was presented—probably in 1632, though the date is disputed—at her Harefield estate to honor the Countess Dowager of Derby, grandmother of the children who were later to participate in *Comus*.[57] Like the masque, this earlier piece represents a careful adaptation of received conventions. Milton retained conventional structural patterns, images, and themes, incorporating them as basic compositional units into his work, while redefining them. His changes developed naturally out of a basic shift in focus. Discarding the usual social and political assumptions of the estate entertainment—its justification of the traditional aristocratic life, its defense of noble privileges as natural, its picturing of the estate as a harmonious community—Milton provided a theological framework for "Arcades" and thus expanded its significance.

The estate entertainment developed out of the institution of the progress. A progress involved the visit of royalty or high-ranking aristocrats and their retinue to the country homes of their subjects. There the distinguished visitors were to be lavishly and lovingly entertained. Because of the estate entertainment's relation to the progress, the movement of visitors toward the manor and their reception into the life of the estate naturally served as the central structural pattern. Normally this movement was given the fictional character of a journey to a place that is in some sense a home, a congenial setting for visitors and hosts.

Milton, however, gave his journey the character of a spiritual quest with the Countess Dowager, seated in state, as its object, a fully realized model of human wisdom and virtue. Our perceptions, however, are allied with those of the "Arcades," itinerant shepherds who have left the old Arcadia to find a more worthy pastoral home. We follow in their wake as they move toward the Lady, gaining gradually as they approach her a comprehension of the ideals she represents and moving ever closer to the adoption of her values.[58]

As was usual, Milton praised the estate itself as a *locus amoenus*, but he made it something less and more than the idyllic and fully realized vision of perfection depicted in conventional entertainments. On the one hand, Harefield is governed by powers that transcend social and political orders. It is a sacred precinct guarded by a local spirit who serves the Countess Dowager at divine behest. The Genius of the Wood, the local guardian, is thus an instrument of the divine will, extending grace to Harefield and to its virtuous owner. Yet, Harefield is not the wholly beneficent paradise of most estate entertainments. Evil is present, though the Genius as a protective force modifies or cures the effects of evil, supervising the growth of his plants and preserving them from disease, storms, and the malice of a Satanic "worm." As he explains:

> I am the pow'r
> Of this Fair Wood, and live in Oak'n bow'r,
> To nurse the Saplings tall, and curl the grove
> With Ringlets quaint, and wanton windings wove.
> And all my Plants I save from nightly ill,
> Of noisome winds, and blasting vapors chill;
> And from the Boughs brush off the evil dew,
> And heal the harms of thwarting thunder blue,
> Or what the cross dire-looking Planet smites,
> Or hurtful Worm with canker'd venom bites.
>
>   [ll. 44–53]

The Genius also involves himself in human growth as he guides the Arcadians into the Countess Dowager's immediate presence, explains in song her virtues, and urges the young shepherds to join her household and adopt her way of life. He cannot efface the ills of the fallen world, but he does remedy some of their effects. Although not a prelapsarian paradise, Harefield is a place where nature has been at least partially redeemed.

In offering the compliments the occasion required, Milton focused on moral worth rather than beauty, power, or titular nobility, and he made the praise emerge naturally out of the dramatic situation. The Countess Dowager is a favored mortal inhabiting a favored place and, as the goal of the Arcadians' quest, represents a realistically attainable level of moral excellence. Reciprocally, the traveling shepherds are praised for having undertaken a spiritual quest toward so worthy a goal. In the final song of the entertainment, the Genius presents the shepherds to the Countess Dowager and leaves them to make their choice as to whether they will join the community at Harefield. In the actual performance, the young aristocrats would certainly have accepted the invitation to become part of the life of the estate. They would have become the automatic recipients of praise by making what the device of the entertainment points to as the right decision. The Countess and the Arcadians, thus, neatly complement each other as worthy objects of a quest and successful questers.

An adaptation of the entertainment tradition in its own right, "Arcades" is also important as a forecast of *Comus*. In both

works, younger family members styled as travelers are engaged
in a journey that leads finally to their reception and absorption
into an idealized aristocratic milieu, which is treated as a divinely favored place. In *Comus*, as in the earlier entertainment,
the noble adults who do not actively participate are given central places in the fiction as the goal of the journey-quest. *Comus*
has no tutelary spirits who divide between them the functions
the Genius of the Wood serves in "Arcades": Sabrina, like the
Genius, is associated with the locality and possesses curative
powers; the Attendant Spirit, like the Genius, serves as a guide
to young travelers, counseling them in the choices they are to
make and directing them to their moral "home." But *Comus*
goes beyond "Arcades." It focuses on a dramatic encounter of
the travelers with forces of evil and ends with an epilogue that
suggests the many journeys that must be made by the virtuous. It thus presents a far more complex moral vision than
the earlier work, although "Arcades" does point to Milton's
interest in reforming modes of entertainment.

The recreation controversy had a massive and complex impact on Milton's writing of his masque. As we shall see in
subsequent chapters, he made extensive formal revisions, ad-
justments of subject matter, and expansion of scope, which the
more modest "Arcades" had only foreshadowed. He also introduced recreation as a central theme, developing it in a way
that suggests he was responding directly to arguments raised
in public debate.

Masques usually spoke to national and international issues.
However, most extolled or justified the established government; Milton's reflected his sympathy with the government's
opponents. Through his villain, Milton made his most direct
attack on the Caroline support of recreation. For while Comus
is obviously Milton's version of an antimasque figure, as numerous critics have remarked he has little in common with
other antimasque characters, bearing more resemblance to
denizens of the idealized world of contemporary main masques.[59]
In fact, he is even far more closely allied with royalist attitudes
and practices than has been noted.

His speeches are fully of imagery, themes, and rhetorical
devices that recall the visions of proper revelry projected in the

main masques of Stuart court productions. The pose of gentle-
manly shepherd, which Comus adopts to prevent the Lady's
suspicions, evokes the political pastoralism that was increasingly used during the decade to disguise the less benign side
of absolute monarchy. The elaborate flattery addressed to the
Lady and her brothers, in which Comus implies their quasi-
divine status, uses much the same patterns of elevation as those
conventional in praising masquers and monarch.[60] Milton's
villain inhabits a brightly lit palace, although such brilliance
was usually reserved for masquers and their aristocratic milieu.
Further, Comus's offer to the Lady of a life lived in an eternal
spring with unending pleasures and perennial, undiminishing
vitality (ll. 667–71), evokes the delightful stasis depicted in
the visions of universal order with which royalist masques often
concluded. In the debate between Comus and the Lady on the
proper use of nature, his insistence that nature intends men to
consume her goods without stint rehearses the doctrine of natural aristocratic and monarchical privilege and the ethic of
conspicuous consumption.

The conventional language and themes of the masque so
pervade Comus's speeches, that his opening monologue can be
read as a miniature, verbal masque. He begins the speech with
references to nightfall and pastoral surroundings that provide
an acceptable fiction for the temporal and spatial locus of his
revelry. Next, he banishes uncongenial elements in a manner
that recalls the expected exorcism of forces in the conventional
antimasque, and he also invokes the spirits that inspire his
celebration:

> Mean while welcom Joy, and Feast,
> Midnight shout, and revelry,
> Tipsie dance, and Jollity.
> . . . .
> Rigor now is gon to bed,
> And Advice with scrupulous Head,
> Strict Age, and sowre Severity,
> With their grave Saws in slumber ly.
>   [ll. 102–4, 107–10]

Most of the remainder of the speech is devoted to developing
a central device, or controlling fiction, for Comus's revelry—

one that will provide complimentary roles for his revelers. He tries several devices used in contemporary masques, though without focusing exclusively on any one. Since he is attended by his herd, the pastoral metaphor is a natural choice. But he also tries out the fairy motif, casting his revelers as nymphs and elves, as well as the stellar device that had become extremely popular in Caroline masques. His claim for his revelers—"We that are of purer fire / Imitate the Starry Quire" (ll. 111–12)—contains a distinct verbal echo of the description of the masquers in *Coelum Britannicum*, who were cast as stars:

> These must in the unpeopled sky
> Succeed and governe Destiny;
> Jove is temp'ring purer fire,
> And will with bright flames attire
> These glorious lights.[61]

As his speech comes to a close, Comus projects that his festivities, which began with nightfall, will end with the approach of dawn. The natural alternation of night and day thus serves as a framing device for his celebration, just as it frequently did in royal masques of the time.[62]

Milton did not gratuitously associate these conventional elements with his villain. Rather, his examination of sports in *Comus* proceeded by much the same means he used in his later reappraisal of the heroic ethos in *Paradise Lost*. Much as he was to attribute to Satan "the conventional trappings of superlative virtue" for the purpose of "discrediting a popular, but inadequate conception of heroic virtue,"[63] so he discredited existing governmental policy on sports by making it the policy of his antimasque figure. He thus moved beyond parody to satire,[64] not simply ridiculing the aesthetic conventions of the court masque, but also attacking on moral, theological, and political grounds the form's underlying habits of thought.

The subtle undercutting of the conventional devices contained in Comus's opening speech, which we have seen works as a miniature masque, provides an index to Milton's satiric intent and technique. Comus's companions wear "glistering" costumes and bear torches, both usual properties of masquers;[65] but even spangled clothing lit to best advantage does not hide the fact that they are grotesque, beast-headed monsters, whose appearance is evidence of their depravity. Comus also violates the conventions of the pastoral metaphor he invokes. On sighting "the Star that bids the Shepherd fold" (l. 93), he proves himself a bad shepherd by calling his monsters out to play. Milton persistently contrasts the personifications alien to their revelry and those that inspire it—a contrast that recalls the usual opposition of antimasque and main masque, but reverses the expected moral associations so that Comus's festivities are shown to be licentious. Rigor, Advice, Age, and Severity, all smacking of an unwelcome discipline, are dismissed, and their places are taken by Joy, Feast, and Jollity with raucous noise and drunken dancing. In addition, the sorcerer admits that his revelers merely "imitate" celestial motions, that their claims of heavenly similitude are playacting. It is clear finally that his celebrations will cease with the approach of day, not because the participants need to return to the active pursuits of their everyday lives, but because their revelry is too shameful to bear scrutiny.

As a satiric embodiment of contemporary masquing practices, Comus justifies Puritan criticism of the form. The revelry he supervises shows masquing at its worst, reflecting its encouragement of immorality, its false elitism, its self-congratulation, and, perhaps most dangerous, its superficial elegance, which obscures the moral bankruptcy of its participants.

Comus is associated, however, not only with aristocratic recreation, but also with the traditional festivities of the common people sanctioned by the *Declaration*. James Taaffe has pointed out specific links between Milton's villain and various Michaelmas customs of misrule which would have been apparent to Milton's original audience on Michaelmas, 1634. One traditional practice was "ganging," which involved the rough, though essentially playful, assault of passersby by groups of revelers. Another custom followed in southwest England, near Ludlow, was the "lawless hour," when rowdy citizens took over the town.[66]

Comus may well have recalled to Milton's audience the misrule given play on Michaelmas; but the poet also took pains to link him with other seasonal festivities. The Lady, hearing his revels at a distance, identified them as:

> . . . the sound
> Of riot, and ill manag'd Merriment,
> Such as the jocund Flute, or gameson Pipe
> Stirs up among the loose unleter'd Hinds,
> When for their teeming Flocks, and granges full
> In wanton dance they praise the bounteous *Pan*,
> And thank the gods amiss. I should be loath
> To meet the rudenesse, and swill'd insolence
> Of such late Wassailers.   [ll. 171–79]

The Lady's reference to large flocks and a well-stocked barn associates Comus's celebration with the traditional Harvest Home, a movable feast that took place some time in late summer or early autumn. Her description makes reference to specific elements of this feast: its music, shouting, dance, pagan rites, and threat of intemperance.

Seventeenth-century commentaries indicate that harvest home festivities retained vestiges of pagan customs, such as the procession of the Kern Baby, representing the spirit of plenty.[67] A sixteenth-century visitor to England reported that "men and women, and men and maid servants, riding through the streets . . . shout as loud as they can till they arrive at the barn." Music was so crucial a part of the festivities that, as John Brand commented, a family might keep "a piper, to play to shearers all the time of harvest." The high point of the celebration was the harvest feast on the evening after the last of the crops had been brought in. The master provided for his workers a "plentiful supper," after which they spent the night "in dancing, singing, &c." Because the festivities often became the occasion for misconduct, some method of punishment frequently had to be devised to maintain order. In Suffolk, for example, the custom of "ten-pounding," which involved beating offenders on the posterior with a hob-nail shoe or a work-hardened hand, was used "to prevent or punish loss of time by laziness, drunkenness . . . and to correct swearing, lying, or quarreling amongst themselves or any other kind of misbehaviour which myght slacken the exertions, or break the harmony of the reap."[68]

The loudness of Comus's revelry, the sound of shouting, and the raucous music of pipe or tabor make the Lady assume she hears the traditional festivities of harvest time and that dancing, false worship, and intemperate behavior, other elements of the celebration, are also taking place.

The Lady's allusion to harvest celebrations would have been timely since *Comus* was performed in late September, but Milton made no attempt to tie Comus's revels exclusively to a single feast. Indeed the sorcerer's language often recalls springtime rituals, as in his reference to the season "When the fresh blood grows lively, and returns / Brisk as the *April* buds in Primrose-season" (ll. 670–71). And he elsewhere describes the dance he and his companions perform as a "morris," traditionally connected with May and Whitsun customs.[69]

Milton's association of specific festivals with Comus was, thus, less occasional than topical. He established a general connection in the minds of his audience between his villain and the celebrations promoted by the *Declaration*. He suggested this connection not only by introducing details that recall actual customs, but also by placing in his villain's mouth arguments that ally him with the royalist attitudes that inspired official policy and figured prominently in its defense.

First, Comus tries to convince the Lady of the legitimacy of his festivities by appealing to the traditional humanitarian argument. He urges her to consider her weariness, hunger, and thirst when she hesitates to drink in symbolic acceptance of his revelry. But he also makes it clear that her compliance means accepting his moral assumption: ". . . the unexempt condition / By which all mortal frailty must subsist, / Refreshment after toil, ease after pain" (ll. 685–87). His argument here is identical with that offered by supporters of the *Declaration*: men cannot possibly spend twenty-four hours a day in devotion or seven days a week in labor; recreation provides essential respite from duty.

Comus also uses the second argument developed by proponents of the official recreational policy, that sports can serve as a tool of government. To begin with, he conceives of his confederacy of revelers as an established social order with himself as ruler. When he vows to make the Lady his queen (l. 256), he implies the existence of a monarchical state. Later, condemning the Lady's resistance as violating "the canon laws of our foundation" (l. 808), he assimilates his revelers to an ecclesiastical order. Then by his choice of language, he casts the Lady as a force for social destruction, a violator of the basic principles, minor and major, necessary for social stability. He appeals to etiquette: there are certain ways a pretty girl is expected to behave (ll. 745–55). But he also implies that she disrupts the economic order by acting like "an ill borrower," by hoarding, by inverting the covenant of nature's trust (ll. 682, 683, 739). She subverts domestic law by behaving like a bastard rather than a legitimate heir (l. 727). He also suggests her failure in the realm of what we might call universal politics. The restraint and nonparticipation she advocates would lead to revolution: "The herds would over-multitude their Lords" (l. 731), and inanimate objects, having lost proper awe for their superiors in the chain of being, would look up with "shameless brows" (l. 736).

Milton further attributed to Comus an exaggerated version of the royalist appeal to liberty. In view of man's "mortal frailty," Comus argues for the freedom to alternate work with sport. Man may enjoy the pleasures of his body and use the elements of the natural world as he wishes. Carrying to its logical extreme the Anglican argument of freedom to pursue morally indifferent acts, Comus admits no limitations on his liberty to enjoy. Indeed, he insists that the unimpeded exercise of this liberty is in itself a moral imperative, since in his role as governor of the natural world man expresses his dominion by using nature.

In exploring Comus's relation to royalist views on sports, I do not mean to minimize his role as a manifestation of evil. The context of the day made the recreation controversy anything but trivial. As we have seen, Prynne, his prosecutors, and his judges were convinced that the cosmic forces of good and evil were engaged in the struggle over sports, though the two sides differed as to whom God supported. The involvement of Milton's masque in the recreation controversy allowed it to speak at once of present occasions and transcendent truths. Attributing to his villain royalist views, Milton gave evil a concrete form, immediate and relevant. Comus enabled Milton to satirize fundamental royalist attitudes; but Comus also represents the evil of a life devoted to mere entertainment—and thus to self-gratification, self-deception, and worldliness—without reference to man's larger responsibilities. The fact that he remains at large and presumably free to go on tempting travelers speaks to Milton's conviction that improper sports can corrupt society. Although stated in more temperate and vastly more artistic terms, it is not wholly unlike Prynne's conviction.

Comus and his arguments do not go unanswered. Throughout the masque Milton offered counterarguments that reflect his general sympathy with Puritan attitudes. He responded to the royalist-Anglican position in part through the speeches of characters who actively oppose or stand firm against Comus's blandishments. But he did far more than that. As I shall suggest in more detail in later chapters, *Comus* embodies a detailed and coherent effort at reform that required a revision of the form's underlying assumptions and far-reaching formal changes.

The conceptual and formal reformation of the masque that Milton undertook in *Comus* set the pattern for his stand on recreation and closely related matters throughout the rest of his career. In his prose works, he continued to express much the same opposition to traditional sports and much the same desire for better forms of entertainment that shaped his masque. The only major change he was later to make in his stand concerned Sunday sports. In his earliest political and ecclesiastical tracts, Milton advocated a strict Sabbatarianism, but by 1643 in the *Doctrine and Discipline of Divorce* he had begun to interpret the Fourth Commandment more flexibly.[70] Although he appears to have performed a startling about-face, his position actually demonstrates a deeper consistency. Two factors remained firm: his underlying faith in *jus divinum* as a guide to conduct (he became increasingly convinced that neither Old nor New Testament specifically prescribed a rigidly observed Sabbath, at least not a seventh-day Sabbath) and his unyielding dedication to Christian liberty, which he viewed in Puritan terms as freedom to pursue spiritual edification.[71]

More obviously consistent than his view of the Sabbath was his position on recreation in general. He judged sports, not according to any inflexible dogma, but case by case, giving weight primarily to the ultimate end or purpose of a recreational activity. Although he had not managed to reconcile sports and serious responsibility in "Prolusion VI," he did achieve a fusion in "Arcades" and *Comus* by making his entertainments lessons in virtuous living. And in *Of Education* (1644), he explicitly stated his method. The instructional system he proposed here has serious ends: first, the moral and spiritual aim of helping students to become good Christians—"to repair the ruins of our first parents"—and second, the practical end of enabling them to become contributing members of society—"to perform justly, skilfully and magnanimously all the offices both private and publike of peace and war" (*CP*, 2:366–67, 378–79). Although he did not introduce the terms, he clearly intended to prepare young men for what might have been called by his Protestant contemporaries their general vocation as Christians and the particular vocation of their life work.

Despite his elevated aims, Milton did not consider it necessary to exclude sports, but neither did he advocate recreational activities as diversions. He provided for alternating periods of study and recreation; however, the specific provisions of his educational plan suggest that, far from being mutually exclusive, the two are nearly identical. He repeatedly named ease and delight as the key to learning.[72] He hoped to instill in young students a joy in acquiring knowledge that would make learning a habit that continued long after they left the academy for the practical affairs of adult life. Just as learning is to be recreational, so recreation is to be educational. Milton allowed sports to play an important part in his program, assigning far more time to physical exercise, music, and similar activities than was usual in contemporary schools.[73] The recreational activities he prescribed, like the formal studies, were intended to prepare young men for their responsibilities as Christians and as useful members of society. He advocated bodily exercise to promote their physical health and stamina, to train them for military service, and to strengthen their moral fiber. Similarly, musical recreation would "smooth and make them gentle from rustick harshness and distemper'd passion," encouraging moral balance and social refinement (*CP*, 2:409, 410–11).

That recreation is not intended as diversion becomes particularly clear from Milton's plan for springtime, when formal classroom learning might cease and students and their guides might take to the outdoors (*CP*, 2:412–13). While sympathetic with the lure of the spring, Milton did not look to leading his students a-maying. His vernal sport is far different from the release from duty represented by official recreations. Nor does it have anything in common with the "too oft idle vacancies" of contemporary schools and universities, which he condemned as a waste of time (*CP*, 2:371). Rather his recreational outings are to provide instruction in religous and practical matters. The boys may gain useful knowledge of the natural world, aided by the clement weather of the season; but by leaving aside man-made volumes they will also come to read universal truths in the Book of the Creatures, perhaps even learning to join the creation's spontaneous song of springtime praise.

In the course of his tractate, Milton broke down the distinctions between sport and study. Prescribed activities do not alternate from education to recreation, but from recreational education to educational recreation. Play is a necessary element in Milton's scheme, since he sought to "draw them [i.e., students] in willing obedience, enflam'd with the study of learning (*CP*, 2: 384–85). He did not use recreation as a "carrot-on-the-stick" to lure boys to their studies. Instead, as Irene Samuel suggests, Milton—like Plato, whom he invoked as one model for his program—assumed that learning is itself pleasantly engaging.[74] Reciprocally, recreation does not draw the student, even temporarily, from important pursuits, but in fact provides the occasion for effective learning. We are given a cautionary example of what happens to badly educated students who come to view recreation and learning as opposed rather than interrelated. Disappointed by their tedious and empty lessons, those who have not had the opportunity to benefit from the sort of plan Milton devised may ignore their callings and choose to "retire themselves knowing no better, to the enjoyments of ease and luxury, living out their daies in feast and jollity" (*CP*, 2:376).

The assumption about sports which influenced *Comus*—that recreational activities can be learning experiences—informs not only the reconciliation of the serious and the playful in *Of Education*, but also Milton's interest in encouraging acceptable alternatives to existing sports. He expressed this interest, foreshadowed in "Ad Patrem" and the *Commonplace Book*, with increased force and clarity in the *Reason of Church Government*:

> Because the spirit of man cannot demean itself lively in this body without some recreating intermission of labour and serious things, it were happy for the Common wealth, if our Magistrats, as in those famous governments of old, would take into their care . . . Our publick sports and festival pastimes, that they might be, not such as were autoriz'd a while since, the provocations of drunkennesse and lust, but such as . . . may civilize, adorn, and make discreet our minds by the learned and affable meeting of frequent Academies, and the procurement of wise and artful recitations sweetened with eloquent and gracefull inticements to the love and practice of justice, temperance, and fortitude, instructing and bettering the Nation at all opportunities, that the call of wisdom and vertu may be heard everywhere. . . . this may not be not only in Pulpits, but after another persuasive method, at set and solemn Panegyries, in Theaters, porches, or what other place or way may win most upon the people to receiv at once both recreation and instruction. [*CP*, 1:819–20]

Although Milton admitted the need for time away from the demanding work of daily life, he was careful to distinguish his from the royalist position. First, he allowed for intermission of labor but not of the exercise of virtue; the pastimes he suggested are intended as moral exercises. Second, the specific examples of reformed recreation he listed differ from the court theatricals of the Stuarts and the traditional festivities prescribed by the *Declaration*, both of which he surely had in mind when he condemned the sports under Charles as occasions for "drunkennesse and lust." His proposed pastimes do not sanction time away from duty to God, but are specifically intended to help fulfill that duty. And the allurements to the virtuous

life he suggested are the appeals of skillful rhetoric, used in all possible forums to reach people in all areas of their lives.[75] Thus, there need be, Milton implied, no inherent conflict between the pulpit and the theater, if entertainment complements religious teaching. He had no sympathy with the Anglican notion, on which the *Declaration* rests, that once one has fulfilled his responsibility to God by attending services one is free to play. In marked contrast, he assumed that there is no such separation between worship and recreation and that, in fact, recreation can and should be used to serve man's responsible development.

In addition to addressing theoretical issues raised by the debate on sports, Milton's prose also contains frequent references to the masque. His comments reflect an abiding interest in this kind of courtly entertainment, a genuine comprehension of contemporary practices, and yet a sympathy with Puritan feelings. He patently agreed with objections to contemporary masquing practices based on moral grounds.

In his attacks on Charles I during the 1650s, Milton focused on court theatricals as symbolic of the king's failures as governor. He accused Charles of sexual immorality, specifying his theater as the forum where he exhibited his licentious behavior (*CP*, 4:408). Such personal misrule, Milton charged, was paralleled by political misrule. Caroline theatricals were marred by luxury and excess, and the king's inability to govern himself and his court bespoke a larger failure to rule the commonwealth efficiently and fairly (*CP* 4:520–21). Like other Puritan commentators, Milton saw in extravagant court performances an example morally corrupting to the nation, as well as a waste of time and money by a king who turned to diversions while neglecting those monarchical duties he claimed to have been divinely chosen to fulfill.

Milton also objected to the masque's conventional orientation toward worldly rather than godly ends, to its use as an instrument of propaganda in support of the religious and political policies of the Stuarts. As John Demaray has argued, Milton's antiroyalism in *Eikonoklastes* and *A Ready and Easy Way* extends to a condemnation of Caroline masques as idolatrous homage. Milton claimed that "the tyrant rules through deception," employing masques and other forms of pageantry to present false images that disguise the disorder and ugliness for which he is responsible.[76] Charles encouraged an adoration of himself, in effect a civil religion, based not on revealed principles of true religion "but [on] quaint emblems and devices, begged from the old pagentry of some Twelfth-night's entertainment at White hall."[77]

Milton recognized in contemporary masques not only their dedication to royalist political doctrines but also their support of the policies of Laudian Anglicanism. He viewed the Established church's concern with the external forms of worship as analogous to the masque's use of elaborate spectacle to conceal real abuses of monarchical power, savagely ridiculing prelates as "Church-maskers" who "hide Christ's righteous verity with the polluted cloathing of . . . ceremonies to make it seem more decent" and use "gaudy glisterings to stirre up the devotion of the rude multitude" (*CP*, 1:828). Both the Laudian church and the court masque, Milton concluded, were more concerned with appearance than truth. He also recognized that the masque served to exorcise religious dissent.

In *Eikonoklastes*, he described the royalist treatment of Puritanism in a metaphor that reveals his knowledge of contemporary masquing patterns: "On the scene he [i.e., the author of *Eikon Basilike*] thrusts first an antimasque of two bugbeares Noveltie and Perturbation; that the ill looks and noise of those two may as long as possible drive off all endeavors of a Reformation" (*CP*, 3:533). Milton obviously understood the conventional relation between main masque and antimasque; he may also have been familiar with the antimasques of *Love Restored* (1611) or *Coelum Britannicum*, which demonstrate royalist unwillingness to take Puritan religious or political concerns as anything other than hypocrisy or petty malice.

Because sports played a crucial role in the conflict between Puritans and Royalists and between the various Puritan factions, Milton naturally considered them in some detail in his religious and political polemics of the civil war and the Interregnum. Recreation remained a central concern in his later poetic works as well. As both sides in the recreation controversy had argued, when, where, and, most importantly, how people choose to play is an index to their moral and spiritual state. In *Paradise Lost*, *Paradise Regained*, and *Samson Agonistes*, Milton used sports as a way of defining person and place. Because sports can represent the lure of the world, they may be, if not correctly used, an enemy of faith. Milton thus gave recreation a part in the temptations at the heart of each of his later works.

John Demaray demonstrates how sports in *Paradise Lost* help to illustrate Milton's visions of Heaven, Hell, Eden, and the postlapsarian world. The spiritual distance between Heaven and Hell is reflected with particular clarity in the recreations practiced in each place.[78] When Satan leaves Hell for his moral assault on Eden, his followers amuse themselves in his absence in various ways: some perform military exercises, others devote themselves to music, poetry or oratory, and still others explore the distant reaches of their gloomy world. Milton emphasizes that their sports are diversionary in the profoundest sense, meaningless exercises intended to help the fallen angels forget their loss of Heaven and the absence of their leader. Such exercises merely delude, lend "truce to . . . restless thoughts," ravish the soul, enthrall the senses, and in the case of the oratorical contests "charm / Pain for a while or anguish, and excite / Fallacious hope." Though designed as release from a physically and psychically painful reality, they do not prove restful. The fact that the "ranged powers / Disband, and wand'ring, each his several way / Pursues" indicates the social fragmentation that results from collective disobedience to God. Because each individual's "inclination or sad choice" determines his recreational activity, their sports become divisive (2:521–628). The implication is that apart from God unity, coherence, harmony, and true recreation (understood in its profoundest sense as "re-creation") are impossible.

In contrast, the angels in Heaven entertain themselves with activities that recall triumphal pageantry: "That day, as other solemn days, they spent / In song and dance about the sacred Hill, / Mystical dance" (5:618–27). As Welsford suggests, "they danced the figured ballet which was one of the chief attractions of the masque all over Europe."[79] Significantly, the angels' festivities do not represent time out from work or from devotion to God, for heavenly bliss means that delight equals devotion equals duty. The first Sunday, as Milton depicted it, is "not in silence holy kept," as strict Sabbatarians urged the Sabbath should be, nor observed with the diversionary recreations allowed by the Established church once worship was concluded; rather the entire day is spent in joyous praise of God. Unlike the sports in Hell, which separate the devils into dissociated groups, heavenly recreation unites all the angels in a collective harmony: "No voice exempt, no voice but well could join / Melodious part, such concord is in Heav'n."[80] Indeed something like Charles I's idea of the perfect society, unified and harmonious as its members engage in sports expressing their allegiance to their sovereign, though never realized in Caroline England, finds expression in Milton's vision of the social order in Heaven.

Sports are also important in Milton's account of the human condition in *Paradise Lost*, for the delights of Edenic life are defined by their similarities to and differences from the recreations of fallen man. Demaray has examined the echoes of Renaissance theatrical practices in the Edenic revels of *Paradise Lost*,[81] but the epic offers broader comment on sports in general. As in Heaven, Edenic recreation does not serve as a release from toil or spiritual responsibility. Prelapsarian life is wholly integrated, without a separation of activities into the serious and the playful. Because man had not yet been condemned to earn his bread by the sweat of his face, his work is delightful, intended to provide variety and to enhance the pleasures of sense and appetite. Adam and Eve perform "no more toil / Of thir sweet Gard'ning labor than suffic'd / To recommend cool *Zephyr*, and made ease / More easy, wholesome thirst and appetite / More grateful" (4:327–31). As Adam observes, God intended their work together to encourage love-play, the "sweet intercourse / Of looks and smiles" (9:238–39). Neither do Edenic recreations divert the primal couple from their devotions to God, for they learn God's goodness and at the same time praise him in the very process of gratefully enjoying his creation. Their spiritual growth is also a delightful experience. Raphael's tales have the serious purpose of teaching Adam about his adversary, but they are initiated during his midday rest and are designed to entertain. Adam declares that he listens to his instructor with "delighted ear."

Other distinctions between Eden and the fallen world are illuminated by references to sports. Eden's recreations are characterized by simplicity, spontaneity, and an absence of artifice. The animals disport themselves before Adam and Eve like comic players, with no need of theater, set time of performance, or any formal prearrangements. The young couple find amusement in discourse or an exchange of endearments. Even on so exalted an occasion as Raphael's visit, they have no need, Milton pointedly noted, of the contrivances used by fallen men to give their movements dignity. Adam walks forth to greet his angelic guest:

> . . . without more train
> Accompanied than with his own complete
> Perfections; in himself was all his state,
> More solemn than the tedious pomp that waits
> On Princes, when thir rich Retinue long
> Of Horses led, and Grooms besmear'd with Gold
> Dazzles the crowd, and sets them all agape.
>
> [5:351–57]

So, too, Milton contrasts the sexual delights enjoyed by Adam and Eve with the perversions encouraged by false modes of recreation:

> Here Love his golden shafts imploys, here lights
> His constant Lamp, and waves his purple wings,
> Reigns here and revels; not . . .
>   . . . in Court Amours,
> Mixt Dance, or wanton Mask, or Midnight Ball,
> Or Serenate, which the starv'd Lover sings
> To his proud fair, best quitted with disdain.
>
> [4:763–70]

Milton condemns, along with the romantic distortions of love in his own world, the masques and other kinds of entertainment that fed them. Appropriating the hymenal imagery of the conventional marriage masque—the winged Cupid, the symbolic lamp of constancy—he offers the direct and natural relations between Adam and Eve as a model for what we may call reformed amorous sport.

Eden can provide the model for right recreation in the fallen world because the same principles govern both. Pleasure, for example, if pursued as an end in itself, conflicts with obedience to God. Thus, in the vision of postlapsarian sports that Michael offers the fallen Adam, the sons of Seth are tempted from upright conduct by the daughters of Cain:

> . . . to the Harp they sung
> Soft amorous Ditties, and in dance came on:
> The Men though grave, ey'd them, and let thir eyes
> Rove without rain, till in the amorous Net
> Fast caught, they lik'd, and each his liking chose;
> . . . then all in heat
> They light the Nuptial Torch, and bid invoke
> *Hymen*, then first to marriage Rites invok't;
> With Feast and Music all the Tents resound.
>
> [11:583–92]

Convinced by an over simplified understanding of his Edenic experiences that pleasure is pleasing to God, Adam is comforted by the nuptial festivities and has to be reproved by Michael:

> . . . Judge not what is best
> By pleasure, though to Nature seeming meet,
> Created, as thou art, to nobler end
> Holy and pure, conformity divine.
>
> [11:603–6]

Milton asserts that "God and Nature bid the same," but to the natural man, insufficiently girded by faith and reason, what *seems* best on the basis of immediate sensory appeal alone may conflict with nobler ends. The perceived tension between what is good in God's eyes and what may at the moment feel good—though it is perhaps felt more acutely in fallen world—also troubled the prelapsarian Adam. The sons of Seth thus recreate Adam's own fall. Adam had confessed to Raphael his weakness against "the charm of Beauty's powerful glance" and complained—wrongly, as Raphael pointed out—that God had be-

stowed on Eve "too much ornament." Although he attributes
the fault here to God and later to Eve, it is Adam himself who
is finally to blame for his fall, for he chooses immediate pleasure in the society of Eve over God.

What would have been loosely categorized in the seventeenth century as sports also play a part in the temptations of
Jesus in *Paradise Regained*. In his second temptation, Satan offers the courtly delights of luxurious festivities conducted in
extravagant settings with magnificently dressed courtiers in
attendance. Jesus dismisses them: "Nor doth this grandeur and
magestic show / Of luxury, though call'd magnificence, . . .
allure mine eye, / Much less my mind" (4:110–14). He is
equally unimpressed by elaborate praise of the sort purveyed
in masques and other kinds of formal panegyrics: "what honor
that, / But tedious waste of time to sit and hear / So many
hollow   compliments   and   lies, /   Outlandish   flatteries?"
(4:122–25).

Later, in an episode that has provoked extensive critical controversy, Jesus spurns Satan's offer of the pleasures of learning,
which include musical, literary, and oratorical recreations. As
he distinguishes between the mere knowledge Satan offers and
true wisdom, he also distinguishes between excessive and proper,
harmful and instructive uses of leisure.[82] His unspoken premise is that learning is shallow and pleasure empty when pursued in isolation from God. In his insistence on spiritual liberty
as the freedom to work for communion with God, not the
license to engage in morally indifferent acts, and in his assertion that nothing is indifferent to God, that all man's ways
have meaning only in reference to God, he makes much the
same assumptions that moved Milton earlier in his masque.

Samson Agonistes reflects similar attitudes to sports. Although William Kerrigan probably overstates the importance
of recreation in the tragedy when he asserts that its theme is
the conflict between godly and blasphemous play, still sports
do serve in *Samson* as a means of defining character. Samson
identifies the flaw that caused his downfall as pride, expressed
in his indulgence in amorous and other sensual delights.[83]
Choosing pleasure over his vocation as a judge in Israel, he

broke his pledge to God in order to please his wife. Their views on festivities also serve to define the limitations of Dalilah and Manoa. Dalilah's vision of herself as the object of a heroic cult, venerated as the savior of her country in "solemn festivities," reveals, as Radzinowicz suggests, her false understanding of a nation: for her it is a political structure rather than a community shaped by godly principles. Similarly, Manoa's resolve to raise a monument where his son will be honored as a cultic hero on appropriate feast days gives evidence of his incomplete understanding of what Samson's final act means.[84]

Finally, the Philistines are revealed as an iniquitous people largely through the descriptions of their religious festivals. Puritans had argued that the popular behavior on feast days of those partaking in officially approved sports revealed the moral bankruptcy of Caroline religious and civil institutions. Samson in a comparable vein finds the Philistines "on thir Holy-days / Impetuous, insolent, unquenchable" (ll. 1418–22). Like the pastimes sanctioned by the *Declaration*, the Philistine celebrations are instituted by the church; they take place in the Temple of Dagon, described as a spacious theater "where all the Lords and each degree / Of sort, might sit in order," like the audience at a masque (ll. 1607–8). In countless tales about immoral revelers struck down with their iniquities on them, contained in *Histrio-mastix* and *Divine Tragedies*, William Prynne had warned that the day of reckoning would eventually come and that God's hand would strike down those who delight in improper sports. In much the same vein, the Semichorus in *Samson* claims that the Philistines destroyed themselves, literally by bringing Samson to entertain them, and morally by their sins:

> While thir hearts were jocund and sublime,
> Drunk with Idolatry, drunk with Wine
> . . . .
> Among them hee [God] a spirit of frenzy sent,
> Who hurt thir minds,
> And urg'd them on with mad desire
> To call in haste for thir destroyer;
> They only set on sport and play

Unwittingly importun'd
Thir own destruction to come speedy upon them.
                    [ll. 1669–70; 1675–81]

Milton may have intended us to contrast with the kinds of
sports detailed in *Samson Agonistes*—Samson's, Dalilah's, Manoa's and the Philistines'—the recreational experience that play
itself affords. He argued in the critical statement prefacing the
play that tragedy is "the gravest, moralest, and most profitable
of all other Poems" and that because of its cathartic power it
has a truly recreating effect on its audience (*CPP*, p. 549). The
case can be made that not only *Samson* but all Milton's mature
works are examples of reformed recreation.

Acutely aware of the instructive capacity of his art, Milton
believed in the poet's responsibility to inform, enlighten, and
reform his readers. He also recognized that literature is recreation, that, as Renaissance critics so often emphasized, literature teaches by delightful examples. Thus, he argued that
together with the cathartic effect, the pleasure of tragedy depends on successful poetic mimesis. Tragedy "by raising pity
and fear, or terror, purge[s] the mind of those and such like
passions . . . and reduce[s] them to just measure with *a kind
of delight*, stirr'd up by reading or seeing those passions well
imitated" (*CPP*, p. 549; my italics). Literature, in general,
can offer compelling moral instruction, "teaching over the whole
book of sanctity and vertu through all the instances of example
with such delight to those especially of soft and delicious temper who will not so much as look upon Truth herselfe, unless
they see her elegantly drest" (*CP*, 1:817–18). In "Ad Patrem,"
composed roughly during the period when Milton was writing
Comus, he explained that the intellectual content of the lyrics
makes music, wedding voice and verse superior to any other
because it is more pleasing: "Denique quid vocis modulamen
inane iuvabit / Verborum sensusque vacans, numerique loqua-
cis?" ["And now, to sum it all up, what pleasure is there in
the inane modulation of the voice without words and meaning
and rhythmic eloquence?"] (*CPP*, p. 84). The delightful aspects of poetry were of immense importance to Milton, but he
never divorced delight from profit.

The same union of pleasure and instruction that he sought in his other works informs his masque. The Ludlow masque is indeed entertaining, even at points amusing. The original audience would have been pleased by the neat parallels Milton draws between the world of his fiction and their own. That it was acted by children probably made some episodes comic, particularly the philosophic debate of the two little Egerton boys. The use of dance, music, and spectacle surely heightened the charm in performance. The masque contains other delights for those sensitive to its poetic beauties. Henry Wotton praised its "Dorique delicacy," and more recent critics have commented on the musical qualities of its verse.

In characteristic fashion, Milton invested the masque with instructive value: as Ben Jonson had prescribed, it speaks to higher mysteries as well as to the immediate occasion of a festive gathering. Masques commonly transcended their limited occasions; as we have seen, Charles I even conceived of the masque as a vehicle for promulgating his politics. But the particular fusion of delight and instruction that Milton achieved in his masque was something new, in aesthetic terms even revolutionary. The truths he wished to convey required a radical reformation of the form, a revision of its conventional patterns of thought and structure, and a new kind of recreational experience.

CHAPTER TWO

The Journey: Transformations in Character and Plot

PROBABLY THE MOST RADICAL CHANGES MILTON MADE in received generic tradition grew out of his daring treatment of the aristocrats who participated in *Comus*. In view of the parts they assumed, the Egerton children can scarcely be considered masquers at all. Milton freed them from the conventional muteness and dignified passivity, allowing them to speak and in their roles as the Lady and her Brothers to make choices that determine the action. This in itself was a bold innovation. Although in French entertainments, the nobility habitually took speaking parts (even the parts of villains), the attempt to introduce the practice in England had met with such resistance that it never replaced the native convention of more decorously restricted roles.[1] Milton took a further step in removing the protection of propriety that surrounded masquers: he released them from their traditional psychic immobility.

William Empson has suggested that "all characters are on trial in any civilized narrative."[2] But the masque—highly "civilized" as an elaborate and encompassing expression of late Renaissance culture—hardly bears out Empson's maxim. Its most important characters are not in any sense on trial. The masquers are not submitted to the critical judgment of the audience, but unambiguously represent the values and ideals that the masque as a whole glorifies. The very social, political, and occasional context of the work ensured that the performers would be immune from criticism. As a ritualistic affirmation of shared convictions, the masque encouraged complicity, not a judgmental tension between spectacle and spectator.

Milton saw the form as it was handled at court, not as civilized at all, but as the corrupt product of a perverted society. He made a principle much like Empson's basic in his reform

of the masque. Unlike the usual masquers, his do not unequivocally represent the assumptions of the masque in its entirety.
The critical debate about his masque demonstrates that it is
not immediately evident, as it would have been in a conventional masque, which of the characters is "right." Certainly
Comus is not the poet's spokesman. But are the Brothers in
their long philosophical musings? Is the Lady? Or are we to
believe only the Attendant Spirit and to assume that the truth
of the matter is presented only in the prologue and epilogue?[3]
The problem is that masques normally speak in stark contrasts, in black and white; but Milton's demands that we perceive an extended range of intermediate grays. We cannot simply
ask, "Is he or she right?" We must ask, "How right?" and
"Right in what sense?" as we test veracity against dramatic
context.

In my view, the Lady and her brothers, while not completely mistaken as Comus is, have only an incomplete and
imperfect perspective. During the course of the masque, they
undergo an educational experience that alters their basic assumptions about themselves and their world.[4] They are, like
dramatic characters, to be judged against the larger thematic
patterns developed poetically throughout the work but fully
articulated only by the Attendant Spirit, who alone has true
vision. In the children's development, Milton offers a paradigm of the moral life and by manipulating our aesthetic response involves us, his audience, in a parallel development.

Milton's shift to a more dramatic conception of character in
the masque parallels his more dramatic handling of incident.
Traditional masques, as Rosamund Tuve put it, "do not have
plots, but designs, 'devices.'" Unlike plays, which develop according to a narrative sequence, masques are iconic, or to use
Jonson's term they operate like a *hinge*.[5] The controlling myth
unfolds from a contrast of antimasque and main masque. Much
as a hinge enables a door to open, so the stock devices of the
masque open its myth to reveal a figurative identification of
the fiction with real people and the real life of the court. Since
a masque is a dynamic emblem, the very process of unfolding
in itself constitutes a slight but distinct plot. Milton goes beyond such minimal action to create what approaches dramatic

narrative. That his masque does not develop iconically is clear when readers try to assign symbolic meanings to its elements and incidents. Particularly troublesome are Sabrina, the children's reception at Ludlow, Ludlow itself, and the earl who, while he takes no active part, as the ranking dignitary present demands some place in a reading of the work.[6]

The practical problem Milton faced was this: if the Lady and her brothers were to be developing characters, the simple opening out of an emblem would not do for the plot. He needed a more elaborate handling of action that offered adequate motives for the changes in his central characters and gave them the opportunity to express their gradually expanding comprehension. His solution was to design a series of linked episodes that comes close to plotting of the sort we expect in drama. After the introductory matter of the Attendant Spirit's opening speech and Comus's self-revelation, the episodes follow in rapid succession: the Lady's experience of her isolation; her encounter with Comus; the brothers' experience of isolation; their encounter with the Attendant Spirit disguised as Thyrsis; the temptation scene; the brothers' intrusion into Comus's palace and their expulsion of the sorcerer with the aid of the Attendant Spirit and his magical herb, haemony; the Sabrina episode; the final celebration at Ludlow; and, the Spirit's parting advice.[7]

The plot Milton developed in *Comus* shows the same kind of "decentering of the crisis" that Patricia Parker has noted in *Paradise Lost*.[8] The traditional masque has two climactic moments: the first when forces of the main masque either dispel or reform elements of disorder; the second when the revels begin, the masque opens out to encompass the world of the court, and the distinction between fiction and reality is obliterated. Milton dissipates the impact of these two conventional highpoints in a way that forces us to focus less on the turning points themselves than on the means whereby they are effected. First, he does not sharply distinguish antimasque from main masque. The representatives of each meet and interact extensively as they do verbal battle. The outcome of their encounter is not decisive. Although Comus is finally banished, the effects of his magic are overcome, not directly by the pres-

ence or even the actual exertions of the aristocratic participants, but indirectly by agents of release. The process of release
is itself prolonged by the use of multiple agents: the Attendant Spirit, haemony, and Sabrina. Second, by the time the
masque opens out into the real world at Ludlow, the process
of simply getting there has so absorbed our interest that the
arrival is anticlimactic. By giving his masque so involved a
structure, Milton gave up the startling contrasts and conver-
sions of other masques; he chose a more subtle development
that allowed, among other things, a testing of his characters
against the settings and circumstances in which they are placed.

Although far more dramatic in its handling of person and
plot than other examples of the form, Milton's masque remains
in important respects very much a masque. As Samuel Johnson
recognized, the brothers make speeches instead of engaging in
dialogue, and even the most exciting scene in the masque, the
debate between Comus and the Lady, needs "a brisker recip-
rocation of objections and replies" to rank as successful dramatic exchange. The speeches are as much oratorical as dramatic.
Milton uses the presentational techniques traditional in the
masque as well the representational tactics of drama.[9] His
work is also masquelike in the special way it reflects its occasion. The Egerton children, Henry Lawes, the earl, and the
guests gathered to enjoy the masque remain essentially themselves, and the Ludlow within the masque is nearly identical
to the real Ludlow. In addition, the work performs the masque's
two occasional functions of complimenting and myth-making,[10]
although Milton changes the grounds for praise and creates a
myth that does not draw on the usual royalist verities.

Although he did not wholly transform masque into play,
Milton evidently marked two elements, person and incident,
for what approaches dramatic development. The reasons for his
selective application of dramatic technique are not hard to find.
First, as we have seen, he objected to the inflated praise of
noble and royal participants in contemporary masques, which,
he felt, cast men as veritable gods exempt from the frailties,
responsibilities, and moral demands that pertain to other men.
His masque illustrates the practical limitations of human power,
even of the power of virtue, as well as the resilience and ulti-

mate invincibility of the resolved soul. The Lady and the Brothers submit themselves to dramatic process. We need not, as we must with conventional masquers, accept their moral character on the basis of such slender evidence as the beauty of their costumes, the skill of their dance, the grandeur of the scenes through which they move, the harmony of the music that attends them, and the speeches of praise addressed to them. Instead, we judge their speeches and actions much as we do those of dramatic characters.

Milton's increased dramatization of the masque also derived from an intensely dramatic moral vision, a conviction that life does proceed according to the stark and facile contrasts of good and evil or the triumphant revelations of virtue that occur in conventional masques. Milton consistently assumed that good and evil are not self-evident, that the world is a baffling place in which moral judgments are hard to come by. The *Commonplace Book* contains several passages that reveal his early preoccupation with the deceptiveness of appearances: "In moral evil much good can be mixed and that with remarkable cunning"; good men often "at first glance seem to be of no worth"; and reciprocally "Whatever seems pleasing at first view must not immediately be called virtue" (*CP*, 1:362–65).

Because of the moral complexities he faces, the virtuous man cannot expect to sustain himself solely through faith and a commitment to upright living. Virtue demands acute powers of reasoning and a store of practical knowledge, and these survival skills must be acquired and kept finely honed by continuing practice. As Milton recognized, temptation—if resisted— is beneficent and even necessary for spiritual growth. The virtuous life is an ongoing dramatic process. One must struggle to live by moral ideals, which finally can be realized only imperfectly in this life. In addition, virtuous living demands a search for truth, an effort to discern the divine—that is, a struggle against falsehood and a continuous testing of apparent truths. Because truth reveals itself imperfectly in the fallen world, it can be perceived only piecemeal, one tentative step at a time.

Throughout his writings, Milton consistently portrayed the lives of those who strive for virtue and for truth as a sequence of conflicts that shape character. The thematic insights contained in the early poems, "On the Morning of Christ's Nativity" and "Lycidas," are not set forth as fully apprehended from the outset. The persona in each traces a pattern of trial and error, undergoing a process of development as he gropes slowly for truth. In the "Nativity Ode," the speaker must discard his mistaken hope that the coming of Christ will immediately initiate a golden age in order to achieve a more realistic sense of how the Incarnation affects the interaction of nature and grace in the world. Similarly, in "Lycidas," the persona must readjust his notions about fame, the relation between man and nature, and the significance of Edward King's loss before he can achieve the consoling and illuminating vision of Lycidas apotheosized and then move on to new pastures, new problems.

Much the same sort of dramatic process takes place in the late poetry. Adam, Eve, and Satan in *Paradise Lost* are developing characters shaped by experiences that force them to crucial choices. Milton's dynamic view of virtue is reflected in his portrayal of the prelapsarian state as involving "radical growth and process."[11] The perfection of Milton's Heaven is also, according to Arnold Stein, an evolving state that includes choice and trial—a conception of bliss that he sees as a reflection of the inward "spiritual striving of post-Reformation man." Moreover, the narrator of *Paradise Lost*, in the view of Ann Ferry, and the reader himself, according to Stanley Fish, undergo a gradual process of enlightenment, as they are tried by the aesthetic and moral experience the epic offers. Most discussion of *Samson Agonistes* focuses on the spiritual development of the title character. In *Paradise Regained*, even Christ comes only gradually to understand his special vocation and to prove himself through his conflict with Satan; for, as Mother Mary Christopher Pecheux explains, "Christ, the sinless man, must show intellectual acumen in a moral context."[12] Milton consistently links virtue with knowledge and treats the virtuous life as a process rather than as a fixed state of being.

The prose, too, incorporates moral dynamism as subject and rhetorical strategy. *Of Education*, for example, treats learning as a lifelong program of personal development that is not simply the passive accumulation of facts and skills, but instead something that demands the active testing and refining of knowledge through experience. John Huntley's perception that Milton in the *Reason of Church Government* casts his readers as developing characters—they are slowly educated as they presumably gain insight from reading the tract—is probably applicable to his other controversial works.[13] Milton frequently treats his persona as a developing figure who offers in his own gradual growth toward understanding a model for the reader's response. In his *Christian Doctrine*, he explicitly describes the spiritual life as a process of growth that demands a continuing struggle between faith and sin (*CP*, 6:508–13).

Perhaps Milton's most memorable statement on the moral ambiguity of the world and man's consequent need to struggle to attain truth and retain integrity occurs in the famous passage in *Areopagitica* in which he finds a use even for bad books: "It was from out of the rinde of one apple tasted, that the knowledge of good and evill as two twins cleaving together leapt forth into the World. . . . As therefore the state of man now is; what wisdome can there be to choose, what continence to forbeare without the knowledge of evill? He that can apprehend and consider vice with all her baits and seeming pleasures, and yet abstain, and yet distinguish, and yet prefer that which is truly better, he is the true warfaring [wayfaring?] Christian" (*CP*, 6:482–84). Implicit here is the concept of the good temptation that remains throughout Milton's writings basic to his explanation of why evil exists in a divinely ordered world. In the *Christian Doctrine*, he elaborated the point more fully: "Good temptations are those which God uses to tempt even righteous men, in order to prove them . . . to exercise their faith or patience, . . . or to lessen their self-confidence and prove them guilty of weakness, so that they may become wiser, and others may be instructed" (*CP*, 6:338). Another theme expressed in *Areopagitica* which pervades the masque is the idea—distinctively Protestant in inspiration—that virtue is derived from living in the world rather than apart from it.[14]

In the light of his consistency on the matter, it is not surprising that we see in *Comus* the same moral assumptions apparent in works produced before and long after it. As Stanley Fish points out, we confront in the masque a world in which good and evil are almost indistinguishable. The reader is intentionally confused, is tempted into false judgments, and comes to know truth and to understand virtue (though incompletely) only through having experienced their contraries.[15] But Milton's protagonists, as well as his readers, undergo a process of development.

Although *Comus* does not include the chivalric *materia* that pervaded conventional masques of the time, it uses some themes and perspectives associated with the romance. If we define the romance as "a form which simultaneously quests for and postpones a particular end, objective, or object," as a literary mode that occupies "that liminal or preliminary space of 'trial' which is the romance's traditional place of testing," then Milton's masque with its tangled forest, its wanderers, and its postponements is romantic in inspiration. Like Bunyan, Milton transmutes the knight's quest into a pilgrim's progress, and the reader himself, along with the protagonists in the fiction, is implicated in typical romantic fashion as a fellow pilgrim.[16]

Milton did not attribute to the Egertons the uncontested, fully achieved virtue of conventional masquers. The Lady and her brothers are at the outset of the masque morally incomplete. Theirs is a youngling virtue that is converted through trial by what is contrary into a force more active, more informed, and more capable of defending itself in a threatening world. The children are not given the elevated but falsifying roles that masquers conventionally had been granted; neither are they praised for titular nobility, hereditary honors, or such trivial achievements as elegant posture and fine dancing. *Comus* offers a standard of heroism attainable by anyone, the heroism of personal sanctity.

Milton's dramatic vision of life found vivid expression in the central device of the masque—the journey. As Maynard Mack suggests, the masque depicts a spiritual pilgrimage: it "is clearly in some sense an emblem of the perplexity and obscurity of mortal life, which constitutes God's trial of the soul."[17] The journey that is central to Milton's *Comus* draws on the religious motif of the pilgrim's progress, a motif as old as the wanderings of the Children of Israel and most familiar in the travels of Christian in Bunyan's paradigm for the life of the pious

Protestant. In selecting the device, Milton followed the lead of the literary master whom he was to pronounce a better teacher than Scotus or Aquinas. The quests of Spenser's knightly Virtues for moral fulfillment have their counterpart in *Comus*. The travels of Milton's young heroes toward their father's home provide the basic plot. The physical journey of the fiction offers occasion for and indeed becomes a metaphor for an inner progress of psychic growth. *Comus* reflects the postmedieval understanding of the image of the pilgrimage, which Donald R. Howard has described: it has "turning points and crossroads, and a return"; it "is marked off by moral crises and choices; its goal is growth in character." [18]

The religious journey is a venerable motif that has had relevance to many ages and cultures, but Milton's use of it in *Comus* was particularly timely. Coolidge argues that the wayfaring, warfaring believer's continuous trial is a stock element in the general Protestant "rhetoric of suffering," and he cites examples to show that Anglicans on occasion, as well as Puritans, had recourse to the device. Lewalski has identified some of the biblical sources for the metaphor and shown that it was incorporated not only into narratives but also into introspective lyrics of the seventeenth century. But as Haller has eloquently demonstrated, the device was particularly identified with Puritans during the anxious years before the war. [19] Emphasizing the special relevance of the motif to their trials, prewar Puritan divines embroidered the pilgrimage with endless detail and ingenuity, counseling and comforting, as they advised how to prepare for the journey, what companions, provisions, and weapons to take along, how to find one's way, what obstacles would appear and how they would be overcome. *Comus*, with its central device of the journey and its focus on companions, obstacles, and aids, draws on what had become a commonplace in religious and moral writings.

Transferring the motif from religious to secular art posed fewer problems than we might expect. By introducing the journey into a masque, Milton did not so much innovate as exhume, revitalize, and to some degree reshape an early masquing practice that had long been in disfavor but had recently regained acceptance among his contemporaries. The masque's origins in the festive pastimes of mumming and disguising linked it with the literal fact of a procession or a journeylike progress.[20] The practical problem of moving revelers in to dance, offering gifts, or engaging in games and then removing them found a convenient artistic solution in the fiction that they were travelers who had arrived from distant parts and needed to move on. The journey remained an important feature in the earliest Jacobean court productions. Samuel Daniel's two masques, presented early in James's reign, are little more than processionals of masquers who dance and offer gifts to the monarch. In both pieces, the masquers' entry and exit are explained as stages in a journey that brings them to court and then necessitates their sudden departure.

Jonson's first two masques, like Daniel's, are processional in structure. He, however, understood more fully than his predecessor the implications of the device. A journey needs a motive, a desire for some end which will, when achieved, presumably change the traveler in some way. In *Blacknesse* (1605) and its sequel, *Beautie* (1608), the journey is treated as a quest for self-perfection and thus implies character development. In the first of the two masques, Ethiopian nymphs (the Queen and her ladies) after reading what poets have written about beauty become dissatisfied with their dark skins. They are advised by an oracle that a remedy will be found in a land the name of which ends in TANNIA. After a long quest, the nymphs approach their destination, Britannia. The masquers' darkness is blanched, not in this work, but in its sequel three years later. In *Beautie*, after the travelers have overcome various obstacles, they finally arrive at the English court where their blackness is transformed to beauty by King James's presence. As D. J. Gordon has demonstrated, both masques draw extensively on Platonic and Neoplatonic thought, and the journey takes on the significance of a Platonic ascent. The nymphs' quest represents Love's striving for Beauty, a striving that purifies the lovers.[21]

The central device of the masque, the quest for perfected beauty, posed practical difficulties for Jonson. Although it has the obvious advantage of giving the monarch a central place in the fiction—as destination—without requiring his direct involvement, it denigrates the masquers by positing a flaw in them that needs repair. Apparently aware of the unflattering implications, Jonson ingeniously argues near the conclusion of *Beautie* that the masquers' blackness is in fact beauty when viewed in the light given off by the English sun-king. The Ethiopian nymphs thus do not need a new skin but only a new scene in which they can be properly beheld.

Jonson's effort to set things right did not entirely convince his audience. Not only did it play havoc with the Platonic scheme, but considerable feeling remained that it was indecorous to cast noble personages as black nymphs. Dudley Carleton, for one, complained that "Theyr black faces, and hands . . . was a very lothsome sight, and I am sory that strangers should see owr court so strangely disguised."[22] In part, Carleton was reacting to the fiction of the masque itself. Obviously unimpressed by Jonson's explanations, he was convinced that blackness is an imperfection. At the same time he revealed a basic assumption about the nature of masquers that was to affect the entire development of the form: masquers must possess an unobscured beauty and grace that bespeaks their nobility and the glory of the English court; they cannot therefore be treated dramatically.

Jonson himself was apparently sensitive to the question of decorum raised by *Blacknesse* and *Beautie*. In his preface to the *Haddington Masque*, a wedding entertainment presented at court several months before *Beautie*, he spoke directly to objections of the sort that Carleton had raised: "The worthy custome of honouring worthy *marriages*, with these noble *solemnities*, hath, of late yeeres, advanc'd it selfe frequently with us; to the reputation no lesse of our *court*, then nobles. . . . It behooues then us, that are trusted with a part of their honor, in these *celebrations*, to doe nothing in them, beneath the dignitie of either."[23] Social decorums thus complicated the artistic task of devising a masque. Jonson needed some sort of dramatic interest, some kind of tension or conflict. Daniel's pallid processionals had failed to please, but subjecting the masquers to a process of development—even in the most minimal way as in *Blacknesse*—was not an acceptable alternative.

Jonson found the solution to his dilemma in the development of the antimasque, foreshadowed in *Hymenaei* (1606) and realized in *Queenes* (1609). Stephen Orgel has demonstrated the nature and importance of the pattern Jonson uses in the latter masque: a moral and thematic distinction is drawn between the opening episodes of disorder in the antimasque and the aristocratic revelry of the main masque, with the transformation scene providing a central dramatic moment.[24] After *Beautie*, Jonson abandoned the journey as a main principle of structure and focused on the narrative and thematic development inherent in the process of ordering disorder. The masquers could stand as static manifestations of fully realized ideals, unchanging and largely insulated from direct contact with their opposites.

This masquing pattern using static masquers and the transformation plot was characteristic of nearly all Jonson's mature masques. Even *Neptunes Triumph* (1623), which is about the return journey of Prince Charles from Spain after the abortive attempt to arrange a Spanish marriage, depends on a central transformation rather than on a progress. The pattern Jonson developed in *Queenes* elaborated in his subsequent masques was observed by other writers of the period such as Campion, Marston, Chapman, and Beaumont.

The only major masque, appearing after *Beautie* but before the new Caroline style took hold, to deviate from the transformation pattern was Jonson's *Pleasure Reconciled to Virtue* (1618). The protagonist of the opening episodes is Hercules, presented not as a strong man but as a moral hero whose journey through life is temporarily interrupted when he pauses to choose between the ways of vice and virtue.[25] After Jonson's hero withstands two temptations and receives praise for his virtue, he is dismissed and the masquers appear. Prince Henry and his entourage, described as young knights who have just completed their education on Mount Atlas ("the *hill* of *knowledge*"), descend to court ("*Hesperides*, faire Beauties garden") to display their moral accomplishments as they perform their parts in the main masque.[26]

The central pattern of *Pleasure Reconciled* is a journey rather

than a central transformation. But while it results in an epi-
sodic plot not unlike that in Milton's *Comus* (the multiple
temptations in Jonson's have their counterpart in Milton's
multiple incidents of release), it does not imply character development on the part of the masquers. Jonson observed established decorums instead of following the device of the journey
to its logical conclusion. The young prince and his fellows
remain static; they do not themselves come into contact with
vice. Only Hercules, serving as a surrogate or stand-in for them,
undergoes temptations that try and strengthen his integrity.[27]

The masquers enter only after Hercules has proved by the
successful completion of his trials that pleasure need not be
vicious but can be reconciled with virtue. For them there are
no temptations to face because through Hercules' efforts a
"cessation of all iars / 'twixt *Vertue* & hir noted opposite, /
Pleasure" has been declared for the duration of the masque.[28]
Even before the masquers enter, we are assured that they are
already virtuous and that their participation in the masque
will not in any way change them. Jonson thus allowed for a
mere display, not a test, of the young nobles' characters.

Pleasure Reconciled concludes with an exhortation to all participants—masquers and spectators—to return to the hill of
virtue once the masque has ended, to strive for increasing wisdom, and to continue their moral growth. Jonson observed the
generic decorums to the extent that his masquers are not developing characters within the masque itself; but he bent them
enough to suggest that human virtue is never perfect and that
the masquers need to continue their development in real life.

Milton's masque, like *Pleasure Reconciled*, concludes with a
reminder of the further journeys that the moral life entails.
But it also recounts a journey that shapes and changes its aristocratic travelers who do not merely display their virtue. In
dramatic confrontations their moral fiber is tested and
strengthened by trial. Although *Comus* and *Pleasure Reconciled*
have much in common—so much that it seems most unlikely
that Milton did not know the earlier work[29]—a comparison
between the two reveals the advances Milton made in plotting
and characterization and the extent to which he deviated from
established aesthetic, social, and political conventions. In *Co-*

mus, Milton neither resorted to the usual transformation plot nor observed the decorums of person that Jonson maintained.

With the exception of *Pleasure Reconciled*, *Comus* has less in common with Jacobean than with Caroline masques, which Milton could have come to know through performance and presentation copies in the possession of Henry Lawes or the Egerton family. Critics have noted resemblances in central mythic device, theme, and language between Milton's masque and Caroline productions, particularly *Tempe Restored*; but the most striking point of similarity is the use of the journey motif as the basis for characterization and plotting.

Caroline masques revived the scheme that Jonson had tried in *Blacknesse* and *Beautie* but discarded as unworkable: the device of a Platonic ascent, with traveling masquers who seek Beauty personified by a royal figure and eventually undergo a purification. In those masques in which Charles participated, the queen, seated in state, was cast as the end of all quests, the embodiment of Divine Beauty. The masquers, unlike their Jacobean counterparts, are not static embodiments of achieved virtue; but they are not tainted by the obvious imperfection of Jonson's blackened nymphs either. They are carefully presented as incomplete rather than flawed, attaining thus a compromise between the dignified stasis expected of Jacobean masquers and the character change demanded by the Platonic scheme. The Caroline masquer is fully virtuous, at least in intent, and yet becomes even better by his participation in the masque. As Charles danced his journey toward the ideal beauty of his queen, he generally played a Heroic Lover, who demonstrates his superiority by undertaking his quest but achieves his virtuous ends only during the course of the performance.

Occasionally the development of the Heroic Lover was the central action of the Caroline masque, as in Townshend's *Albion's Triumph* (1632). As embodiments of Heroic Love, Charles and his fellow masquers undergo a process of character development, which was repeated with minimal variation in other masques of the time. Wounded by the arrows of Diana and Cupid, the masquers are conquered by Love and subdued by Chastity. Their apparent defeat is paradoxically a triumph, for they are freed from sensual strivings and rendered obedient and receptive to a higher love. The king himself becomes divine through successfully completing his Neoplatonic journey of psychic growth.[30]

The masquers, however, were not the only developing figures associated with Caroline masques. These works actively tried to involve their audiences in a journey, to encourage on the part of the spectators a Neoplatonic ascent. At the conclusion of *Coelum Britannicum*, for example, the royal couple, seated together in state, become the appropriate goal toward which the onlookers should strive. Carefully interweaving the moral and political implications of the Platonic journey, a presenter praises as successful questers those courtiers whose participation in the masque—whether as masquers or as admiring spectators—presumably signals their devotion to the royal couple. They are "Brave spirits, whose advent'rous feet / Have to the mountain's top aspired."[31]

In *Tempe Restored*, Townshend goes even farther in drawing spectators into a loving journey toward Beauty and submission to the monarch. The main masque offers a series of spectacles that constitute stages, or episodes, in the audience's ascent. Following an antimasque dominated by Circe and her beasts, our attention is drawn away from corrupting and inferior objects of earthly love to the heavens. First, there is a dance by young aristocrats, who appear as Influences. They represent the forces of heavenly bodies that affect life on earth and mediate our movement to higher spheres. Next, singers seated on a mechanical cloud appear as the eight spheres. Above them, we then see lady masquers who play the fixed stars. Finally above all sits Divine Beauty, that is, Henrietta Maria playing the Primum Mobile. As the sequence suggests, the very act of seeing the masque leads the spectators upward toward the apotheosized queen, and the visual journey culminates with the theatrical image of the royal couple united in love.

This final spectacle of royalty signals the conclusion of the journey for masquers and spectators, and indeed the end of all journeying. Caroline masques inevitably end with peaceful vistas—pastoral, celestial, architectural—which imply stability. Portraying the royal couple as figurations of Ideal Forms not only afforded acceptably elevating praise, but also asserted the inviolable fixity of the monarchy as an institution. The poetry with which Caroline masques conclude affirms that time, evil, and disorderly passions have been conquered and immutable perfection achieved. Thus *Chloridia* closes with the triumph of an eternal spring over inclement weather. In *Tempe Restored*, as in *Albion's Triumph*, unpredictable and uncontrolled appetites are quelled. The *Triumph of Peace* ends with the thought that the royal couple, attended as they are by personifications of Truth and Eternity, can through their favor conquer the process of aging. In the final scene of *Coelum Britannicum*, those who have completed their ascent toward the royal couple are liberated from further strife: "Here from the toiling press retired, / Secure from all disturbing evil."[32] The traditional moral and spiritual implications of the Neoplatonic quest are subordinated to political aims. The royalist message is clear: the individual's struggle for self-perfection, for apprehension of God and goodness, finds its proper end in devotion to the king.

Caroline masques habitually assume that a compromise between the Neoplatonic extremes of Ideal Forms and the diminished reality of earthly appearances is embodied in the institution of the monarchy. A monarch mediates between extremes, since, according to the traditional doctrine of the king's two bodies, the monarch is at once timeless and temporal; further, according to the principle of divine right, the king is God's ruling agent among men, bringing together heaven and earth in his very person.[33] The journey traced in Caroline masques ends with a vision of sovereignty because the king is a reflection of eternal truth—as royalist apologists urged, the most accurate reflection available on earth.

The Caroline treatment of the journey has important parallels in *Comus*. Milton, too, cast his aristocratic participants as questers who are not flawed but incomplete, and who grow during the course of the masque. He made a similar attempt to extend the fictional journey to include his audience by locating them in reference to the Lady and her Brothers.

But his masque contains significant deviations from the conventional formula—deviations that signal basic changes in his thematic intent. First, the journey of his protagonists is far more difficult and complex than those traced in Caroline masques. It involves an extended trial by what is contrary and demands repeated judgments and deeds on the part of the travelers. The plot of Milton's *Comus*, in short, transcends the simple Neoplatonic strivings depicted in contemporary productions. Second, Milton placed far less of a premium on stasis. Only the antimasque figure, Comus, offers an end to travels and a residence in a realm of timeless pleasure. As the Attendant Spirit's epilogue indicates, the children's arrival at Ludlow does not mean a conclusion to life's journeying. Ludlow can offer little more than a temporary resting place, since virtue requires unending struggle. Royalist masques conclude with an appeal to authority that assumes that truth—completely revealed—is embodied in existing institutions. Milton's *Comus*, however, is the work of a Protestant radical who rejected absolute institutional authority, emphasized the primacy of the individual's pursuit of enlightenment, and posited that stasis is impossible in the fallen world, that individual and collective organisms must either grow spiritually or die.

The most profound and encompassing change of all involves Milton's handling of his Neoplatonic materials. Royal masques turned these materials to political ends; but Milton's prime concerns were moral and theological, not political. Neoplatonic thought figures importantly in Milton's masque; as Sears Jayne notes, references to that currently popular doctrine would have been expected by the original audience gathered at Ludlow and would have made *Comus* more acceptable to spectators accustomed to unraveling the erudite mysteries of Caroline masques.[34] In creating his dissident masque, Milton rejected the politicized philosophy and instead integrated his Neoplatonic *données* into a larger Christian context developed in terms of Puritan concerns of the day. In chapter 4, we will examine Milton's reaction against the epistemological assumptions of Caroline masques, assumptions based on a distinctive blend of political expediency and Neoplatonism. And in chapter 5, we will find that, while Milton bridged the gap between the Platonic extremes of Form and Appearances, he did not offer the monarch as his mediating principle. He instead described a world in which the divine infuses the natural and grace is immediate and available to those who know how to recognize and use it. In addition, Milton characterized the masque's central journey in Christian and Neoplatonic terms, but his classical materials are ultimately modified by and subordinated to his larger theological and moral concerns.

The induction to the masque, which presents the journey as its central device, reveals Milton's method of fusing Christian and Neoplatonic thought:

> Before the starry threshold of *Joves* Court
> My mansion is, where those immortal shapes
> Of bright aereal Spirits live insphear'd
> In Regions milde of calm and serene Ayr,
> Above the smoak and stirr of this dim spot,
> Which men call Earth, and with low-thoughted care
> Confin'ed, and pester'd in this pin-fold here,
> Strive to keep up a frail, and Feaverish being
> Unmindfull of the crown that Vertue gives
> After this mortal change, to her true Servants
> Amongst the enthron'd gods on Sainted seats.
> Yet som there be that by due steps aspire
> To lay their just hands on that Golden Key
> That ope's the Palace of Eternity.   [ll. 1–14]

In the Bridgewater and Trinity Manuscripts, the speaker of these lines is called a "daemon." Although Milton removed this obvious Platonic reference in later versions of the masque, making the heavenly emissary simply a spiritual guardian whose philosophical/theological roots are left vague, the Platonic resonances of the passage as a whole remain.

The Attendant Spirit's evocation of the two realms, "Regions mild of calm and serene Air" and "the smoke and stir of this dim spot / Which men call Earth," may, as B. A. Wright suggests, recall Plato's descriptions of Earth and True Earth in the *Phaedo*. However, it is more likely, as Irene Samuel argues, that Milton was not at this point directly influenced by the Dialogues, and that the masque instead reflects his immersion in Neoplatonic doctrines that would have been accessible to any Renaissance writer.[35] The contrast of the two realms was highly conventional, as was their equation with heaven and earth. The Attendant Spirit draws further on commonplaces in his description of the two ways that men can choose to live

in a dualistic world. While he ignores the first stage in the
Neoplatonic view of human life, the soul's initial descent into
the body, he explains the soul's continuing struggle against its
confinement in the flesh and its victorious reascent to heaven,
the habitat of pure spirit. In effect, the Spirit offers two exis-
tential alternatives: one may accept bodily bondage, or one
may strive to escape the enslavement and regain his heavenly home.

Although the Neoplatonic references are unmistakable, the
induction also contains significant Christian echoes. "Jove" is
a conventional poetic correlative for the Christian God. The
Spirit's description of the regal glory of heaven ("Court," "en-
thron'd," "Palace of Eternity") accords with Biblical renderings
of the Kingdom of Heaven and seems more Christian than
Platonic in inspiration. The soul's struggle with the flesh and
the world is a pervasive theme in Pauline thought. But the
most unambiguously Christian references occur in the terms
for those who aspire to immortality: having lived as "true Servants," paradoxically deriving from service the freedom to proceed to heaven, they will be granted after death "the crown of
Virtue" and will succeed to "sainted Seats."

In his mention of heavenly rewards and the life of service,
Milton evoked New Testament topoi of the Christian believer
as servant, soldier, and athlete. The "crown of Virtue" recalls
the honor accorded the spiritual runner who completes his course
or the good soldier who successfully battles temptation. In
James 1.12, the man who is tried by temptation will obtain
"the crowne of life." According to 1 Peter 5.4, pastors who
faithfully perform their ministerial duties will receive "an incorruptible crown of glory." Second Timothy 2.5 promises that
those who suffer affliction as soldiers of Christ and remain constant in adversity will be crowned. In 1 Corinthians 9.24–25,
Paul urges the congregation to live temperately to win the race
that earns "an incorruptible" crown. In 2 Timothy 4.78, he
brings together the topoi of athlete and soldier, conflating the
prizes for winning a race and for military victory into a single
symbol of spiritual triumph. "I have fought a good fight and
have finished my course: I have kept the faith," Paul exclaims,

and he looks forward to a "crown of righteousness" as his ultimate reward.[36]

Milton's vision of the "true Servant" draws on another biblical commonplace. Christ's parables frequently describe the relation between God and man as that between a king and his servant and the relations among men as those of fellow servants. In Ephesians 6, when Paul offers the practical advice that children should obey their parents and servants their masters, he tempers his support of secular authorities with the reminder that we are all spiritual servants to our heavenly master. Also in this chapter, Paul moves easily from the motif of servant to that of Christian warrior, implying by the association the inherent compatibility, in fact, the near identity, of the two roles.

Milton made frequent use of all three motifs in writings preceding and following *Comus*. He was aware that the three overlap, that the Christian life requires man to be at once a servant to God and not to the world, a warrior staving off spiritual adversaries, and a runner who does not pause in the race but keeps on toward his heavenly goal. Milton also recognized that these three topoi could be subsumed within the larger figure of the spiritual pilgrimage. The famous passage in *Areopagitica*, which I have cited in part above, brings together references to Psyche's labors of service, to a race, and to either warfaring or wayfaring as elements in the journey of spiritual development. Similar Christian allusions in the induction to *Comus* imply that the life of the spiritual pilgrim is at once a race, a series of battles, and a continuing act of service.

The central device of the masque, presented by the Attendant Spirit in his opening speech, thus hinges on the journey motif, which is given Neoplatonic and Christian overtones. As Woodhouse has suggested, the sequence of ideas in the induction implies a movement from the pagan philosophy of the early lines to the theological allusions of the later.[37] In a manner typical of the Renaissance humanist, Milton developed his device in classical terms where the terms are consonant with his theology; but he turned to Christian references at the point where theology departs from or transcends philosophy. The Spirit's Neoplatonic visions of heaven as pure and unchanging, of earth as corrupt, and of worldly-minded men as trapped in vain and futile endeavors are all reasonable versions of their Christian equivalents. The shift comes with the Attendant Spirit's description of the lives of the just. Men need not choose between the Neoplatonic extremes of imprisonment in the body or spiritual ascent, for the tensions between body and soul, heaven and earth, find resolution in the lives of believers who as spiritual pilgrims live in this world but by heavenly ideals.

The implications only introduced and hinted at in the induction are further amplified by poetic and dramatic means throughout the rest of the masque. The spiritual journey not only provides the narrative substructure; it pervades the poetry of the masque as a vital and coherent image pattern summarizing central themes. The repeated poetic references to ambulation and other kinds of bodily motion—which must have been visually reinforced by the movements of the performers—provide an index to inner spiritual states. Mother Mary Christopher Pecheux argues that Milton frequently conceived of sin in the Hebrew sense as a misstep or error.[38] In *Comus*, characters are distinguished morally by the way they walk. For example, Comus's "hatefull steps" obviously contrast with the Lady's "different pace / Of . . . chast footing." The Lady is afforded a glimmer of light to illuminate her pathway through the forest; but as the Elder Brother insists, the vicious soul forever "benighted walks."

The crucial contrast in the work—between those who journey and those who do not—depends on the figure of physical movement. As we have seen, the Attendant Spirit establishes the distinction between men who choose to remain "confin'd and pester'd" in corruption and those who "by due steps aspire" to reach heaven. Comus and the children obviously fall into opposing categories; but as Milton reveals the moral complexity of the world in *Comus*, it becomes apparent that there is no facile opposition between absolute stasis and clear, linear progression.

Comus, though once a traveler himself "roaving the *Celtick* and *Iberian* fields," currently devotes himself to disturbing the travels of others. His lineage as son of Circe is obvious not only from his genealogy but also from the significance Milton attached to him. His ability to effect a bestial metamorphosis indicates that he is to be understood through the principles of faculty psychology and the ethic of rational control that were familiar in classical and Renaissance treatments of Circe.[39] Leonora Brodwin has shown that Comus is also associated with an enervating idleness that had been part of the Circe myth from its Homeric beginnings. Certainly in Milton's other uses of the myth, the sorceress represents a threat to the individual's vocation.[40] Similarly, he made his Circean antimasque figure the embodiment of a life spent in defiance of man's spiritual calling.

Georgia Christopher has suggested that Milton may have drawn on Luther's treatment of Comus as belly god and patron of carousing—a characterization based on the false etymological derivation of *comessatio* (carousing or revelry) from the god's name. She further demonstrates that carousing or concupiscence was a conventional Protestant figure for the life of the flesh. Milton conceived of the Pauline notion of the flesh in the light of the distinction common in Reformed theology between the unregenerate Adam and the man made new in Christ. Luther, for example, consistently refused to accept the limited orthodox equation of the flesh with sexuality and other physical drives, and instead spoke of the flesh as "the entire realm of sin, which struggle[s] against the realm of the Spirit in the godly." Calvin argued much the same point. Milton, too, asserted that sins of the flesh do not have to do only with the body. When he spoke of the conflict between the flesh and the spirit that confronts all believers, he had in mind the saints' struggle to pursue their calling and to resist allurements to repeat through sin the primal fall.[41] As Comus holds out his cup and offers physical and psychic relief from the toil of spiritual questing, he is advocating that wayfarers remain immersed in the flesh, that they give up trying to live according to God's precepts.

Beyond the obvious moral-spiritual threat he presents, Comus also reflects a recognizable set of social and political atti-

tudes. He is not a vile debauchee who figures forth licentiousness
in its most distasteful form. Brodwin suggests that he represents the drive for personal security and comfort, for "ordinary,
if aristocratic, happiness."[42] The point Milton made by not
depicting Comus as a disgusting belly god is that complacency
is in itself evidence of moral failure. As a reflection of an aristocratic vision of happiness, Comus signifies the immediate
and the extended occasion for the masque. He embodies a moral
threat of particular relevance to the Egertons and their fellow
aristocrats gathered at Ludlow. In the light of the growing
dissension between Loyalists and Puritans, Comus reflects more
specifically the Puritan sense that the upper classes, because of
their obsession with comfort and position, failed to fulfill either
their specific callings as traditional governors or their general
callings as God's righteous people.

The social and political implications of Comus make him a
foreshadowing of Milton's later handling of the Circe myth in
the political tracts. In *Eikonoklastes*, he condemned as victims
of Circe those who did not reject Charles's tyranny because
they feared to upset the status quo. In the *First Defense*, he
again attacked a portion of the English population, as well as
his opponent, Salmasius, as willing victims of Circe for having
preferred personal security before truth and virtue.[43] His underlying assumption is that men confederated in social groups
must, like individuals, continue their journey. Their collective
journey is the process of reformation; they must demand and
use, often at some risk to themselves, the freedom necessary to
evolve toward a reformed state.

Thus, Comus's claim that he can provide relief from the
pain of the spiritual quest has political and moral implications. The language in which he couches his offer—the references to endless pleasure, eternal spring, continuous youth—
pointedly recalls the rewards that royalist masques of the period held forth to onlookers. Comus's message resembles the
propaganda that Charles's poets set forth for him in court productions: submit to my authority, and your quest for truth,
goodness, happiness is over; you will have completed your
journey, for I am your destination, the end of all. On the social
level, Comus urges a compromise of principles for the sake of

stability and order. For the individual, he advocates—as did the king according to Puritan opponents of his policy on sports—sloth and worldly ease in place of the grueling adventures of the *miles Christi.*

Milton, however, tested Comus's promises against his own assumption that life should be a journey toward the divine telos to demonstrate that the pleasant stasis Comus describes is impossible in this life. To ignore the goal of life's journey does not enable anyone to break free of continuing effort and achieve fixity; rather one loses what gives life meaningful direction.

Comus and his followers (and evil in general) perform circular and futile movements. Mimicking the figured dances of conventional masquers, the sorcerer and his monsters enact their own rowdy version as they "beat the ground, / In a light fantastic round" (ll. 143–44). When Comus figuratively links his followers with the unending flux of stars and planets, he is asserting, as Rosamund Tuve suggests, that universal process is purposeless, that "the vast skiey system is nothing but one grand and idiotic whirligig."[44] In view of this undirected activity, we naturally associate Comus and his rout with those who, choosing not to live as pilgrims, "Strive to keep up a frail and Feverish being, / Unmindful of the crown that Virtue gives" and with the Elder Brother's optimistic vision of evil as a self-destructive force that wears itself out in frenzied movement:

> . . . evil on it self shall back recoyl,
> And mix no more with goodness, when at last,
> Gather'd like scum, and setl'd to it self
> It shall be in eternal restless change
> Self-fed, and self-consum'd.   [ll. 593–97]

The Lady and her brothers are, in contrast, defined as travelers with a destination and purpose: they "are coming to attend their Fathers state." Their way leads them along "perplex't paths"; they are "forlorn and wandering passengers." Their movements are uncertain, not because like Comus they have no goal, but because they do not possess the practical knowledge necessary for reaching it. Not knowing is what makes them vulnerable. As the Attendant Spirit explains, Comus and his fellows prey on the uninformed and innocent; they "inveigle and invite th' unwary sense / Of them that pass *unweeting* by the way" (ll. 538–39, italics mine).

Indeed, the Lady and her brothers are guilty of repeated mistakes that so delay and complicate their journey that Milton obviously intended to portray their fallibility. Just as Comus's purposeless whirlings reflect his spiritual life, so their wanderings reflect theirs. The indirections of both reflect the realities of life in the fallen world that make exact straight paths unlikely. But although the children digress from their intended quest, they do not join in the narcissistic involutions of the villain. The Lady and her Brothers never give up the commitment to their destination, and this commitment reflects their continuing belief throughout the masque in the virtuous ideals of the Christian sojourner. Their wanderings indicate not active immorality, but the limitations of uninformed virtue.

Their naiveté leads them into situations that could precipitate a fall from virtue into vice, but that in fact test and strengthen them, refining their untried virtue into a knowledgeable and resilient force. Trials sharpen their ability to judge moral situations, to articulate their judgments, and to act on their choices. Since these matters are the subjects of chapters 4 and 5, here I wish only to suggest the main principles of character development in *Comus*.

The children undergo an educational experience involving conflict and a trial-and-error process. At intervals they gain illumination, but each illumination, while representing a moral advance, leaves them unprepared for the next challenge. Their situation as the masque begins is itself the result of an error. Disoriented and alone in unfamiliar and hostile surroundings, the Lady blames her plight on the "wand'ring steps" of her young escorts and on her own inexperience in what one popular spiritual guidebook of the day called "exact walking."[45] "O where els," she asks, "Shall I inform my unacquainted feet / In the blind mazes of this tangl'd Wood?" (ll. 179–80), and her phrase summarizes the whole subsequent action: it will consist in informing unacquainted feet.

Drawing on the familiar tradition of the Christian wayfarer, Milton cast his Lady as a pilgrim who needs, like the travelers described in contemporary religious writings, various kinds of companions and aids. First, as she inventories her available resources, she realizes that she is defended by her moral integrity, that the "Vertuous mind . . . ever walks attended / By a strong siding champion Conscience" and by Faith, Hope, and the problematical Chastity (ll. 211–15). But such internal aids alone do not enable the Lady to resume her journey, since she lacks certain crucial skills, and needs, in her own words, "the best Land-Pilots art" and "well-practiz'd feet" to navigate the tangled forest. She seeks external help, initially turning to God. Her decision at this point to look beyond herself represents an important phase in her development, a phase paralleled in her two brothers' progress; she tempers her youthful faith in her abilities with a realistic sense of the limits of self-sufficiency.

Her advance in awareness is typically followed by a lapse, when she accepts Comus as a guide. In spite of her mistake, she remains committed to the journey of the virtuous life, trusting herself to Comus only because she believes that he offers a temporary shelter "till further quest." As she leaves with the villain, she prepares herself, not for release from toil, but for the next test her journey will bring.

The brothers' trial by what is contrary is softened into the dialectical process of their philosophic exchange. As the debate begins, the two hold positions that are opposed, but not mutually exclusive. The Younger Brother is a literalist; the Elder Brother, an idealist. While the younger one experiences their isolation in the forest as a separation from friendly social converse, the elder one has a profound sense of alienation from a universe that seems morally chaotic. The Younger Brother is primarily concerned with his sister's physical safety, her discomfort in the cold harsh forest, and her danger from the hunger of possible cannibals or from the lust of rapists. The Elder Brother, however, focuses on the state of his sister's soul, entirely confident that her virtue will not be shaken by whatever temptations she may meet. Their positions shift as each begins to take into account the arguments of the other. The elder

remains convinced that the Lady's moral integrity will survive
intact, but he responds to his younger brother's fears by recognizing his sister's physical insecurity:

> . . . I do not, brother,
> Inferr, as if I thought my sisters state
> Secure without all doubt or controversie:
> Yet where an equall poise of hope and fear
> Does arbitrate th' event, my nature is
> That I encline to hope rather than fear,
> And gladly banish squint suspicion.
>
> [ll. 407–12]

His optimism rests on no simple-minded disregard of physical
reality, but on a logical weighing of possibilities. In turn, the
Younger Brother remains intensely aware of "th' unarmed
weakness of one Virgin / Alone, and helpless" (ll. 582–83),
but he admires his older brother's perspective: "How charming" he exclaims, "is divine Philosophy!" (l. 476).

Although they move toward agreement, the brothers do not
finally take a single position that synthesizes their earlier stands;
their dialogue does not in any sense mark a stopping point in
their personal development either, for further trials await them.
The appearance of Thyrsis now tests their judgment, much as
the appearance of Comus had tested their sister's. Once informed of her danger, they are further tried by the role of
savior-defender that is thrust on them. When the Elder Brother
vows single-handedly to vanquish his sister's abductor, the Spirit
corrects him with kind but firm words:

> . . . here thy sword can do thee little stead,
> Farr other arms, and other weapons must
> Be those that quell the might of hellish charms,
> He with his bare wand can unthread thy joynts,
> And crumble all thy sinews.   [ll. 611–15]

Like his sister, the Elder Brother learns the limitations of self-
sufficiency. The boys manage to drive off the sorcerer, but they
fail in their first attempt to release the Lady and need further
help from the Attendant Spirit as well as from Sabrina.

Presented in the masque as a local goddess and curative force,
Sabrina would have been recognized by Milton's audience from

popular mythology and from the poetry of Spenser and Drayton as a personification of the Severn River. Since the Severn is the traditional border separating the Marches and Wales from the rest of England,[46] the appearance of Sabrina indicates that the children's journey homeward has brought them within the lands governed by their father. But while Sabrina can enable the Lady to regain her mobility, the children do not continue their journey to Ludlow Castle on their own. The Spirit leads them on their remaining journey and protects them lest they again go astray.

The children's repeated mistakes and their need for continuing education are a necessary part of their "trial by what is contrary." Not only is their youngling virtue tested and purified by its encounter with vice, but also truth gradually emerges through experience with error. The children learn a series of lessons regarding their abilities, the nature and power of evil, and the aids and weapons available to them. Their virtue intact and strengthened by trial, they are finally welcomed triumphantly into their parents' presence. Their virtue has not given way under pressure, but their preservation has been due in large part to the assistance of their heavenly guide.

Already at work in *Comus* are certain assumptions regarding free will and personal responsibility that foreshadow Milton's mature stand, which Maurice Kelly has defined as Arminian: "[Arminianism] rejects both the autonomous man of Pelagius, independently working out his own salvation, and the arbitrary God of Augustine, Calvin, and Beza, unconditionally impelling man to an end predestined from eternity. For these it substitutes a synergism wherein the human will cooperates with divine grace to attain an earned rather than a bestowed election to eternal life" (*CP*, 6:80). In his *Christian Doctrine*, Milton explicitly took the Arminian position, rejecting the traditional Protestant doctrines of justification *sola fide* and of good works as merely the product of faith or the evidence of salvation but inessential to justification. He redefined faith and good works to achieve a fusion: "We are justified, then, by faith, but a living faith, not a dead one, and the only living faith is a faith which acts" (*CP*, 6:490). He did not argue for the moral legalism of Thomistic thought or for a doctrine of merit alone; rather he asserted that all man's works are imperfect and are accomplished only by the grace of God. Still, Milton balanced faith against works, merit against free grace, to insist that God's justice and the very existence of a moral system demand that man have some part in effecting his own salvation: "Obviously if religious matters were not under our control, or to some extent within our power and choice, God could not enter into a covenant with us, and we could not keep it, let alone swear to keep it" (*CP*, 6:398).

Several recent critics have shown that Milton's Arminian principles inform *Paradise Lost* and *Samson Agonistes*.[47] Although he did not explicitly espouse the position until fairly late in his career, it is not fair to assume, as some readers have done, that earlier in life he was a strict Calvinist. True, in his religious tracts of the 1640s, Milton specifically attacked Arminians by name (*CP*, 2:293, 519–20). But others of his early writings reflect much the same doctrine of synergistic cooperation between man and God—albeit in a germinal form—that characterizes his later theology. In his introduction to Milton's *Complete Prose*, Kelley suggests that the Arminian position on free will is assumed in *Areopagitica*: "Otherwise, Milton's second argument . . . —his argument from principle—would be an empty one, for trial can purify only those who have freedom of choice." Similarly, in "At a Solemn Music" (1633), Milton suggested that just as man by his fall broke the universal harmony, so he may choose to "answer" the angelic music and "keep in tune with Heav'n."[48] Personal responsibility is also implied in "Elegy VI" (1628), for the vatic poet must prepare himself to receive spiritual and aesthetic inspiration by maintaining purity of life.

Comus, too, depends on Arminian assumptions regarding the moral nature of man and divine involvement in human affairs. The references to indwelling divinity, which Christopher notes, testify to Milton's sense of human virtue as a gift of God. Comus and the Attendant Spirit recognize the infused grace that speaks through the Lady's song and speech.[49] And, as the Elder Brother asserts, her virtue, "if Heav'n gave it, may be term'd her own" (l. 419). Although the children need superhuman aid to sustain them on their way, they are not in

Calvinist terms depraved, for they reveal a remarkable moral strength by remaining unswervingly constant to their destination.

The masque concludes appropriately with the Attendant Spirit's summary of the interaction of human effort and divine grace:

> Mortals that would follow me,
> Love vertue, she alone is free
> She can teach ye how to clime
> Higher than the Spheary chime;
> Or if Vertue feeble were,
> Heav'n itself would stoop to her.
>   [ll. 1018–23]

Man achieves salvation by a combination of virtuous behavior and divine aid, through the struggle and toil of a lifelong spiritual pilgrimage, and through God's gracious involvement in human affairs. The masque begins with the double action of those who "by due steps aspire" and the Attendant Spirit's descent into "the rank vapors of this Sin-worn mold." It closes with a reference to the identical dual action—when the virtuous climb and Heaven stoops—although this time the Spirit's description is couched in hortatory rhetoric, as he urges his auditors to participate in the synergy of divine and human effort.

The virtuous journey through this world to the next does not apply to the Egerton children alone but is extended as a paradigm for Milton's broader audience. He drew his audience into the fiction of the masque, or, perhaps more accurately, he annihilated the distinction between reality and fiction by speaking directly to his audience and thus located the premises on which his fiction is based in real life itself. He cast his initial audience and his subsequent readers as travelers whose wayfaring roughly parallels that of the Lady and her brothers. The parallel is only approximate, since the precise relation Milton established between protagonists and audience-readers, their journey and ours, is a complex one that reflects the poet's sensitivity to fine nuances of response.

The masque traditionally depended on an assumed empathy

between aristocratic performers and spectators. With the revels, audience and masquers literally demonstrated their sense of shared identity; but even before this, indeed from the outset of the masque, spectators participated vicariously in the spectacle they watched through their belief in the ideals it advanced. But Milton did not create a sense of involvement by invoking the standard royalist assumptions; instead he involved his viewers by using wholly unconventional means. Manipulating point of view so that the audience watching the Lady and the brothers saw youthful versions of themselves, he characterized his audience as—and thus made them—receptive to his morality.

Throughout most of the masque, the audience's perceptions do not coincide with the children's, but involve what Jean Martin aptly calls "a bifurcation" of vision.[50] Milton deliberately created a dramatic irony. The audience, who has heard the Spirit's induction and overheard Comus's self-revelations, knows far more about the moral world of the masque than do the Lady and her brothers. They see behind the pastoral disguises of the Spirit and Comus the forces of good and evil working on the children's lives.

For the original audience at least, such superior moral understanding was reinforced by the fact that they literally saw what the children did not. When he took on the guise of a harmless villager, Comus did not need a costume change— and probably had no time for one if he remained on stage to overhear the Lady's speech and song. He tosses his "Magic dust" into the air, and apparently becomes to the Lady's eyes a pastoral figure. But he remains for the audience the wanton reveler he had appeared to be from the start. By this means, Milton provided his first audience, not with an actual moral superiority, but with more information. The inexperienced Lady may be fooled by Comus's pose, but the audience, with the vision Milton grants it, is able to recognize evil in its various guises.

Although at the outset the protagonists' perceptions are not those of the audience, the masque does trace a gradual movement toward aligning the two. The audience is identified with and is even in some sense placed at Ludlow, the immediate end of the children's journey, the assumption being that it has already successfully completed the particular stage of development that the youngsters are currently experiencing. The children's progress thus takes on the significance of an initiation into adulthood, a *rite de passage* complete with the traditional elements Van Gennep describes: isolation, trauma, and the final celebratory reception into adult life.[51] Their incorporation into the adult community, composed of their parents and other members of the audience, constitutes a coming of age. Their maturing has moral implications as well. Only after they learn to recognize the evil Comus represents and to free themselves from him do they join the audience at Ludlow Castle. At this point the barriers between spectator and spectacle dissolve, the perspectives of children and audience merge, and all share the applicability of the Spirit's closing advice.

Despite the moral insight that Milton flatteringly assumed in his audience and readers, he did not allow them to remain mere observers. For one thing, the children and their trials are exemplary.[52] This is not to say that the Lady and her brothers are to be viewed as symbols. They remain in the masque very much themselves. Milton preserved their relationship to each other, to their parents, and to their teacher-guide, pointedly reminding us—whenever we might be tempted to slip into the symbolic mode—that the Lady is a sister with youthful brothers, a helpful teacher, and a politically important father. Still, while they perform their special roles in life as siblings, pupils, offspring, and aristocrats, they also pursue a general spiritual calling that they share with all righteous men.

In addition to manipulating perspective and promoting an empathetic response to the children's example, Milton relied on a third method of bringing his lesson home. Audience and readers themselves develop in the course of experiencing the masque. Stanley Fish has argued with reference to *Paradise Lost* that "response is choice," that a reader's favorable or unfavorable reaction to characters or situations reflects a moral decision. When we view Satan as a glorious rebel, God as a tedious old bore, and Adam's choice of Eve over obedience to God as an act of romantic heroism, we reenact the fall of our primal parents.[53] As we have seen, the premises of affective stylistics, as Fish calls the theory, were not alien to masque-makers, who habitually assumed that aesthetic reaction implies moral, social, and political choices and ingeniously contrived to direct the spectators' response into the service of royalism.

Drawing on the masque's conventional capacity to shape audience response and foreshadowing to a remarkable extent his skilled manipulation of the reader in *Paradise Lost*, Milton created for his audience in *Comus* a series of trials. The small but vocal group of critics who delight in Comus's festivities and are repelled by the Lady's insistence on purity fail the most preliminary test. For those who are initially more successful, other less obvious tests remain. Like the children, the audience is offered experiences that try their ability to make and articulate moral judgments and their ability to use properly the things around them. Again, I postpone further consideration of these two operations, and here trace only the way Milton implicated his audience in a journey of psychic development.

In essence, Milton assumed that his audience begins with notions regarding the nature of reality, which their previous experience with masques leads them to expect his masque will confirm. But far from satisfying such expectations, the masque reveals the inaccuracy of conventional assumptions and, thus, forces a revision of the very world view that had come to define the masque as a genre. The treatment of human virtue is a case in point. When we are told at the beginning of the Ludlow masque that the Lady and her Brothers are nobly born, "nurs't in Princely lore," and "favor'd of high *Jove*," we are invited to think of them in terms of the aristocrat's common assumptions about himself. We therefore expect the children to be conventional masquers, their class—as reflected in their appearance—to be the evidence of their moral integrity, their very presence to be enough to conquer or dispel the antithetical forces of the antimasque. As the masque unfolds, it becomes clear that in the world Milton created things are not so simple; virtue often proves inadequate and needs the sustenance of grace; in short, the aristocrat's conventional notions about his nature and power do not hold true.

A similar shift away from conventional perspectives also affects Milton's treatment of the ranking dignitary in attendance at the original performance, the earl himself. He is initially characterized by his place in an allegory of interrelated sea gods and their dominions:

> . . . *Neptune* besides the sway
> . . . .
> . . . to grace his tributary gods
> By course commits to severall goverment,
> And gives them leave to wear their Saphire crowns,
> And wield their little tridents, but this Ile,
> The greatest, and the best of all the main
> He quarters to his blu-hair'd deities,
> And all this tract that front the falling Sun
> A noble Peer of mickle trust, and power
> Has in his charge, with temper'd awe to guide
> An old, and haughty Nation proud in Arms.
>
> [ll. 18, 24–33]

How precisely the allegory translates into the actualities of contemporary British government is not entirely clear; but the earl, unmistakably the "noble Peer," is by implication a sea god delegated his power by a superior deity. Orgel has noted that such ocean deities were highly conventional governing figures in Stuart masques.[54] In *Neptunes Triumph*, for example, King James is cast as "the mighty Neptune," who commands "waters and isles," controls powerful fleets and the riches of the deep, and "'mongst the winds' suffer[s] no debate." He is sole sovereign of the forces of nature and of his subjects' hearts.[55] In the light of this tradition, our first expectations are that the earl will function within Milton's *Comus* as an absolute ordering principle, controlling the destructive forces of nature within and without.

However, the maritime motif is abruptly dropped, not recurring until the appearance of Sabrina. At this point, not only has there been a shift from salt water to fresh, but the underlying myths have been revised so that the earl is no longer unqualified ruler of water and isle. Sabrina has become the governing force:

> . . . oft at Eeve [she]
> Visits the herds along the twilight meadows,

> Helping all urchin blasts, and ill-luck signes
> That the shrewd meddling Elfe delights to make,
> Which she with pretious viold liquors heals.
>
> [ll. 843–47]

Sabrina cures the effect of evil not only on plants and animals, but also on the children, who come within range of her healing waters. The earl, when he reappears in the masque, is simply a resident of Ludlow Castle and father of the Lady and her brothers. Although he profits from Sabrina's beneficent powers, he does not in fact control them. Conventional masques, in extravagant hyperbole, credited earthly governors with veritable omnipotence; but, in a masque specifically designed to celebrate the earl's increased rule, Milton ironically chose to demonstrate the limits of government and to emphasize the governor's dependence on forces beyond his influence. As in his treatment of the children, so in his handling of the earl, Milton subverted conventional expectations; instead of providing the occasional artist's usual flattery of his patron, he offered a realistic vision of fallen man's place in a fallen world.

Milton's revision of the masque's standard assumptions regarding character is revealed gradually to his audience, so that experiencing the masque becomes an educational process. His changes in the traditional plot also encourage a step-by-step rethinking, for the masque forces us to confront the very fact of the journey itself. The work consciously disappoints our expectations that it will inevitably culminate in a perfectly static vision, that it will support existing institutions as inviolable elements in a fixed cosmic order.

Comus offers us what initially appear to be conventional closures that hint at an imminent vision of fixity but that prove not to be so. The Lady's vision of Faith, Hope, and Chastity, followed by her prayerlike song, might normally be expected to introduce a main-masque world, ordered by these particular virtues and sustained by divine sanction; but what we next see is Comus in disguise. Likewise, the blaze of glory that greets our first view of Comus's palace does not signal the defeat of the dark forces of the antimasque and the triumph of order. The brothers' philosophical exchange recalls the debates in other

masques, such as Jonson's *Hymenaei*, which preceded the emer-
gence of the masquers and generally concluded with the triumph
of virtue, reason, beauty, or whatever ideal was to be celebrated in the main masque. But the debate in Milton's masque
does not resolve either the central thematic tension or the com-
plications of plot. The brothers' dramatic expulsion of Comus
with the aid of haemony does not prove conclusive either; Sabrina must be invoked for further aid. Even then, the Spirit
and the children remain for a time in a hostile environment,
instead of moving immediately to the serene, secure surroundings of a conventional main masque. After the children have
returned to their parents at Ludlow, the Spirit makes explicit
in his closing advice what we have already learned through the
repeated experiences of having our expectations of closure
thwarted: the demands of virtue make stasis impossible. The
children have scored an initial triumph, but Comus remains
free, and protagonists and audience may expect further skir-
mishes.

In specifying that the children have won at least a preliminary victory over "sensual Folly and Intemperance," Milton
detailed the two operations—the epistemological and the ethical—that make up moral life. Although the two overlap,
Milton for the most part described them separately. In the
Christian Doctrine, for example, he made a traditional distinction between the virtues and vices of the understanding and
those of the will, wisdom and folly falling into the former
category, temperance and its opposite into the latter. Similarly,
the results of regeneration are two-fold, including a heightened understanding of spiritual affairs and a greater holiness of
life as expressed in good works (*CP*, 6:478–79).

Comus attempts to promote in its audience and performers
an increased skill in these two basic moral operations. Although necessary for spiritual pilgrims of any era, both skills
were, from the Puritan perspective, particularly essential for
wayfarers of the 1630s, assailed as they were by the general
godlessness of the times and by such specific instances of depravity as the official policy on sports. Without losing sight of
the occasion of his masque, Milton tied the moral issues raised

by the contemporary debate over entertainment to the larger, timeless problems faced by all believers. In the next two chapters, I will examine the two skills—judging and choosing—that must be mastered for the successful pursuit of man's general calling and for deciding when, where, how, and whether to participate in recreation.

CHAPTER THREE

Poetry and the Other Masquing Arts: Toward an Integrated Rhetoric

MILTON'S SENSE OF MISSION AS A VATIC POET CONVEYING divine revelations to his society was difficult to reconcile with his view of the world as a baffling place where good and evil, truth and falsehood are subtly intertwined. From the artist's perspective the problem was rhetorical: how can the artist most effectively communicate his insights? His difficulty lay in depicting people, situations, and things in a way that was true to life (and thus realistically confusing), yet at the same time ensured that moral values were recognizable enough to make the poet's point. A further complication was added by the practical necessity of attracting an audience and holding its attention while setting forth a serious message. The well-worn Horatian dictum that literature be *dulce et utile* lay behind much of the poetic and rhetorical theory of the Renaissance, but the didactic techniques it inspired were not flawless. Although a work's pleasant qualities might draw prospective members of the audience into teaching range, they could also prove so alluring that the audience neglected to penetrate the surface to the truths contained within. How could an artist ensure that his audience would make the requisite shift from delightful exterior to thematic core? A few Puritans of the period weighed *dulce* against *utile*, and, deciding that literature was too dangerously seductive to be an effective way of conveying knowledge, condemned it wholly or in part. On similar grounds, Plato had banished poets from his *Republic*. Milton—as poet, humanist, and Puritan moderate—retained a supreme faith in the didactic force of his art and sought a balanced rhetoric capable of true teaching, true delight.

The problem of artistic communication that Milton confronted in *Comus* is not unique to that work alone. His struggle for answerable style throughout his career involved, at least partially, the search for an accommodation that took into account the delusory and seductive nature of appearances and fallen man's inherent tendency to mistake surface for substance. In the masque, he made the problem of accommodation a central concern, incorporating it as a theme and as a key to his rhetorical tactics.

The reasons for his interest in effective rhetoric in the Ludlow masque are historical, having to do with the history of the masque as a form and with the larger religious and political controversies of the time. Almost from its inception as an independent genre, the masque was marked by an inner tension among its various rhetorical means. In writing a masque, Milton necessarily confronted this tension and was forced to choose among the available modes of expression. In the light of contemporary debates about the way the monarchy expressed itself and about the rhetoric of religious worship—debates that became particularly heated during the 1630s—the artistic problems of the masque took on a broader significance.

The inner tension that Milton inherited along with the masque tradition arose out of the form's synthetic nature. A multimedia form combining the visual arts of scenery, costume, and lighting with dance, music, and poetry, the masque strove to integrate the arts into a unified aesthetic experience that persuaded by all possible means and appealed to as many of the senses as possible—sight, sound, smell (through the use of perfumes), and kinesthesia. As Jean Hagstrum suggests, this merging of the arts was based on the Renaissance notion that "when several arts worked together to create a harmonious whole," thereby appealing to several senses simultaneously, the impression was more powerful "than temporally separated appeals to one sense after another."[1] The harmonious union of collaborating arts was an ideal not always attained in actuality. Producing a masque required, in Angus Fletcher's words, "poetical diplomacy."[2] Arguments could arise over which art was to be granted prime responsibility for communicating a masque's meaning and which artist was to make command decisions.

Almost from the masque's inception as an independent form, the greatest threat to harmonious integration of the arts was the rivalry between poetry and the visual arts. Samuel Daniel maintained that masques were not primarily designed to teach—"*Ludit istis animus, non proficit*"[3]—but even he claimed that when games have serious significance poetry must be the prime vehicle. In the commentary Daniel appended to the *Vision of Twelve Goddesses*, the last major Elizabethan masque, he defended his introduction of a presenter who explains the spectacle verbally, arguing the superiority of poetry to pictures as a means of expressing truth, and of ear to eye as a faculty of apprehension: "that the eyes of the Spectators might not beguile their eares, as in such cases it ever happens, . . . therefore was it thought their descriptions [of the masquers] should be delivered by the Sybilla [i.e., the presenter figure]."[4]

The tension between word and spectacle became most acute during the uneasy alliance between Ben Jonson, poet, and Inigo Jones, architect and production designer. For twenty-five years the two worked together. Indeed the history of the masque is largely the history of their partnership. By the late 1620s the collaboration faltered, in part because of a clash of personalities. More important, while the two agreed to a remarkable extent on the fundamental nature of the masque, as D. J. Gordon has shown, they diverged on one crucial point: the rhetorical issue of whether the masque speaks its meaning primarily by literary or extraliterary means.[5]

Jones understandably championed the visual arts as the best means of communication, basing his argument on the Neoplatonic assumption that earthly forms perceptible to the eye provide reflections of ideal forms. A word is simply the name of an idea; pictures are the means by which men are able to think. To Jones's mind, it was through its sophisticated visual tableaux that the masque presented its thematic content. Consequently, an audience's comprehension depended on the power of visual images. Jones had the dominant opinion of Renaissance dramatic theory behind him when he assumed that, far from being "mere distraction," spectacle "was in fact the substance of theater."[6]

A self-proclaimed literary critic, Ben Jonson issued numerous theoretical statements relevant to the masque—far more than Jones. Although his comments are scattered and frequently contradictory, he finally moved toward opposition to the architect's preference for the visual arts over poetry. Jonson based his argument in part on an aesthetic judgment regarding the proper hierarchy of the arts. In the body-soul metaphor he developed in his famous preface to *Hymenaei*, he drew not only on the technical language of emblem literature,[7] but also on the common assumptions of Christian dualism. Poetry, as the soul of a masque, Jonson claimed, transcends the extraliterary arts, which provide its formal body, both temporally (since the soul is eternal, the body mortal) and essentially (since the soul partakes of the divine). Jonson's figure also plays on the Christian-Aristotelian view of the soul as the form of the body and thus implies that poetry and the poet should provide the central inventions, or themes, that shape a masque.[8]

Jonson's insistence on the dominance of poetry also rested on certain epistemological assumptions that he worked out gradually over a period of time. His comments in *Discoveries* on the relative effectiveness of poetry and the visual arts as conveyors of truth are conflicting and ambiguous. Under the heading *"Poesis, et Pictura,"* he argued that poetry is superior to painting because it speaks to the highest of man's faculties: "Yet of the two, the Pen is more noble, then the Pencill. For that can speake to the Understanding; the other, but to the Sense." In the passage immediately following, he offered a contradictory judgment: "Picture is the invention of Heaven: the most ancient, and most a kinne to Nature. . . . Yet it doth so enter, and penetrate the inmost affection (being done by an excellent Artificer) as sometimes it orecomes the power of speech, and oratory." Elsewhere in the *Discoveries* the account of one popular view of the thought process seems to accord language the derivative function of merely providing the verbal tags for pictures: "The conceits of the mind are Pictures of things, and the tongue is the Interpreter of those Pictures."[9]

Discoveries does not necessarily present Jonson's finished judgments. As a commonplace book, it records his thoughts and readings over a period of time on subjects that interested him and should not bear the critical weight it is often given. All that we can deduce from his contradictory notations on the relative merits of poetry and the visual arts in *Discoveries* is that

Jonson was thoughtfully considering the issues raised by his quarrel with Jones and carefully weighing opposing arguments.

From the beginning of his involvement with pageantry, Jonson was a champion of poetry. In comments appended to his coronation entertainment for James I, he spoke approvingly of spectacle that can communicate without the need for verbal labeling: "Neither was it becoming, or could it stand with the dignitie of these shewes . . . to require . . . one to write, *This is a Dog* or *This is a Hare*: but, so to be presented, as upon the view, they might, without cloud, or obscuritie, declare themselves to the sharpe and learned: and for the multitude, no doubt but their grounded judgments did gaze, said it was fine, and were satisfied." [10] Jonson appears willing to concede the esoteric nature of the masque and to accept a distinction between levels of comprehension, similar to the contrast of plebian and patrician understanding that Jones himself was to make in *Albion's Triumph*. But this passage reflects a concern that words not be demoted to simply providing the names for concepts conceived of and communicated in pictorial terms, that they not become mere crutches for the unlearned.

By the 1620s Jonson had moved away from this defensive posture. During the later years of his collaboration with Jones when their quarrel had become bitter, an insistence on the superiority of poetry dominated. Denigrating Jones's attempt to communicate by visual means as a vain effort "to make Boardes to speake," he commented sarcastically on the subordination of poetry to art:

> O Showes! Showes! Mighty Showes!
> The Eloquence of Masques! What need of prose
> Or Verse, or Sense t'express Immortall you?

Jonson also objected to the Neoplatonic esotericism basic to Jones's use of theatrical emblems in his masques, caricaturing the assumption that only "certeyn politique Eyes / . . . can pierce into ye Misteryes of many coulours!" [11] When Jonson prefaced *Loves Triumph* with a description of the work's themes entitled "To Make Spectators Understanders," he meant not only to assert that seeing and understanding are far from being the same thing, but also to undercut Jones's intentional hermeticism by educating those spectators who would otherwise have been left unenlightened.

Jones's assumption that boards could speak to those capable of understanding is not in fact so foolish as Jonson made out. For almost two decades he and Jonson had managed through their cooperation to develop the masque into a form that communicated by verbal and nonverbal means. A series of conventions allowed the nonliterary arts to function almost as a language. Some of the basic assumptions were readily comprehensible: harmonious order conforms to divine intents; reciprocally, the disorganized movements of antimasque figures and the irregular, clamorous music that accompanies them reflect the opposite;[12] beauty, brightness, richness, and symmetry are manifestations of virtue, both personal and communal; conversely, what is dark, grotesque, stark, or disorderly, while not always vicious or evil, is in some sense morally limited or incomplete. In short, there was an implied equation of aesthetic and moral values that grew out of the premise that perceptible exteriors offer an accurate index to intangible qualities.

Even after the antimasque had been expanded into a series of dramatic interludes, as in Shirley's *Triumph of Peace*, the masquers and their values continued to be presented by nondramatic, nonverbal means. The assumption that kings manifest their kingliness, nobles their nobility, and gentlemen their gentility by their mere presence placed the matter of their inherent superiority beyond the realm of verbal discourse.

The underlying equation of aesthetic qualities with moral values and with political positions, thus, did make it possible for boards to speak and for politic eyes to perceive profound meanings. Despite Jonson's criticism, his partnership with Jones contributed to the development of a nonverbal rhetoric that operated in cooperation with poetry. The history of Jacobean court pageantry, as Orgel traces it in the *Jonsonian Masque*, was shaped by an ongoing effort to teach audiences to see something more than boards by emphasizing the conceptual principles behind costume, scenery, music, and dance.[13]

Just as Jonson ultimately repudiated visual rhetoric by insisting on its limitations, so Jones moved deliberately toward an increasing reliance on esoteric theatrical emblems. By the early 1630s, he had won the quarrel by default, since Jonson did not contribute to masques after *Chloridia* in 1631, and even this last production followed Jones's principles rather than his own. Jones, because he worked in subsequent court productions with poets who allowed him to dominate, was free to consolidate his gains by developing a theoretical justification for the primacy of the visual arts.

Of Jones's relatively few theoretical pronouncements about the masque, most followed his break with Jonson and reflected his conscious effort to devise a means of expression that would lessen the masque's reliance on words. The often quoted comment that Jones attached to *Tempe Restored*—"these shows are nothing else but pictures with light and motion"[14]—indicates his sense of the masque as a pictorial rather than a literary art form. We sense in the first few masques Jones produced independently of Jonson his effort to put his conception into practice, a straining beyond verbal confines to create a visual language capable of expressing complex meaning yet intelligible to his viewers.

The first court masque that appeared following the split with Jonson, *Albion's Triumph*, teaches his elite audience how to use their eyes to reach understanding, how to see Neoplatonically. An opening song, which prepares us for the systematic downplaying of words in the entire piece, asserts that in presenting the triumphal entry of the masquing king, "We speak in acts, and scorn words' trifling scenes."[15] The explicit lesson in perception takes the form of a debate between an incomplete, unsophisticated way of seeing and true insight. In this confrontation, the plebian, Publius, who sees in the elaborate display of the triumphal entry only pleasing and varied appeals to the senses, finally gives way in argument to the Neoplatonic apologist, Plotinus, a patrician who does not even need physically to see the pageantry to intuit its deepest significance: "know I have seen this brave Albanactus Caesar [i.e., the masquing King Charles], seen him with the eyes of understanding, viewed all his actions, looked into his mind, which I find armed with so many moral virtues that he daily conquers a world of vices."[16]

This contrast of complete and incomplete vision is informed by the complex elitism about which students of Renaissance symbolic technique have often remarked.[17] The emblems Jones presented in his masque must be arcane enough to remain mysteries inaccessible to literal-minded common men of Publius's sort. The aristocrats gathered at court to participate are urged to take the view of Plotinus, to see with something more than brute sense, lest the royal triumph not be meaningful. Plotinus's assertion that "outsides have insides, shells have kernels in them, and under ever fable, nay under almost everything, lies a moral"[18] points to a realm of meaning accessible only to the cognoscenti.

Subsequent court masques of the 1630s reveal Jones's continued reliance on visual language, in spite of the occasional difficulties he faced in making his aristocratic spectators see the kernels beneath the shells. The revelation of the masquers, expressed primarily in dynamic tableaux, provided a logical point at which he attempted to move beyond words. Thus a presenter in *Tempe Restored* asserts that he does not expect attention to his speech once the masquers have revealed themselves:

> I cannot blame ye if ye gaze,
> And give small ear to what I say,
> For such a presence will amaze,
> And send the senses all one way.[19]

In *Coelum Britannicum*, Jones deliberately subordinated ear to eye to imply the near self-sufficiency of visual rhetoric. At the moment of supreme insight when the masquers dance their entry, sight becomes the all-encompassing sense that precludes the need for any other. A chorus sings after the masquers' first dance, "And had the music silent been, / The eye a moving tune had seen."[20]

Although Jones used visual rhetoric successfully in presenting the heroic dimensions of the masquers, he apparently found it difficult to communicate less familiar ideas. As Orgel has shown, the *Triumph of Peace* was misunderstood by its royal spectators, who mistook correction for praise. Similarly, in the published version of *Tempe Restored*, Jones felt it necessary to attach a multiparagraph explanation of his allegory, presumably because his audience had not understood the masque in performance.[21]

By the time Milton wrote his masque the Jonsonian principles regarding the primacy of poetry and the need for making spectators understanders had been firmly supplanted by the intentional hermeticism of Jones's visual rhetoric. Still, the underlying tension between poetry and the visual arts remained an element of the masque tradition as Milton received it, and played a part in the aesthetic choices he was to make.

Milton's stand on the issues raised by the Jones-Jonson debate has received a fair amount of critical attention. The general consensus has been that Milton followed Jonson's lead, making his work a "literary masque" in which the extraliterary arts—though not entirely eliminated—derive their significance from the verbal framework.[22] Modern readers naturally view *Comus* as a literary work, almost a semidramatic poem: its text is longer than every other masque except *Coelum Britannicum*; as we have seen, Milton continued to revise the text after its performance was long past; only a handful of songs are extant; and we have no records of performances. Even in production the poetry no doubt dominated. Ludlow was too far from London for much equipment to have been transported, and the Great Hall where *Comus* was presented was too small for elaborate scenic effects.[23] Yet Milton did not devalue the contributions of the nonliterary arts or use poetry to substitute for nonliterary effects. Rather his masque reveals a deliberate and consistent effort to modify and control the contributions of the extraliterary arts, often by poetic means. His aim was to develop a masquing rhetoric.

Milton's preference for a literary rhetoric cannot be explained entirely in terms of Jonsonian precedent. In fact, his handling of the arts owes less to Jonson than to Jones, who provided his point of departure. Jonson's beliefs regarding the proper hierarchy of the arts and the essential superiority of literature were apparently of little interest to him. Like Jonson, he was concerned with artistic epistemology and effective communication. He differed from the elder poet in that for him the question of how a masque speaks was inextricably intertwined with matters of individual and political morality. But he differed no less from Jones, whose visual rhetoric he also repudiated as immoral and misleading. He rejected the whole simplistic equation in Caroline masques of inner and outer, of aesthetic quality with political status and moral worth.

For Milton, as for other men of his day, far more was at stake in the argument over the predominance in the masque of word or image than an isolated matter of aesthetic form. For one thing, Royalists of the period attributed great importance to images and appeals to the eye. A firm believer in monarchical imagery, James I had explained to his son and heir in *Basilikon Doron*: "A King is as one set on stage, whose smallest actions and gestures, all the people gazingly doe behold: and therefore although a King be never so praecise in the discharging of his Office, the people, who seeth but the outward part, will ever judge of the substance, by the circumstances."[24] As Orgel has observed, the Stuart emphasis on the image of the king was a natural outgrowth of the belief in monarchical absolutism.[25] Since subjects played virtually no part in the inner workings of government, they viewed it and the king himself from the outside.

James specifically defended richness of display as a royal necessity: "Remember then, that this worldly glorie of Kings, is given them by God, to teach them to preasse so to glister and shine before their people, in all workes of sanctification and righteousness, that their persons as bright lampes of godliness and vertue, may, going in and out before their people, give light to all their steps."[26] The conventions that underlie the nonverbal rhetoric of the masque are here given broad political application. A king has a right to the splendor traditionally associated with his office because it is God-given and because it is morally functional, providing *visibilia* that heighten his effect as a model of behavior. Ideally, a monarch's pomp and circumstance are reminders that he must coordinate inner with outer, and thus serve as a sword of Damocles, though notably without the sword's threat of immediate punishment for abuse of power. In fact, such abuse was a real possibility, for James intended control of the monarch's splendid image to remain in his hands. Subjects were to see, respond respectfully, and accept without considering whether there was any disparity between the image of the kingly "lamp of virtue" and the reality of his accomplishments or whether it was beneficial to devote national wealth to elaborate image-making in the first place.

Following his father's advice with a single-mindedness that James himself had been too politic to undertake, Charles made his faith in the monarch's glorious image a cornerstone of his reign. The heroic visions of kingship set forth in the numerous portraits he commissioned and in the great Caroline masques testify to his belief that he could control events by manipulating the way he and his government were seen.[27] Charles's obsession with image is manifest in his official communications, as well as in his patronage of the arts. After dissolving Parliament in 1629, for the third time in his short reign, he issued an explanation. But lest offering an explanation be construed as an acknowledgment of any qualifications to sole prerogative and monarchical absolutism, Charles carefully outlined his intentions: "Howsoever princes are not bound to give account of their actions, but to God alone; yet for the satisfaction of the minds and affections of our loving subjects, we have thought good to set down thus much by way of declaration, that *we may appear to the world in the truth and sincerity of our actions, and not in those colours in which we know some turbulent and ill-affected spirits . . . would represent us to the public view.*"[28] His statement was not a self-justification, but Charles's revelation of his image, a clarification of that external manifestation of himself, which his people perceived as their monarch.

Caroline England saw like developments in religion. William Laud's emphasis on ritual, the sacraments, and external *visibilia* at the expense of preaching inspired heated debate over the relative merits of ear and eye as means of apprehension. As apologist for the more traditionally Catholic wing of the Anglican church, Richard Hooker developed the underlying epistemology for the increasing reliance on visual rhetoric. The eye, he claimed, is the most acute sensory organ; and although visual statements speak less directly to the reason than do words, they can have a more intense and lasting effect on the average man.[29]

Laud himself paid frequent tribute to "the beauty of holiness." While the term is psalmic in origin, his understanding of it was informed by two Neoplatonic commonplaces. First, beauty comes from order imposed on chaos; in its highest form it reflects the ordering of God's creation and his government of the world. Second, beauty can have a calming effect on those who perceive and make themselves receptive to it. A beautiful and ordered setting can encourage a detachment from the daily routine and reverent attitude toward God. The physical beauty and planned disposition of the sanctuary, ceremonial movements, and splendid music were thus not mere decorations, but enhanced religious experience.[30] Laud's faith in the power of beauty was the religious analogue to Charles's reliance on icons as means of governing.

It was precisely Laud's external forms of worship that Puritans opposed, although they differed on how to redress the hated "innovations." Some wanted to eliminate from worship services all nonverbal means of expression—music, visual arts, the choreography of ceremonial movements. John Philips has documented the extremes to which Puritan iconoclasts went in eliminating what they perceived as debasements of the Word.[31] Others—the majority perhaps—argued not for complete exclusion of nonverbal rhetoric, but for an end to what they saw as an overemphasis on external forms of worship. Their aim was a return to a balance of rhetorical means that preserved the traditional Protestant preference for rational modes of religious experience and for an emphasis on preaching and Bible reading as the principal aids to faith.[32]

With this latter group Milton allied himself. In her discussion of Protestant emblematics, Barbara Lewalski has suggested something of the context for Milton's treatment of the visual and verbal arts in *Comus*. Protestant commentators often described physical symbols in the Bible as God's own emblems. Protestant emblem-makers and poets felt justified in producing emblem books or poetry that drew on the images contained in contemporary emblem books and "for highlighting the visual, emblematic qualities of those images, since they have their origin in . . . God's creation and God's Word." But Protestant writers also made changes in the emblem tradition, moving "resolutely away from the Neoplatonic esotericism" of their Catholic forerunners, toward biblically based emblematics. Among the kinds of emblem books favored by seventeenth-century English Protestants were those organized around the theme of the pilgrimage of spiritual life or the love relationship between the soul and Christ.[33] We have seen in chapter 2 how imagery based on the former theme, derived from the Old Testament and the Pauline epistles, dominates the figurative texture of *Comus*; in chapter 4 we will examine the motif of the spiritual love affair in the masque's imagery.

Milton was clearly not among those Puritans who abhorred the nonverbal arts and the use of visual rhetoric for religious and political expression. As Roland M. Frye has shown, he was neither unaware nor unappreciative of the great wealth of Renaissance art available to him in tapestry, painting, and sculpture. For its effect on his imagination we need only look to the descriptive imagery of his two epics.[34]

Milton did repudiate the use of nonverbal rhetoric to deceive or limit understanding. In *Eikonoklastes*, he attacked the traditional icons of kingship, still compelling to his contemporaries even in the wake of civil war, as dangerous threats to national reform. Tacitly accepting Charles as the author of *Eikon Basilike*, Milton satirized the king's efforts to rule by manipulating images. He hammered at the point with an insistent use of theatrical imagery, referring to "Court-fucus," "vizards," and "painted feathers," and with repeated contrasts of outward show and inner motives.[35] He cast Charles as a player-king: beneath the display of majesty lies the reality of a man, foolish and immoral, a public official who has proved himself inept, self-serving, and tyrannical. He ridiculed as ineffectual Charles's effort to avoid rational scrutiny by taking refuge in a contrived, quasi-religious system of mysteries, arguing that the English are a thinking people, not to be fooled by hollow images: "But quaint emblems and divices . . . will do but ill to make a saint or martyr" (*CP*, 3:343). Acutely aware that words, too, can be used to create false images, he attacked the king's abuse of verbal rhetoric. He mercilessly demonstrated that Charles's arguments frequently do not make sense but use words only for image-making, for "ostentations."

Finally, Milton justified the execution of Charles by two interconnected strategies. First, he undercut the traditional *ikon basilike* and the sympathetic image of Charles as hapless martyr: these became illusions designed to hook those incapable of critically assessing images. Second, he substituted faith in rational discourse for ungrounded faith in images. In his version, the execution of Charles occurred because truth marched forth triumphant to destroy all false appearances.

On similar grounds Milton objected to the obsessive and misleading use of nonverbal means of expression in religion, as well as in politics. He saw in Laud's innovations an overemphasis that had no biblical sanction and violated the proper aims of worship. In his antiprelatical tracts, he condemned the Caroline church's overreliance on the senses: "Faith needing not the weak, and fallible office of the Senses, to be either Ushers, or Interpreters, of heavenly Mysteries, save where our Lord himselfe in his Sacraments ordain'd." The visual rhetoric that Laud introduced as devotional aids was a "new-vomited Paganisme of Sensuall Idolatry" that succeeded only in increasing man's carnal ties to the world and diminishing his ability to comprehend the spiritual. Essentially, Milton's objection was that reliance on externals perverts the basic principles of Christianity, inasmuch as it undervalues God's word given in Scripture and denies the meaning of Christ as logos: "Grosser ceremonies now in force delude the end of Christs comming in the flesh against the flesh, and stifle the sincerity of our new cov'nant which hath bound us to forsake all carnal pride and wisdom especially in matters of religion."[36]

Although he objected to an overuse of nonverbal rhetoric, Milton recognized that words, too, can be abused. The false icons behind which Charles hid were as often verbal as visual. So too in the ecclesiastical satire of *Lycidas* Milton condemned the abuse of language by the clergy (ll. 123–27). Some of the more obscure expressions in the satiric passage have eluded the efforts of modern explicators. Even so, Milton clearly attacked the devaluation of the word in the Laudian church, and the objects of his satire are specifically the false pastors who preach only infrequently ("when they list"), whose sermons are decorative rather than substantial, whose "blind mouths" do not achieve an enlightened preaching of God's word, who do not edify but corrupt.[37]

It is not surprising that Milton should have concerned himself in *Comus* with verbal and nonverbal rhetoric both as a technical matter and as a theme. The Jonson-Jones debate over the nature of the masque had ended with the victory of Jones and the nonverbal rhetorical means he supported. In the areas of religion and politics, controversy on much the same issue was particularly heated during the 1630s. Milton himself saw a connection between the earlier conflict over masquing rhetoric and the ongoing and far more consequential debates over the rights of the king and the forms of worship. As we have seen, he explicitly condemned Laud and his prelates as "Church-maskers," linking the "carnal" language of the Caroline church with the elaborate, intentionally esoteric language of court productions of the period. He also associated masquing with the current political controversy. Milton's assault on Charles in *Eikonoklastes* as a player-king reached its peak with his ridicule of the portrait of the king in masquing dress that prefaced *Eikon Basilike*.

Because he associated conventional Caroline masquing practices with religious and political positions he opposed, Milton found it necessary to devise a more congenial masquing rhetoric. The result was a revised rhetorical collaboration in which poetry is the major contributor, providing continuity and coherence to the masque's artistic statement, with the other arts seeming to enhance, to clarify, and to extend what the words express.

This interaction of poetry with the other arts determines the function of the music in Milton's masque. All that remains from the original music Henry Lawes provided are five songs, but even the extant music is important to the word's persuasive power. As Sabol has remarked, the very style of the songs ensures a wedding of sound and sense: "The music seldom soars to impassioned heights, nor does it obscure the lyrics with ornamentation. Most of the songs are musical recitations in which the nicest balance is maintained between declamation and melody."[38] The songs are not declamatory; they do not to any extent use musical techniques for the motive intensification of the word, that hallmark of the *recitativo* style. But since the lyrics are intellectually complex, the music is helpful in bringing out their significance. The rhythms and tonal inflections underline shifts in argument, clarify complicated syntax, and emphasize conceits. Lawes merited the tribute Milton was later to pay him for the artful manner in which he set poetry to music so that the music spans "words with just note and accent" ("To My Friend, Mr. Henry Lawes, on His Aires," l. 3).

There are far fewer songs in *Comus* than one would expect in a masque of its length, but they occur at critical points in the action. In his handling of the musical episodes, Milton drew on well-known traditions regarding *musica mundana* and *musica humana*. *Musica mundana* might signify the music of the spheres or a concord of the elements or of the seasons, but was always regarded as a demonstration of world harmony. *Musica humana* reflects man's ordering of his own being and of his society to bring himself into tune with the world harmony.[39] Significantly, Comus is not allowed a song. In contrast, the Lady's song, in the tradition of *musica humana*, proclaims her a well-tuned instrument.

The most vital function Milton accords music is as an aural-oral vehicle, mediating between the supernatural and the natural. The Attendant Spirit's song, which in an early version began "From the Heav'ns now I fly," became in the final text "To the Ocean now I fly." In both versions, the song is associated with the Spirit's movement between heaven and earth and reflects an effort—if not to bring *musica mundana* and *humana* together in harmonious concert—at least to coordinate the two. Sabrina is also invoked in a song, which Louis Martz suggests represents "nature and spirit . . . brought into a rich union."[40] The Lady's song is addressed to the nymph Echo, "Sweet Queen of Parley," who mediates the parlance between heaven and earth. Although Echo is literally a product of the human voice, produced by the Lady's singing, she also conveys utterances of some transcendent voice. Echo may give "resounding grace to all Heav'n's Harmonies," making supernatural music available by gracious means to human ears. She may also as a manifestation of the Lady's voice "be translated to the skies," the process of translation being understood here not only in its etymological sense of "borne across," but also in its common linguistic sense. Milton granted the power of translating between the natural and the supernatural realms to song, that is, to music that heightens the force of the word.

The educational process in which Milton involved his audience throughout the masque requires among other things, learning how to understand the reformed rhetoric of the piece. To begin with, the poet directed his audience to "unlearn" the lessons derived from experience with conventional masques. He went to particular lengths to subvert expectations regarding visual rhetoric in the masque. His preservation of traditional elements from the myth of Circe leads us initially to assume that he also preserved that assumption, conventional in the masque, that there is a consonance between inner and outer. The "human count'nance" is "th'express resemblance of the gods" (ll. 68–69), and "reasons mintage [is] / Character'd in the face" (ll. 529–30). Conversely, to live by one's lower faculties is reflected in a visible descent in the chain of being: "the visage" is transformed into "the inglorious likeness of a beast" (ll. 527–28). As the masque proceeds, however, it becomes apparent that the equation of appearance and moral state does not hold. Instead *Comus* undercuts the visual language, which audiences educated by Jones's court productions had learned to read, by invalidating the essential linguistic link between iconic sign and its referent.

There are three settings, a tangled wood, which is Comus's haunt, a glorious palace, also Comus's, and finally a scene depicting Ludlow town and the Earl of Bridgewater's castle. The first scene, the dark labyrinthine forest, is a typical antimasque vision. The Lady and her brothers do not at first recognize it as such; but they are youngsters, not yet fully initiated into the mysteries of adult society and certainly not into masque conventions. But those of Milton's original audience and readers familiar with Jonson's *Oberon* or *Chloridia*, Campion's *Lord's Masque*, Chapman's *Memorable Masque*, or any number of other masques would easily have made the association of rough terrain and darkness with moral lassitude, social chaos, and cosmic disorder.

Since the first setting follows convention, the second scene comes as a shock. We move from a dark wood to a brightly lit palace peopled by revelers dressed in spangled costumes; but we do not progress from antimasque to main masque. Herford and Simpson comment with obvious critical frustration:

> The sudden and decisive change of scene and temper which regularly comes with the apparition of masquers has only a formal parallel in the change of scene from the gloomy wood to the splendour of Comus' . . . palace. . . . For this change normally announced that the dramatic conflict between higher and lower powers has now issued in the decisive triumph of the good. . . . But Milton, while offering something superficially like the splendid apparitions to which his audience were accustomed, has altogether detached these elements from their original purpose.[41]

By offering the palace as a second vision of disorder and evil, Milton demonstrated in theatrical terms that beauty and richness of appearance do not signal moral worth. Further, the fact that Comus dominates forest and palace implies an equation between the rude and the elegant that is wholly alien to the conventional masque with its elitist assumptions. There is no difference between the brutishness of a primitive forester and that of the sophisticate; a moral savage can exist even at court.

Although Milton consciously repudiated conventional political iconography by undercutting the equation of visual splendor, social position, and moral value, he did not take refuge in simplistic reformulations. The Lady mistakenly accepts Comus's offer of guidance:

> Shepherd I take thy word,
> And trust thy honest offer'd courtesie,
> Which oft is sooner found in lowly sheds
> With smoaky rafters, then in tapstry Halls
> And Courts of Princes, where it first was nam'd,
> And yet is most pretended.   [ll. 321–26]

In her preference for the unostentatious, the Lady has merely inverted the values underlying conventional royalist icons. In fact, her judgment of Comus is grossly in error, for *Comus* offers us no reliable, systematic relation between inner and outer.

The third scene of *Comus*, specified as "Ludlow town and the President's Castle," is not further described in either stage directions or the poetic text. Milton did not give it a fictional identity of the sort conventional in main masques. Instead he emphasized a return to unadorned reality. Such a depiction of actual architectural sites in masquing scenery was not usual. Throughout the early seventeenth century, court productions occasionally included as a setting a place such as White Hall or the Banqueting Hall. But as Orgel has shown, from roughly 1620 onward, such realistic scenes invariably occurred at the beginning of masques and were transformed into peaceful pastoral visions within which the monarch became the tamer of nature. Masques organized in this way functioned as Platonic revelations leading spectators on a perceptual journey from surface realities to the higher reality of informing ideals.[42] Milton, however, did not follow this pattern, probably because he would have seen in the theatrical revelation of the court as a benign, well-governed place another example of flattery.

The simplicity of his final scene—which was probably evoked by little more than a backdrop—is the highest compliment Milton could have paid to the earl and his family. The Egertons apparently did not need or desire elaborate and deceptive visual display. The implication that their senses were properly regulated is a more creditable reflection of the earl's powers as a governor than conspicuous consumption would have been. Again, as with Comus's brightly lit palace, Milton revised the common visual language.

Milton's creation of a revised masquing rhetoric goes beyond a mere repudiation of received conventions to redefine and in some instances expand the role of the extraliterary arts. Since dance was the raison d'etre of the ordinary masque, its treatment by Milton is often viewed as casual. Milton does include a few incidents of dance: the "measure" performed by Comus and his rout, the rural jig, and the children's dance as they are presented to their parents. Revels may also have been part of the original performance, if the country dancers "took out" members of the audience,[43] or if the children danced and then performed the "asking out" themselves. But clearly it is the literary episodes that bear the dramatic weight of the work. For example, the children's "triumph in Victorious dance" before the seat of state offers a closure, not a climax; it is the happy ending pursuant to the Lady's temptation.

Milton denied dance its usual function in the masque. Dancing—traditionally the gentleman's accomplishment—normally served as an indicator of the moral, social, and aesthetic superiority that the upper-class masquers claimed for themselves. Court masques achieved their climax with the glorious revelation of the masquers. As they descended to the dance floor and performed, they confirmed the initial impression of beauty and order. The Lady and her Brothers, however, do not dance until after it has become clear that virtue cannot just be presented but must be proved through active choice. By postponing his protagonists' dance and expanding the preliminary dramatic matter, Milton achieved a far more complex and intense impression of dance as an expression of virtue than was ordinarily possible.

Further, he added to the vocabulary of the masque by exploring the implications of stasis. William Blake brilliantly captured the choreographic possibilities of the temptation scene, particularly in his second series of illustrations. In the third design, Comus appears almost to be dancing, stepping from one foot to the other, balanced lightly on the ball of one foot. His rod in one hand, potion-filled glass in the other, he stands over the Lady, who is by contrast rigidly static. Blake eliminated the Lady's theatrical gesture of arms crossed over her breast, which he had used in his first illustration of the scene. In the later version she sits erect with her hands on her thighs, her neutral and fixed position indicating her detachment from the dancelike activities of Comus and from the activities of the beasts who sit around a feast table with food or drinks held in their hands. As Blake recognized, the Lady's stasis in the midst of movement is central to the visual composition of the scene. Aristocratic masquers generally demonstrated their virtue in dance. Milton's Lady initially proves hers by not dancing.

The lesson on rhetorical means and their proper use, contained in Milton's work, depends on a careful manipulation of the masquing arts and consequently on the modulation of the way a masque speaks. But it also proceeds by other means. The first two characters to appear, the Attendant Spirit and Comus, embody the contrast between proper and improper rhetoric.

Comus is associated with a false rhetoric. Like Jones in his Caroline masques, the sorcerer relies primarily on appeals to the senses. Comus may be most closely linked with the sense of sight. He indicates the general delights of his realm—"See here be all the pleasures" (l. 668)—and then focuses attention on the potion in his cup—"behold this cordial Julep here" (l. 672). However, he attempts his seduction in a setting designed to appeal to all the senses: "a stately Palace set out with all manner deliciousness" (ll. 658 ff.). Even the gustatory sense is called into play as Comus claims that the Lady will gain enlightenment by receptiveness to his sensory appeals. "Be wise, and taste," he urges; but he implies, "Taste, and be wise."

Milton carefully points out the error of Comus's ways. Comus uses his multisensory appeals not to enhance or expand understanding but to create imprecision and confusion. The sorcerer conjures up an image of his realm as one of youth and *joie de vivre*, but with a vagueness designed to conceal the brutal ugliness of his immorality. "'Tis onely day-light that makes Sin" (l. 126), he claims. If not seen because of the fallibility of the visual sense, sin need not be considered. Conscious that the senses, traditionally the doorways of sin, are what apprise men of the seductiveness of the world and the flesh, Comus preys on the "unwary senses" of passing travelers. The hold he maintains on his victims depends on the inaccuracy of sensory perceptions, particularly on visual distortions that can be produced by psychic aberrations. Not realizing the visible changes produced by their moral fall, his monsters "Not once perceive their foul disfigurement, / But boast themselves more comely then before" (ll. 74–75). The magician understands that appearances are frequently deceptive and contrives to make them more so:

> . . . Thus I hurl
> My dazling Spells into the spungy ayr,
> Of power to cheat the eye with blear illusion,
> And give it false presentments.
>
> [ll. 153–56]

He exploits uncertainties until appearances become wholly il-
lusory as he dazzles, fools, blears, deludes, and generally fal-
sifies.

Just as Comus plays on the fallibility of vision by distorting
appearances, so he exploits the weaknesses inherent in language by distorting the capacity of words for rational communication. He plans to set a verbal trap for the Lady:

> I under fair pretence of friendly ends,
> And well plac't words of glazing courtesie
> Baited with reasons not unplausible
> Wind me into the easie-hearted man,
> And hugg him into snares.
>
> [ll. 160–64]

Significantly, he uses language to support false appearance and
to fool the rational capacity of his victim. Despite the two
instances when he recognizes the divinity manifested in the
Lady's utterances, he repudiates as "moral babble" the truth-
seeking, truth-revealing capacity of language because he does
not wish the truth. He uses verbal as well as nonverbal rhetoric to falsify.

In contrast, the Attendant Spirit uses multiple rhetorical
means to reinforce and clarify each other. He is primarily associated with music and with hearing. Early in the masque his
ears advise him of Comus's approach—"I hear the tread / Of
hatefull steps"—and he makes himself "viewles" (ll. 91–92).
Later, he explains how he witnessed the initial meeting between Comus and the Lady. He heard, rather than saw, their
encounter, and he characterizes each in aural terms. The "bar-
barous dissonance" of Comus contrasts with the Lady's song,
"a soft and solemn breathing sound" so powerful that it figuratively transformed the Spirit into an aural metonymy of himself: "I was all ear" (ll. 550, 555, 560).

As a musician who sings and plays an instrument, the Spirit

(Thyrsis) is a skilled practitioner of the aural arts. The passages that describe his Orphic powers constitute, as many critics have noted, direct praise of Henry Lawes, who played the shepherd; they also serve—somewhat hyperbolically—as tributes to the rhetorical force of word and music. Thyrsis "Well knows to still the wilde winds when they roar, / And hush the waving Woods" (ll. 87–88); his "artful strains have oft delaid / The huddling brook to hear his madrigal, / And sweeten'd every muskrose of the dale" (ll. 494–96). His blending of voice and verse brings disorderly elements to order and enhances existing order.

Within the masque, the Spirit functions explicitly as a truthteller, as one who educates by verbally setting forth necessary information. His long narrative explanations (ll. 1–92, 513–80, 617–56, 824–57, 976–1023) cannot be justified in conventional dramatic terms by situation or by psychological context; they are unambiguously lectures directed at the audience, the children, or both. He reminds us of this at intervals: "And listen why, for I will tell ye now," and "List mortals, if your ears be true" (ll. 43, 997).

The Attendant Spirit is associated not only with poetry and music, but with the visual arts as controlled and extended by poetry. The following exchange with the Elder Brother explains the rhetorical methods he uses:

> ELDER BROTHER: What fears good *Thyrsis?*
> Prethee briefly shew.
> SPIRIT: Ile tell ye, 'tis not vain, or fabulous,
> (Though so esteem'd by shallow ignorance)
> What the sage Poets taught by th'heav'nly Muse,
> Storied of old in high immortal vers
> Of dire *Chimera's* and inchanted Iles,
> And rifted Rocks whose entrance leads to hell,
> For such there be, but unbelief is blind.
>   [ll. 512–19]

One can come to "see by hearing"—a premise implied by his effort to "show" verbally and by his dismissal of those who reject poetic truth as "blind." The Spirit teaches through words, incorporating into poetry the power of visual imagery.

The Spirit also uses a variety of persuasive means to enhance his lesson. He is to some degree a creature of the eye. His guardianship of the children requires a "mountain watch"; he apparently has some ability to manipulate appearances, to become voluntarily "viewles." Occasionally he introduces props, such as his sample of haemony, to reinforce lessons presented verbally. He is associated with dance by virtue of his occasional function as "truchman" or pointer, explaining the significance of his descent and reascent, the frenzied movements of Comus and his revelers, and the children's performance before their parents. Like Milton's masque itself, the Spirit teaches for the most part by literary means; but he is associated with dance, music, and the visual arts, and uses all available rhetorical means to communicate his message.

The contrast between Comus and the Spirit defines the rhetorical and epistemological choices available to us. The lessons in using rhetoric and in ascertaining the realities that may be obscured by misleading sensory evidence or false rhetoric are given further impetus by the trials of Milton's protagonists, the Lady and her brothers. They learn from their experiences (as do we, though more indirectly) that to form judgments on the basis of isolated perceptions is inherently wrong.

Although the children have been taken in by appearances even before the masque begins, by the time the Lady delivers her first speech she has begun to learn how to judge what she sees. The children had previously viewed the dark forest as a "kind hospitable Woods" where food and safe lodging could be found. The Lady has since recognized her surroundings as a "tangl'd Wood," which has not only failed to offer refuge and provisions but has proved so confusing that the brothers have been separated from their sister. Similarly her initial vision of nighttime as a somber but sanctified personification—"the gray-hooded Eev'n / Like a sad Votarist in Palmers weed" (ll. 188–89)—gives way to her denunciation of "theevish Night," an "envious" criminal who has "for som fellonious end" deprived travelers of the light they need to find their way (ll. 194–200). Through their cumulative experience, the children gain a steadily increasing consciousness of the potential danger that surrounds them, and their periodic reckoning of opponents echoes throughout the masque.[44] The Lady looks for help and finds "but single darkness." The Elder Brother, frustrated by the loss of his sister, comes to see in the forest "*Chaos*, that raigns here / In double night of darknes, and of shades" (ll. 334–35). Later, having heard of Comus's threat to his sister, the brother declares: "O night and shades, / How are ye joyn'd with hell in triple knot" (ll. 580–81). First a single, then a double, and finally a triple danger, the forest comes to be recognized as a threatening place in which darkness, dense vegetation, and evil collaborate to subvert the good.

The Lady's opening speech reveals her increasing skill in organizing perceptions into accurate conceptions; it also reflects her recognition that the senses are fallible and that it is difficult to know anything accurately in a complex and confusing world. Because vision is useless in the dark, she chooses to rely on hearing: "This way the noise was, if mine ear be true, / My best guide now" (ll. 170–71). Her ear has indeed proved a true guide—"the tumult of loud Mirth / Was rife, and perfect in my list'ning ear" (ll. 202–3); but in the absence of further clues—either auditory or visual—she remains lost and isolated.

At this point her speech takes the form of a traditional soliloquy, reflecting the subtle modulations of emotion and the associative flow from one thought to the next. Her first reaction to her inability to find immediate help is fright, and she imaginatively evokes visual and auditory impressions of impending dangers, "calling shapes, and beckning shadows dire, / And airy tongues, that syllable mens names" (ll. 206–8). Fear, however, gives way to courage and faith, as the Lady undergoes a visionary experience:

> These thoughts may startle well, but not astound
> The vertuous mind, that ever walks attended
> By a strong siding champion Conscience.—
> O welcm pure eye'd Faith, white-handed Hope,
> Thou hovering Angel girt with golden wings,
> And thou unblemish't form of Chastity,
> I see ye visibly, and now beleeve
> That he, the Supreme good, t'whom all things ill

Are but as slavish officers of vengeance,
Would send a glistring Guardian if need were
To keep my life and honour unassail'd.

{ll. 210–20}

Critics have often seen this as a climactic utterance, as the
Lady's most complete statement of her principles.[45] In fact,
the passage makes sense only if the vision is read as one stage
in a complex process of reaching toward truth, a process that
involves the interplay of sight and sound.

Her vision does not confirm Inigo Jones's theory of the
masque, that seeing is understanding. In other masques of the
period, abstract concepts—such as peace, justice, virtue, and
beauty—were made concrete by actors who assumed symbolic
roles. This is precisely what Milton chose not to do. The Lady
claims to see her virtues "visibly," not symbolically, and describes in physical detail what she "sees." In conventional
masques, a speech like the Lady's would have been accompa-
nied by, indeed would have become mere verbal "window-
dressing" for, a breath-taking spectacle, which would have assumed the primary rhetorical burden.

Obviously no such spectacle is to accompany the lines spo-
ken by Milton's Lady. Her vision is entirely of the inner eye
and is, as such, of considerable psychic importance. Fright-
ened by her isolation and her inability to find refuge, she comes
close to affirming that evil has triumphed. Only her confidence
in the security of her virtue enables her to assess her plight
more optimistically. The ordering of her thoughts at this point
is crucial because it suggests the direction and the import of
her discoveries; the vision affirms her sense of her integrity.
Remembering human goodness reminds her of "the Supreme
good" and renews her faith in a benign God. At the next stage,
she revises her interpretation of the world around her. In the
Trinity Manuscript, immediately after the words "I see ye,"
Milton wrote and then marked out a passage that emphasized
(and perhaps needlessly overemphasized) the Lady's changing
view of her surroundings: " . . . & while I see yee / this dusky
hollow is a paradice / & heaven gates ore my head."[46] Even
without these lines, it is clear that her situation is not hope-

less, that help is available to her, and that she will not be taxed beyond endurance.

The Lady's vision constitutes only one stage in her development, for Milton provided a double climax of sorts. Enraptured vision inspires enraptured song and both build toward an ecstatic affirmation of faith.[47] The Lady had explained her response to her vision, "I see ye visibly, and now beleeve"; but in her song she invokes Echo, who "liv'st unseen," and indicates that she knows, despite the absence of visual evidence, something of the nature and location of the nymph. She moves from faith in what she has to faith in what she has not seen, a shift that reveals a critical advance in her development. As Christ explained to Thomas "Because thou hast seen me, thou has believed: Blessed are they that have not seen, and yet have believed" (John 20.29).

The importance of the Lady's recourse to song as evidence of her heightened spiritual awareness is magnified by the multiple interpretations offered within the masque itself. Immediately after her performance, Comus describes his response, and three hundred lines later the Attendant Spirit describes his in terms that almost exactly repeat Comus's. The sorcerer contrasts her song to the music of his mother Circe:

> Sure somthing holy lodges in that brest,
> And with these raptures moves the vocal air
> To testifie his hidd'n residence;
> How sweetly did they float upon the wings
> Of silence, through the empty-vaulted night
> At every fall smoothing the Raven doune
> Of darknes till it smil'd: I have oft heard
> My Mother *Circe* with the Sirens three,
> Amidst the flowry-kirtl'd *Naiades*
> Culling their Potent hearbs, and balefull drugs,
> Who as they sung, would take the prison'd soul,
> And lap it in *Elysium*.   [ll. 246–57]

Circe's music is associated with an ambiguous blur of pleasure and pain, with enclosure, sleep, poison, and a general deadening or dulling of reason and conscious control. The Lady's, in contrast, is divine in origin and unambiguously delightful.

Her song induces "sober certainty" of pleasure; because the "it" of line 252 is intentionally ambiguous, any number of things are made to smile. Her song is liberating and fulfilling as it makes the silent air express its previously latent capacity for producing sound and evokes a "home-felt delight." It is buoyant, alive, and vitalizing; it floats, fills emptiness, awakens the listener's conscious enjoyment; it calms and orders auditors, both animate and inanimate. The Attendant Spirit describes it as living (a "solemn breathing sound"), as vitalizing (it draws the Spirit from the borders of sleep to a waking state), and as divine (capable almost of creating "a soul / Under the ribs of Death" [ll. 561–62]).

The Spirit's and Comus's marveling descriptions obviously function as praise of the young Alice Egerton, which the immediate occasion demanded. But they also reflect the assumptions behind Puritan objections to the unsanctioned and excessive emphasis of the Laudian church on external forms at the expense of preaching. God himself chose to speak through the Word, and he continues to do so through the voices of his preachers, prophets, and saints. Correctly used, oral utterance vitalizes in that it brings the word to life and awakens men, making them spiritually alive. William Perkins argued that successful sermons should convince an unregenerate listener (much as the Lady's song does Comus) that "certainely God speakes in this man!" The power of her song gains significance in the light of the Puritan belief that "the word of God preached is the life, . . . as well to the body, as the soul."[48] Thus, visual, verbal, and musical means interact, as the Lady, comforted by her vision, her faith renewed by what she has seen "visibly," expresses herself persuasively in song.

Comus, himself awed by her music, resolves that he, too, will use oral means to persuade: "I'le speak to her / And she shall be my Queen" (ll. 264–65). His attempt to beguile the Lady meets with some success, for she is not yet skilled enough to pierce the false rhetoric of others. The Lady is unconvinced by his highly conventional portrait of her as a local goddess, responding: "Nay gentle ill is lost that praise / That is addrest to unattending Ears" (ll. 271–72). She argues that her song was a functional expression, "not any boast of skill" designed to win applause.

The Lady's reproof seems at first to take effect, for the lines immediately following involve a concise exchange that proceeds according to the terse question-and-answer of plain discourse. But Comus soon reverts to decorative, image-making rhetoric as he idealizes the Lady's two younger brothers: "Their port was more than human . . . / . . . I was aw-strook, / And as I past, I worshipt" (ll. 297–302). The Lady either does not perceive the falsity of his rhetoric or is so anxious to find her brothers that she does not bother to correct him a second time. In any case, her lapse at this point foreshadows her far more serious error in accepting his offer of guidance. "Shepherd," she says, "I take thy word" (l. 321), revealing that the ear, like the eye, can be deceived by appearances and that verbal, like visual rhetoric, can seduce.

When the Lady next appears, she has clearly learned that things are not as they had seemed. The humble cottage she had been promised turns out to be a luxuriously appointed palace. Instead of finding refuge, she is subjected to an assault on her physical and moral well-being. Comus is hardly a simple, harmless shepherd. But the Lady does more than readjust her perceptions of specific place, person, and situation; she derives from her experience general concepts regarding rhetoric and epistemology.

First, she comes to realize how an understanding of moral worth is to be derived. Comus assumes the same equation of moral and aesthetic values that was implicit in conventional masques. His exhortation to indulge the appetites and the senses hinges on his belief that beauty and splendor equal goodness and thus must be used, much as virtue is to be exercised. The Lady, however, reverses the epistemological process, asserting with monosyllabic firmness:

> . . . none
> But such as are good men can give good things,
> And that which is not good, is not delicious
> To a wel-govern'd and wise appetite.
>
> [ll. 702–5]

Aesthetic appeal does not determine moral worth; rather intrinsic moral worth should determine aesthetic appeal.

The Lady also comes to a realistic sense of the nature and power of the word. Her final speech in the debate, in which she concentrates her attack on the matter and manner of Comus's arguments, is frequently criticized for its supposed inadequacies, chiefly because it is generally read as a philosophical monologue, with the expectation that it should enunciate a single, uniform position. In fact, it is a dramatic utterance that reveals the thinking process of its speaker. Her argument wavers in its focus to reflect the Lady's uncertainty about whether she should attempt to persuade Comus and even whether it is possible to persuade him.

She has become skilled at recognizing false rhetoric, for she condemns Comus as "this Jugler [who] / Would think to charm my judgement, as mine eyes / Obtruding false rules pranckt in reasons garb" (ll. 757–59). Though outraged at his abuse of language, she has no firm sense of how goodness is to articulate a crushing reply: "I hate when vice can bolt her arguments, / And vertue has no tongue to check her pride" (ll. 260–61). Choosing at this point to give virtue a tongue herself, she launches into an attack on Comus's arguments and offers her explanation of the natural order and man's duties. But her explanation ends with some uncertainty ("Shall I go on? / Or have I said enough?" [ll. 779–80]), for she begins to realize that she has not in fact convinced Comus. The Lady concludes that he is beyond persuasion. One who has revealed his contempt for language and for truth by his "profane tongue" is also incapable of rational hearing: "Thou hast nor Eare, nor Soul to apprehend" (l. 784). She, therefore, leaves him to his empty wit and decorative rhetoric with the dismissal, "Thou art not fit to hear thy self convinc't" (l. 792).

Whether her words and their substance are powerful enough to convert Comus is left a moot question, since the Lady makes no further effort to change him. She explains that if she should try, the force of her argument could make "brute Earth" respond sympathetically, though she offers no assurance that Comus would ever do likewise. Thus, while she credits inspired rhetoric with Orphic power (comparable, though she does not know this, to that exerted by her song and by the Attendant Spirit's music), its effect depends ultimately on the receptive will of the auditor.

The brothers' educational process roughly parallels that of their sister, as they learn to distrust appearances and to use their various senses to check each other. Lost in the tangled forest, they regret the darkness that impedes their vision, a darkness that represents their need of spiritual and moral enlightenment. As their debate makes clear, each boy wanders in his own kind of darkness. The younger boy's perspective is limited. He does not go beyond the literal fact of the darkness or the physical reality of his sister's beauty, which may attract "som ill greeting touch."

The Elder Brother, on the other hand, sees Neoplatonically and during the course of their dialogue tries to bring the younger one around to his own mode of vision. He asserts his faith in the higher vision of the spiritual eye: "the single want of light and noise" will not lead to their sister's destruction, for "Vertue could see to do what vertue would / By her own radiant light" (ll. 373–74). What virtue sees he describes further in his account of angels, who

> . . . in cleer dream, and solemn vision
> Tell her [the virtuous soul] of things that no gross ear can
>   hear,
> Till oft convers with heav'nly habitants
> Begin to cast a beam on th'outward shape,
> The unpolluted temple of the mind,
> And turns it by degrees to the souls essence,
> Till all be made immortal: but when lust
> By unchaste looks, loose gestures, and foul talk,
> But most by leud and lavish act of sin,
> Lets in defilement to the inward parts,
> The soul grows clotted by contagion,
> Imbodies, and imbrutes, till she quite loose
> The divine property of her first being.
>
> [ll. 457–69]

The Elder Brother insists on a link between physical and higher vision and on a consonance between inner and outer that recalls the conventions of contemporary masques. The body that is the temple of the mind accurately reflects a being's moral nature. Those of the virtuous are more luminous ("a beam" has been cast on their external forms) and spiritualized; those of the immoral are dark, impure, heavy.

The boys do not attain their sister's understanding that Neoplatonic assumptions of a correspondence between appearance and moral nature are simplistic or her faith in things unseen. Their dialogue ends inconclusively with the younger boy's delight in his brother's argument. His description of the lesson as "charming" leaves us uncertain whether in his view its magical powers are like Comus's or those of the Attendant Spirit and Sabrina.[49]

That the boys have made some progress in their educations becomes clear, however, as they break off their debate and attempt by a combination of hearing and logic to determine who is moving toward them. First, they recognize a distant noise as a call of some sort. Next the Elder Brother enumerates reasonable possibilities:

> Either som one like us night-founder'd here
> Or els som neighbour Wood-man, or at worst,
> Som roaving Robber calling to his fellows.
> [ll. 483–85]

Finally, the Spirit and the brothers identify each other by voice, and since the Spirit appears in the form of Thyrsis the older boy's second supposition of a friendly rural neighbor is shown to be the correct one. Like their sister, the brothers learn ways of using the senses to gain knowledge in the fallen world, interrelating various perceptions for greater accuracy.

The final teaching the Spirit offers to protagonists and audience, as he turns to reascend to his heavenly habitat, summarizes the rhetorical and epistemological concerns that have pervaded the masque and sets them forth in all their complexity. He urges us to continue in the ways of virtue and tells us what awaits further along in our spiritual journeys:

> There I suck the liquid ayr
> All amidst the Gardens fair
> Of *Hesperus*, and his daughters three
> That sing about the golden tree:
> Along the crisped shades and bowres

Revels the spruce and jocond Spring.
The Graces, and the rosi-boosom'd Howres,
Thither all their bounties bring,
That there eternal Summer dwels,
And West winds, with musky wing
About the cedar'n alleys fling
Nard, and *Cassia's* balmy smels.
Iris there with humid bow,
Waters the odorous banks that blow
Flowers of more mingled hew
Then her purfl'd scarf can shew,
And drenches with *Elysian* dew.

[ll. 980–96]

The graceful movement, splendid colors, dance, sprinkling of perfume, and delightful revelry all evoke characteristics of the traditional main masque. Indeed, the passage reads like an anthology of conventional main masque devices, recalling the eternal spring, the garden of the Hesperides, and other pastoral bowers of the sort that were popular in Stuart masques. The references to Iris, the Graces, and the flowers suggest the complimentary roles often accorded masquers or other main-masque personages. In conventional masques, the Spirit's thirty-line description would scarcely have been necessary, for the earthly paradise would have been rendered in visible, theatrical terms.

No such thing happens in Milton's *Comus* and for good reason. To realize the rich imagery of the epilogue in theatrical spectacle would have violated the consistent rhetorical strategies of *Comus*. The Ludlow entertainment concludes not with a flight into spectacular fantasy, but with a balanced account of the joys of paradise that integrates appeals to all the senses into the poetic texture of the passage. Contributions of the other masquing arts—dance, music, the visual arts—pervade the poetry, which thus becomes their expressive vehicle. Transcending the moral concerns that dominate the rest of the masque, the epilogue offers visionary insight into the joys awaiting redeemed man. The Spirit's epilogue entices, and our response to its beauty and persuasive power measures the effectiveness of the reformed rhetoric of *Comus*.

CHAPTER FOUR

Merriment Well Managed: Chastity as a Rule of Life

ALTHOUGH MILTON'S MASQUE DOES NOT OFFER A SIMPLE contrast between antimasque and main masque, it distinctly opposes the powers of darkness and light. Comus is clearly the villain, and his heroic opponent is chastity, embodied in varying degrees by several characters. The brothers' dialogue turns on the need for faith in the power of chastity. The Lady's comforting vision includes the "unblemish't form of Chastity," and her enraptured response to Comus's libertine arguments culminates in her evocation of chastity and virginity as sublime doctrines and holy mysteries. Sabrina is introduced as a chaste nymph who extricates similarly chaste young people from threatening situations. The Attendant Spirit's stress on his own purity as he descends into an impure world and his dramatic function as Comus's opponent suggest that he, too, is to be counted among the forces of chastity.

There is no doubt about the importance of chastity to the theme and narrative of the masque. Although critics have recognized the Christian and Platonic elements of thought that inform Milton's chastity, what he meant to convey by it has proved a "high mystery" in itself.[1]

A careful consideration of context, however, provides useful clues as to what kind of Platonism and what kind of Christian views shaped *Comus*, and how and why Milton brought the two systems of thought together. His decision to celebrate chastity was in no way eccentric, for the concept figured prominently in the reigning theatrical tradition of the time and in the religious debate between Anglicans and Puritans that provided the background for Milton's developing theological and moral positions. His handling of chastity reflects the same critical attitude toward received tradition, the same process of revising, reforming, and adapting that characterizes the masque as a whole.

As an ideal of conduct in the Neoplatonic cult promoted by Charles and Henrietta Maria, chastity was a frequent theme in Caroline court plays and masques. In most respects, the Caroline love cult differed little from the poetic Platonism that had flourished throughout Europe during the Renaissance. It was a literary style and a style of living and loving—a code of manners, of political behavior, and of courtship.[2] Although indebted to the medieval tradition of courtly love, the cult drew its immediate inspiration from more recent continental and native sources. Henrietta Maria brought with her to England the *préciosité* in vogue in France. She and her ladies attempted to make Honoré D'Urfé's *Astrée*, the literary handbook of the *précieuses* (partially available in an English translation), as "canonical at Whitehall as it was at the Hotel de Rambouillet."[3] The cult also drew support from English literature, particularly from Beaumont and Fletcher. Significantly, Fletcher's *Faithful Shepherdess*, a dismal failure when first presented in 1610, was received with delight by the royal couple on Twelfth Night, 1633. Sidney's *Arcadia*, too, took on new life as a relentlessly mined source for fashionable Caroline dramas.[4]

By the time Milton wrote *Comus*, the Neoplatonic cult was in its heyday. Walter Montagu's *Shepheard's Paradise*, the prototype of drama inspired by the cult, did not appear until 1633 when the cult was already firmly established. Jonson's 1629 play, *The New Inn*, which satirizes the Neoplatonic lady, is evidence that the cult had reached beyond the confines of court to the popular theaters. Jonson's final two masques and those composed by Townshend, Shirley, and Carew in the early 1630s were also inspired by principles of the love cult. It similarly infused William Habington's *Castara* (1634), Suckling's *Aglaura* (1637), and Sir Kenelm Digby's *Private Memoires* (1627). James Howell was describing a fad of wide popularity when he wrote in a 1634 letter: "The Court affords little News at present, but there is a love call'd Platonic Love, which much sways there of late; it is a Love abstracted from all corporeal gross Impressions and sensual Apetite, but consists in Contemplations and Ideas of the Mind, not in any carnal Fruition." As Shackerley Marmion reported, every gentleman could "lie a-bed, and expound *Astraea*, and digest him into compliments," and every lady spoke "perfect Arcadia."[5]

The basic principles of the love cult are the familiar assumptions of romantic Neoplatonism in general. The beloved lady is beautiful in body and soul. The lover attracted to her ascends the traditional ladder of love, moving from a limited physical to a spiritual affection that revels in her moral perfections as reflections of divine goodness itself. More distinctive is the cult's "heroinism," that is, its ideal of the active female heroine who has considerable power in her world, and the cult's increased emphasis on marriage as the aim of love.

Two attributes, beauty and chastity, make the lady the heroic center of her world. Beauty gives its possessor power over her world, serving particularly as a means of communicating with and controlling men.[6] In Walter Montagu's *Shepheards Paradise*, an eight-hour drama that exhaustively reviews the Caroline love cult, the power of beauty is even recognized as a political fact. The ruler of the pastoral paradise is a queen who is elected annually on the basis of superior beauty.[7]

Beauty is not an effective source of power by itself, because it makes a woman vulnerable to the violent and short-lived lusts of the male. Beauty needs the support of chastity. Not limited to the practice of sexual abstinence, chastity (or as it is sometimes called, virginity) is less a physical fact than a state of mind; it is the habit of life that motivates sexual purity. In the *Faithful Shepherdess*, two once licentious lovers become virgins by magical means when they repent and vow to mend their lives.[8] Chastity is related to sexuality, for it expresses itself in sexual conduct. In love relationships, chastity upholds women's control over men by conquering the mutability of passion that destroys women's security in love. If desire is unfulfilled or incompletely sated, then love is never used up, for much as Keats tells the lover depicted on his Grecian Urn: "She cannot fade, though thou hast not thy bliss, / Forever wilt thou love, and she be fair!" Chastity thus ensures that the male remains ever yearning, ever responsive to his mistress.

Beyond its psychological and social advantages, chastity accords the female real control over men and events. The cult encouraged chivalry, with pure-minded young men often rescuing damsels in distress. Ladies do not always simply wait passively to be saved, for chastity can be resourceful and determined on its behalf. A chaste glance is often capable of striking evil dumb and impotent, capable even on occasion of reforming it; ladies can, when necessary, defend themselves with words or weapons. Nearly every Caroline heroine became, at some point, a Britomart. Freed from the restrictions that flesh-and-blood women of the day faced, fictional ladies fearlessly passed through their pastoral landscapes at all times of day or night, secure in the power of chastity. Nancy Pearce notes that in trials of chastity, Fletcher's heroines generally defend themselves. Their self-sufficiency is probably one thing that recommended the Jacobean playwright to the next generation of theatergoers. The lady errant, female counterpart to the chivalric knight errant, became a common figure in Caroline drama.[9]

Chastity has the added power of its special moral efficacy. It renders the love of physical beauty legitimate and even virtuous. Love of a beautiful body, though a mere preliminary step in the Neoplatonic ascent toward the meeting of souls, is necessary to true love, for the senses must be sated by an overwhelming perception of physical beauty before the lover moves on to a higher state.[10] Chastity is a negative attitude in that it requires a restraint of the appetites; but it is also a positive quality that inspires a lover to perceive his lady's physical beauty as a mere reflection of the loveliness of her soul and to strive for spiritual union with her.

Although love according to the Caroline cult is not to be primarily carnal, sexual consummation is not precluded. Physical satisfaction is the reward for lovers who have proved through numerous trials that their relationship is not based solely on physical attraction. The cult doctrine usually required that marriage precede sexual consummation.[11] In his discussion of Renaissance love poetry, Mark Rose comments that, while continental Platonists saw their only choices as either immersion in carnality or asceticism, their English counterparts celebrated marriage as a middle way.[12] Marriage provided the *via media* for fashionable Caroline lovers. An amorous shepherd in Montagu's pastoral offers the representative opinion that love is a union of spirit, emotion, and mind: "two hearts so equall in it [love] as they are measured by one another, are the vessels where it [love] is refined, heated naturally by each others eyes, and joyned by pipes as subtill as our thoughts."

Once lovers have achieved this enraptured union which makes two into one, the joining of bodies—as well as hearts, eyes, and soul—in wedded consummation enhances chaste love by rendering it more stable and permanent: "Love may rise to this transcendent height, that it may seem to look down on all things and despise even enjoying: but, likely, our thoughts in this elevation stay not long, but growing dizzy fall. . . . the possession [in marriage] is a foundation to maintain Love at that height: and such love . . . remaines unmoved. . . . Therefore possession what it takes off from loves summer-prospect in the height, doth recompense it with strength, and security against the change of seasons."[13] Through marriage, chaste love becomes a collective as well as an individual good, by making possible the family bonds that ensure social continuity. Caroline writers often introduced the traditional metaphor of the king's marriage to his people to deliver a political message. Only by loving submission to the monarch could the kingdom remain stable and fruitful.

The love cult provided the basic assumptions in masques contemporary with Milton's. As we have seen, the traditional ascent took the form of a journey by masquers and spectators, and the splendid costumes and scenery that embellished the royal couple and their courtiers were treated as reflections of their moral and spiritual perfections.

The heroism of the Caroline cult produced some changes in masquing patterns. Although not a performer himself, James I regularly served as the artistic ordering principle. In Caroline masques, the queen frequently assumed much of the ordering power. *Loves Triumph Through Callipolis* takes place in "the city of beauty or goodness" where Henrietta Maria reigns as the Queen of Love. The masque tells us, "Love presents a world of chaste desires, / Which may produce a harmony of parts," and this harmony includes a conquest of time, of sensuality, and of political opposition in which the queen figures prominently.[14] In *Chloridia* the queen, cast as goddess of the flowers whose coming brings the stellification of earth, symbolizes the union of heaven and earth made possible by monarchical absolutism. Similarly, *Albion's Triumph*, *Tempe Restored*, and *Coelum Britannicum* all depict Henrietta Maria as the Queen of Love and Beauty who draws toward herself the heroic love of her regal spouse and the chaste and orderly desires of the entire kingdom. She becomes the means for demonstrating the power of chaste love to effect inner and social peace. She does not just share power with her husband; she is a governing agent in her own right. Through her influence she makes the king an effective ruler of himself and of the nation.

The Neoplatonic cult's elevation of marriage also found its way into the masque. The royal couple is constantly celebrated as the exemplar of romantic wedlock. Caroline masques generally conclude with a tribute to their perfect union, praising them as "royal paramours," "Mary-Charles . . . Hymen's twin," "a blessed pair," or "royal turtles."[15] When the king as Heroic Lover submits his passions to the sanctifying government of wedlock, he becomes a model for his people. As we have seen, the lesson for spectators is also political. "Chaste embraces famed" make Britain "the paradise of love," where Peace, Eunomia (Law), and Dice (Justice) are at home.[16] The contrary tugs of flesh and spirit felt collectively by the body politic can find reconciliation in the loving marriage of subject to sovereign.

Milton probably had some familiarity with the popular literary texts that set forth the basic tenets of the cult.[17] His response to it, however, accords with the general objections of contemporary Puritans. As George Sensabaugh has argued, Puritan moralists condemned the cult on the grounds, first, that all the pious talk of chastity merely served as a disguise for licentious behavior, and, second, that the cult fostered the idolatrous worship of women.[18] Milton himself, convinced that Charles's theater encouraged sexual immorality, viewed Neoplatonic spirituality as hypocritical; he abhorred the inversion of sex roles that the cult encouraged. He was later to dismiss Henrietta Maria as an "Idol Queen," including in his condem-

nation her husband's uxorious attachment to her elevation as
the object of the entire nation's devotion (*CP*, 3:335).

He also probably intended an unfavorable allusion to the
Neoplatonic fad in that famous discussion of chastity in *An
Apology against a Pamphlet*, which is frequently used as a gloss
to *Comus*. When Milton speaks of "the divine volumes of *Plato*,
and his equall *Xenophon*," who were the subjects of his youthful
study, he contrasts their teachings with a morally corrupting
lore: "Where if I should tell ye what I learnt, of chastity and
love, I meane that which is truly so, whose charming cup is
only vertue which she bears in her hand to those who are worthy. The rest are cheated with a thick intoxicating potion which
a certaine Sorceresse the abuser of loves name carries about;
and how the first and chiefest office of love, begins and ends
in the soule, producing those happy twins of her divine generation knowledge and vertue, with such abstracted sublimi-
ties as these, it might be worth your listning, Readers" (*CP*,
1:891–92).

Comments on this passage generally assume a simple distinction between love and lust. But Milton's counterpoising of
the charming cup of true philosophy to the killing potion of
the Circean temptress suggests rather that he was developing
a more complex distinction between true and false Platonism.
He carefully defined the chaste love of true Platonism as beginning and ending in the soul. He spoke of "abstracted sublim-
ities" without reference to any means of rendering them concrete:
love in true Platonism leads toward the spiritual perfection of
greater wisdom and virtue rather than toward the sense of total
intimacy and the human offspring desired by Caroline lovers.

Milton may well have had the Caroline love cult in mind
again when he described in his outlines for proposed tragedies
on Old Testament subjects a play on the burning of Sodom
(Gen. 19) to be entitled "Cupids funeral pile." John Demaray
has recently noted certain isolated parallels between the projected play and *Comus* (particularly the similarity between the
vision of profligacy in each), though he has not commented on
the relation of either work to the Caroline love cult.[19]

Milton describes Sodom in his outline as a city that worships "Venus Urania or Peor"; and there are implied equations

not only between the Heavenly Venus of traditional Neoplatonism and the false god of the Sodomites, but also between Sodom and Milton's England. He outlined a choral ode relating the nightly worship of the Sodomites, "every one with mistresse, or Ganymede, gitterning along the streets, or solacing on the banks of Jordan." He also planned a discourse on the difference between love and lust by the angels God sends to judge the city—a discourse that recalls the lengthy debates on similar subjects in Caroline drama. Lot, the intended hero of the play, is persecuted for not participating in obligatory religious festivities, which he has condemned as immoral. The climax of the piece is to come with Lot being saved by the avenging angels, the King of Sodom being punished "for dispising the continuall admonition of Lots," and the entire city being destroyed as a warning to other nations to avoid such godlessness.[20] In representing a society devoted to hedonistic sports in the name of religion and to the persecution of righteous men who refuse to participate in immorality, Milton seems to have designed a commentary on the recreation debate, cast from the Puritan perspective. He also placed the problem of proper and improper sport in the larger context of true and false love in a manner that is thoroughly relevant to the Ludlow masque.

Despite Milton's obvious disagreement with the Neoplatonic cult, he appeared to offer in his masque something that superficially resembles dramas that grew out of the tradition. This much is clear from the substantial number of critics who have found general similarities between *Comus* and various Neoplatonic pastorals, both English and continental.[21] We can see something of the typical heroinism in the Lady's solitary situation, her strength of character, her straightforwardness in confronting Comus, and her own and the Elder Brother's faith in the power of chastity. Some readers have also seen in Milton's *Comus* the celebration of marriage, arguing that the work mediates between Comus's libertinism and the Lady's idealism, advocating the chaste love of wedlock.[22] However, such similarities are only superficial, giving way under scrutiny to reveal Milton's profound disapproval of the fashionable style of loving and his revision of masque conventions to reflect this disapproval and to present a different kind of chastity, a different kind of love.

The revision involves Milton's replacing Caroline love ethics with a theologically based morality. While related to faith, as is hope, Milton's chastity is a virtue distinct from the others. M. M. Ross exclaims in wonderment at the Lady's version of the Pauline virtues, "Faith, Hope, and *Chastity*! And the greatest of these is chastity."[23] Since Milton wrote in an age far more familiar with the Scriptures than our own and was undoubtedly aware that the triad of virtues serves as the very foundation of Paul's practical divinity, he surely intended the Lady's reformulation to startle. By leading us to expect charity and then giving us chastity, Milton draws us into another educational experience. He made his shocking substitution because he specifically intended to clarify the meaning of religious love and what it entails. Chastity is Milton's version of charity.

Milton's conflation of charity and chastity is nothing new in literature of the European Renaissance. A good English example occurs in book 1 of the *Faerie Queene*. Here Spenser synthesized the two in his depiction of Charissa, sister of Fidelia (Faith) and Speranza (Hope), as "full of great love . . . chast in worke and will." Charissa's roles as faithful wife and fecund mother draw on the traditional motif of the Christian soul bound by reciprocal love to Christ and reflecting that love in acts of virtue. Spenser's handling of the nuptial motif and the emphasis on the active life of the devout Christian foreshadow similar elements in Milton's *Comus*. However, Milton toned down the allegorized sexuality of Spenser's charity/chastity, and he focused on a question that had become a point of controversy between seventeenth-century Puritans and Royalists: what kinds of behavior constitute the good works expressive of Christian faith?

When Anglicans of the day answered this question, they drew heavily on Roman Catholic conceptions. They agreed that the prime work of charity should be a love for God. However, their treatises devoted far less space to divine charity than to such works as conforming to established forms of worship, almsgiving, visiting the sick, offering spiritual encourage-

ment to the low in spirit, fraternal correction, and other acts
of philanthropy. They also gave charity an application to civil
and ecclesiastical politics. Aquinas had noted that charity unites
people in a love for God and in a concern for the general welfare that rule out discord, contentiousness, and schism. In his
Ecclesiastical Polity, written to codify and thus fix Anglican belief in the face of growing agitation for continued reformation
by the Puritan faction in the church, Hooker closely followed
Roman formulations. He listed as works of religious love the
proper observance of rites of worship and of the sacraments;
"works of satisfaction," such as prayers, fasts, and almsgiving;
and, not surprisingly, in view of contemporary turmoil, institutional concord. Throughout the treatise he returned to the
latter kind of charity several times, arguing that Christian love
does not divide but unites the church in prayers for the spiritual well-being of all, and he pointedly suggested that in post–
Reformation England the "exercise of charity were safer and
seemlier for Christian men, than the hot pursuit of these controversies."[24]

Reformed thinkers generally objected to the orthodox view
of charity on two grounds. First, they condemned as supersti-
tious the equation of charity with isolated acts of external piety
and rituals of worship. Good works are significant only inasmuch as they are the product of faith, and faith demands a
total dedication of oneself to God. There was a tendency consequently among Protestant theologians to avoid legalistic
prescriptions and proscriptions of specific actions. One's entire
life was expected to be a good work, although the usual qualifications to human righteousness were recognized: man remains liable to sin and his virtue is not entirely his own, but
a gift of God.[25] Protestantism retained a sense of its own origin in revolt that was apparent in its conception of charity.
Though cautions against civil disruption were frequent, reformed thinkers argued that institutional concord should not
take precedence over purity of faith and that loving God often
demands incurring hatred and dissension among one's neighbors.[26] Their emphasis was on charity as an unyielding love of
God that looks to a complete union with him and to personal

salvation. Everything else—social harmony, forms of worship, philanthropy—was to be secondary to this all-encompassing love.

The difference between orthodox and reformed views of charity came to the fore in the debates between Anglicans and Puritans during the prewar period. Appeals to charity were frequent in loyalist calls for ecclesiastical and political obedience. As Coolidge notes, for the conformist love often meant mutual forbearance, civil obedience, and the restraint of individual liberty in order to preserve social order. In his defense of the *Declaration of the Book of Sports*, Bishop Sanderson asks that Sabbatarians exercise "godly charitie" by allowing others to participate in Sunday recreations. In Shelford's "Sermon of holy charitie," charity is equated with upholding existing institutions:

> There is no pride in charitie, but it submitteth it self to all good ordinances, both in Church and Commonwealth. . . . This will say, Come neighbours, let us hold together, we must be subject to our governours for conscience sake, we may not do what we list, we may not be our own judges, we may not make our selves equal with Apostles. . . . And in this Predicament are they which make havoc of Church-discipline: they will not keep holy dayes; . . . to stand up in reverence when *Gloria Patri*, *Te Deum*, *Benedictus*, and the rest are said . . . of them is a needless ceremonie; Confession and Absolution is flat Paperie; and with such all is superstition, save onelie a sermon from the spirit without premeditation, . . . but the true speakers and true hearers are alwayes in charitie.[27]

In contrast, English Puritans of the 1630s argued for a charity toward God that superseded all other commitments. In essence, the Puritan saw himself as faced with a stark either-or choice between God as his rule of life or some substitute that would make him an idolator. Idolatry was for him an all-inclusive sin, in the sense that any evil act was a falling away from God. Since God expects to be loved not just on Sunday, not only in church, and not in isolated acts of piety, but in every speech, action, and thought, any lapse was an act of idolatry and a failure of charity. Richard Sibbes exhorts his congregation to accept their current nickname ("Puritie is become a nickname") so that it may remind them of the world's obloquy, inevitably incurred by true saints, and so that it may recall to their minds the ideals of consistency and purity they should strive to fulfill.[28] A Puritan's priorities were clear: God was to be loved before all else, before the appetites, the pleasures of the world, the king, the church, family and neighbors, and even before personal security. Such single-minded charity demanded considerable courage and self-control; one had to become, if necessary, a rebel against his country's government, all established institutions, his family's welfare, and himself.

Puritans frequently chose to characterize the life of charity in the metaphoric terms of human love. Those who accept the call of Christ and are sealed in grace become his betrothed; they agree to put aside all other lovers, to persevere in constant love during the period of betrothal (that is, for the rest of their natural lives), and they look forward to their marriage to Christ and the final consummation of their love after death in heaven. A popular text for sermons was the Song of Songs, which Puritans read as a narrative of the love between Christ and a human soul or between Christ and his church. They avoided mystical interpretations of the sort common in orthodox commentaries, instead viewing the Canticles as an exposition of the reformation process or of the spiritual pilgrimage of the individual believer.[29]

Although the motif was not unique to Puritans, its popularity among them was probably due to its ready applicability to their theological doctrines. Christ's choice of his Bride reflects the doctrine of election. In addition, the espousal metaphor helped to illuminate the view of sin current among Puritans, who, following reformed tradition, rejected orthodox distinctions between venial and mortal sin in favor of their either-or concept. Sin is idolatry, but the sins committed by those espoused to Christ are also acts of fornication, since the betrothed soul goes a-whoring from its divine lover. Just as a lover either is or is not faithful, so any act either is or is not sinful. Formal distinctions between varying degrees of sin are to no purpose. As Preston explained, "Now hee that loves not the Lord is an adulterer, that is, hee is false to the Lord that

should be his husband. And when he loves not the Lord, he
doth love somewhat else." [30]

Depicting the soul's bond to God as a love relationship helped
to illustrate the Puritan idea of Christian liberty. Charity toward God is not expressed by scrupulous fulfillment of any
legalistic code of conduct that prescribes some things, pro-
scribes others, and permits still others as morally indifferent.
It involves instead a voluntary and wholly engrossing movement toward God that grows out of a desire to possess and be
possessed by the divine lover in perfect and complete union.
Freedom to devote oneself to love of God means that one is
not under bondage to things of the world—either to the senses
and appetites or to man-made laws that impede the free exchange of love between God and the individual soul. Since
charity toward God required forsaking all rival lovers, Puritans frequently spoke of it as chastity, using the two terms
almost interchangeably. Puritans divorced chastity further from
sexuality than had Orthodox commentators, treating it as proper
use not only of one's own body, but of all created things.

There was a general and overriding tendency among Puritans to insist on the interrelation of all virtues and all vices
because all involve the proper use of the world and all flow
from a constant and chaste love of God. In effect, chastity
became an inclusive virtue, often used interchangeably with
virginity, moderation, purity, temperance, sobriety, continence, and frugality. [31] To behave virtuously was to abide by
God's precepts and to preserve in chastity one's love relationship with God. Thus, to be sober, frugal, moderate, or otherwise virtuous was to be chaste.

In addition, for Puritans chastity did not imply asceticism.
Rather, the Protestant doctrine of stewardship made the rule
of chastity a correct use of the world rather than a flight from
it. [32] Puritan commentators often emphasized that it was proper
to love one's spouse and to enjoy a good meal. But commitment to God must inform and when necessary take precedence
over all earthly delights and loves. Puritan clerics recognized
the difficulty in determining how much love of the world was
too much and frequently offered practical guidelines. Making
specific reference to the problems of recreation, Preston offered

a simple test for determining whether enjoyment of things of the world violated chastity: "You may know whether your love to any creature, to any sport or recreation be adulterous or no. A chast wife may love many men besides her husband; but if it once begin to lessen her love to her husband, that is an adulterous love."[33]

Milton consistently expressed general agreement with the Puritan concept of works. In the *Christian Doctrine*, he defined charity in Puritan terms as a chaste love or charity toward God. When describing charity as an effect of regeneration, he specifies: "I am not talking about charity towards one's brother. The love I have in mind is love of God, and not only the love which we have for God, but a love which arises from the instinct and awareness of the love which he has for us." In the second half of the treatise, which is devoted to good works, Milton discussed in an order that probably reflected their relative importance: charity as proper worship of God, charity toward oneself, as expressed in proper use of one's body and of the world, and finally charity toward other men. Charity toward self and fellowman are informed by and, in fact, express a chaste love of God. The nuptial metaphor pervades Milton's entire theology, occurring in his discussions of sin, marriage, regeneration, forms of worship, and the complete glorification to occur after the Apocalypse.[34] A key concept in his theology is the relation between charity and freedom. Under the New Dispensation, God and man are bound by love, not law. Men are free from the Mosaic code, free from all coercion in religious matters, and most important, free to perform works inspired by a chaste love of God (*CP*, 6:535).

The same assumptions inform Milton's other works. In the divorce tracts, he treated fornication as a straying of the spirit. His ideal of marriage derived from his sense that the human couple is a type for the chaste and loving relation between Christ and his Beloved. As Jason Rosenblatt has shown, sin in *Paradise Lost* is described in sexual terms that indicate Milton's sympathy with the Puritan idea of human immorality as idolatry, fornication, a choice of union with the demonic rather than the divine.[35] The Protestant ideal of charity as love of God and purity of life also informs human virtue in *Paradise*

Lost. After the long and dreary preview of mankind's history, Michael speaks comfortingly to Adam of the love between Christ and the human soul, a love that will guide men in righteous conduct and help them resist the satanic Cupid, who would lure them to fix their affection on unworthy objects:

> . . . but from Heav'n
> Hee to his own a Comforter will send,
> The promise of the Father, who shall dwell
> His Spirit within them, and the Law of Faith
> Working through love, upon thir hearts shall write,
> To guide them in all truth, and also arm
> With spiritual Armor, able to resist
> *Satan's* assaults, and quench his fiery darts.
>
> [12:485–92]

Milton's political and religious tracts are also infused with a characteristically Puritan concept of charity as a chaste love of God that informs one's use of secular things. True charity demands a consistency of purpose, and it was on this count that Milton in *Eikonoklastes* disputed Charles I's self-justification that he had behaved according to his kingly conscience. The terms that concluded the Bishops' War, releasing the Scots from ecclesiastical and liturgical conformity, and Charles's willingness to make concessions to the Irish, Milton argued, proved that the king's policies were not inspired by a truly charitable desire for concord, but by a "fals Virginity": "But being once on this side *Tweed*, his reason, his conscience, and his honour became so streitn'd with a kind of false Virginity, that to the English neither one nor other of the same demands could be granted, wherwith the Scots were gratifi'd" (*CP*, 3:487–88). If the king was unchaste, so was the Laudian church. Christ is the church's husband, and he expects "her to be presented before him a pure unspotted virgin." The prelates sullied with idolatry and false doctrine the purity of the Reformed church, dredging up from Catholicism the "gaudy allurements of a Whore." The English church, as wifely vine, Milton insisted, chose to clasp the elm of worldliness rather than her divine spouse (*CP*, 1:755, 557, 555).

Even in the period roughly contemporaneous with the composition of *Comus*, Milton tended to associate a chaste love for God with the good works arising from faith. In the *Apology*, he recalls in some detail his early concern with chastity, which was fed by his reading of Dante, Petrarch, chivalric romances, and finally Plato and Xenophon. Because of the nature of the charges he was answering in his pamphlet (that he frequented bordellos), his comments on chastity refer specifically to sexual relations, but they also have broader implications regarding the Christian ideal of purity of life. As Woodhouse and others have recognized, his discussion of chastity is organized according to a hierarchy of values, as in proper Christian humanist fashion he moved from his naturally chaste disposition to his philosophic commitment to chastity, both of which are finally transcended by the superior chastity of a living faith expressed in the works of personal purity. Drawing on the traditional nuptial metaphor, he exalted the "chaste and high mysteries" contained in the Pauline notion that "the body is for the Lord and the Lord for the body," and he looked forward to the consummation of spiritual marriage with Christ promised to those who persevere in constant and chaste love: "Nor did I slumber over that place expressing such high rewards of ever accompanying the Lambe" (*CP*, 1:892–93).

Milton's early writings reveal an interest in the nature and power of chastity and the importance of the metaphor of spiritual espousal to his poetic vision. The innocent child, whose death was the occasion for "On a Fair Infant," was raped by death but married to immortal life. In the "Nativity Ode," the earth is personified as a Magdalene, who had been accustomed before Christ's coming "to wanton with the Sun her lusty Paramour"; but the new Sun-Son promises to be a superior lover, and in his honor she strives for purity, covering herself with "the Saintly Vail of Maiden White." The nuptial kiss that welcomes the soul into eternal bliss in the poem "On Time" is a symbol of man's escape from mutability and his union with the divine. Similarly, the dead Lycidas is greeted in heaven with "the unexpressive nuptiall Song"; and in his elegaic lament for the death of Charles Diodati, Milton spoke of the divine Cupid and the immortal marriage that will be the young man's reward for virtue.

Comus offers the earliest and fullest poetic development of the figure of spiritual marriage and the related motif of chastity as good works performed out of love of God. Milton's treatment of chastity in the masque is neither straightforward nor simple, for he develops his theme gradually through a series of partial revelations that involve his audience and readers in a process of trial and error. During the course of the masque, he succeeded in disentangling chastity from the romantic associations it was given by the Caroline love cult, in transcending its orthodox implications of sexual abstinence and general asceticism, and in defining it in Puritan terms as ideal for those living actively in the world.

The Attendant Spirit's opening monologue, describing the pure world from which he descends and the impure world that is the testing ground for human virtue, establishes the beginning and end for the spiritual journey of human life, on which the plot of the masque depends. The monologue also poses a question that is the central thematic concern of the masque: how does one bridge the gap between here and there? Various answers to the question are possible, as the mixed Christian and Platonic references would indicate. There are hints in the prologue that Milton's solution in the masque is to be a Christian one, that the two disparate realms are to be reconciled in the lives of righteous men who live in the world but by heavenly values. Since the hints are little more than embedded allusions to the Pauline crown of virtue and to the idea of Christian service, Milton's message is in no sense clear at this point.

The changes he made in the prologue as he revised the masque indicate his attempt at least to point his audience in the right direction. In the version contained in the Bridgewater Manuscript, he placed between what were finally to be lines four and five (and therefore immediately between his descriptions of the pure and the impure realms) fourteen lines that tell of an intermediary place that, like the impure realm, appeals to the senses and yet is, like the pure one, free of darkness, purposeless activity, and corruption. As C. S. Lewis has suggested, Milton omitted this passage from the induction, inserting it instead in the epilogue, because "nothing that blurs the distinction between the region of the Spirit and the region of Comus must be admitted until we have passed the 'hard assays.'"[36] The fourteen-line description of a lush, vernal place raises expectations that a conventional reconciliation of Heaven and earth can be achieved here and now, recalling the bowers of chaste love in Caroline masques, which represent the coming together of king and queen, Heaven and earth, the ideal and the real, subject and sovereign. Since Milton intended nothing of the sort, the lines when placed at the beginning were simply misleading. As he clarified the message of *Comus* through his revisions, he chose to shift the description from the prologue to the conclusion, where it took on an entirely different significance.

The first reference to chastity comes with Comus's perception of the Lady's "chast footing," which impresses him as belonging to "som Virgin sure." Such an introduction, given the Lady's situation as a virtuous, young girl in imminent danger, would lead us to assume that she is to be the conventional heroine familiar in Neoplatonic pastorals. The faith she subsequently expresses in chastity is, thus, not unexpected. There are, however, strong suggestions, implicit in her opening soliloquy, that Milton's chastity is not what we expect: the context for her reference to chastity is distinctly nonromantic; there is not even the vaguest reference to the ideal of political harmony usually associated with chastity in Caroline masques; and the Pauline allusion indicates that the Lady's spirituality may well be more Christian than Neoplatonic.

With the brothers' dialogue, the unexpected religious note sounded by the Lady is temporarily stilled, and we return to the Neoplatonic patterns. The Elder Brother claims to draw support for his assertions from "antiquity from the Old Schools of Greece," but in fact his thought has less in common with the Platonic Dialogues than with contemporary love lore. His speeches reflect the influence of a general sort of Renaissance Neoplatonism but also appear to have more specific links with works inspired by the Caroline cult. In the easy movement from immediate situation to theoretical heights, the sense of dramatic action frozen in place while the brothers pause to debate, the contest between a Neoplatonic and a dissenting perspective, and the focus on the nature of chastity, the brothers' dialogue is very like the endless philosophic discourses standard in Caroline court theatricals.[37] The self-sufficient virgins of contemporary works probably influenced the Elder Brother's vision in *Comus* of militant chastity: "Virgin purity . . . may pass on with unblench't majesty," untouched by any threat; "the huntress Dian" conquered lust and "set at nought / The frivolous bolt of *Cupid*"; and the "wise *Minerva*, unconquer'd Virgin," quelled her foes with "rigid looks of Chast austerity" (ll. 427, 430, 441, 444–45, 448, 450).

The brothers' debate may even be indebted to a particular work that grew out of the Caroline love cult, Thomas Randolph's *Jealous Lovers*. Milton might well have attended a performance of this work at Cambridge in 1632/33. Even if he did not witness the play, there is good reason to believe that, as an aspiring young poet, he knew the writings of Randolph, easily the most celebrated writer concurrently in residence at the university.[38] There are echoes of Randolph's play in the brothers' speeches. Randolph's virtuous heroine, Evadne, when caught in threatening circumstances, responds at first with fear, which she expresses in words recalling those of Milton's Lady: "What strange fancies / My maiden fears present me!" While Milton's heroine turns to faith in her own virtue and in God, Evadne places her trust in Diana, patroness of chastity. Similarly, the Elder Brother defends his optimistic view of his sister's situation by pointing to the powers of the classical goddess of virginity and the hunt. He later vows in the best tradition of Caroline court drama to become a chivalric avenger of the innocent:

> Against th' opposing will and arm of Heavn'
> May never this just sword be lifted up,
> But for the damn'd magician, let him be girt
> With all the greisly legions that troop
> Under the sooty flag of *Acheron*,
> *Harpyies* and *Hydra's* or all the monstrous forms
> 'Twixt *Africa*, and *Inde*, Ile find him out,
> And force him to restore his purchase back,
> Or drag him by the curls, to a foul death,
> Curs'd as his life. [ll. 600–9]

His speech is a possible reworking of a similar vow by Tyndarus, Evadne's Neoplatonic lover:

> Away, foul ravishers! I will teach my sword
> Justice to punish you. Such a troop of harpies
> To force a lady's honour! I will quench
> With your own blood the rage of that hot lust
> That spurr'd you on to base and bold attempts.[39]

Although the brothers' dialogue draws on conventions of Neoplatonic theatrical entertainment, it introduces in germinal form several themes that receive further development in Christian terms and are ultimately fitted into the theologically based morality of the masque. The brothers' choice of language suggests that the virtues and vices are interrelated; they consider the power of chastity to sustain itself; and they touch on chastity not simply as a human attribute but as a quality that inheres in all created things, animate and inanimate.

The masque does not celebrate any specific, isolated virtue or set of virtues. It is about all the virtues—involving use of one's body, use of the goods of nature, and proper worship of God—that are necessary to a consistent life of faith. It does not focus exclusively on those virtues that much criticism of *Comus* emphasizes—virginity, chastity (understood in an orthodox sense), and temperance—but also comments on sobriety, right worship, gluttony, and virtue in general. Much the same is true of the masque's treatment of vice, as my listing below of virtues, vices, and their line references in appendix B indicates.

The virtues and their opposed vices in *Comus* are not arranged in any neat system. The Lady's mention of the "holy dictate of spare Temperance" comes early in her diatribe, "the Sun-clad power of Chastity" later, and still further along "the sage / And serious doctrine of Virginity" (ll. 767, 782, 786), but there is no distinction among these virtues according to relative worth, no suggestion that they are arranged in an ascending hierarchy of value. Indeed, Milton blurs the relation of the various virtues to each other and does much the same with the vices. For example, the Younger Brother worries about his lost sister's virginity and the threat incontinence poses.

The Elder Brother speaks of "true virginity," "chaste austerity," and "saintly chastity," using the terms interchangeably. There is an obvious resonance of terms here since the younger boy's concern for his sister's virginity has to do with bodily integrity and the older boy is clearly thinking of spiritual wholeness. Milton allowed the different views to become explicit in the boys' debate and the debate ends with a balanced concern for bodily and spiritual integrity. There is thus a blurring of the relation between the physical and spiritual states. The Elder Brother asserts, "Vertue may be assail'd, but never hurt, / Surpriz'd by unjust force, but not enthrall'd" (ll. 589–90), and the Lady tells Comus, "Thou canst not touch the freedom of my minde" (l. 663). But the subsequent episodes of the masque are about the Lady's achieving a physical freedom consonant with her liberty of spirit.

The blurring of various virtues and vices in the brothers' speeches occurs throughout the masque. Comus appeals to the intemperate thirst of weary travelers; he attacks abstinence, temperance, and virginity. In his carpe diem argument, he intends an assault on the Lady's physical integrity and on the spiritual chastity that guides her conduct. Similarly, the Lady obscures distinctions when she speaks of the "sober laws" of "spare Temperance," "wanton dance" as evidence of false worship, and gluttony as blasphemy.

Milton's imprecision is intentional, for careful distinctions between vices and between virtues are simply not important to the moral vision of the masque. What he does make precise is the relation between vice and idolatry. Comus declares himself and his beasts "vow'd Priests" of Hecate and Cotytto. When he refers to Cotytto as "goddess of Nocturnal Sport," the more learned members of Milton's audience may have understood by "sport" the sexual excesses attributed to her by Juvenal, Horace, and Virgil.[40] Yet even the less erudite would have comprehended the general implication of immorality and gathered from her association with "Stygian darkness" that devotion to her constitutes devil worship. The Attendant Spirit describes the sorcerer as the practitioner of vicious religious rites, adding to the implications of licentiousness a hint of unholy sacrifice:

> . . . night by night
> He and his monstrous rout are heard to howl
> Like stabl'd wolves, or tigers at their prey,
> Doing abhorred rites to *Hecate*
> In their obscured haunts of inmost bowres.
>   [ll. 532–36]

Mistakenly identifying Comus's revelry as harvest celebrations, the Lady speaks contemptuously of country folk who "thank the gods amiss" for nature's bounty; and she later condemns Comus's libertinism as false worship.

In addition to breaking down traditional distinctions between virtues, the brothers' dialogue considers the power of virtue to influence events in the natural world. Stuart productions habitually assumed the inevitable triumph of chastity, but Milton offered a less simple relation between earth and Heaven and a disquieting vision of human virtue that acknowledges its limitations as well as its strengths. In Stuart masques heavenly forces descend to bring order to earth. In *Comus* divine providence works in less obvious and less comforting ways.

Caught up in the rapture of her vision, the Lady realizes that a benign Providence oversees events on earth and she feels assured that virtue is powerful because God and his forces will directly intervene to protect his people:

> . . . he, the Supreme good, t'whom all things ill
> Are but as slavish officers of vengeance,
> Would send a glistring Guardian if need were
> To keep my life and honour unassail'd.
>   [ll. 217–20]

In the brothers' debate, the younger boy suggests that the Lady's virtue may prove unable to defeat the assaults her beauty attracts. The older boy elaborates an optimistic view: no evil thing can soil a virgin's purity; gods and men fear the chaste Diana's frown; Minerva conquers by a single look. He also expresses a belief, similar to his sister's, that heaven aids the chaste, though he magnifies her single "glistering Guardian" into a veritable army of attending angels:

> So dear to Heav'n is Saintly chastity,
> That when a soul is found sincerely so,
> A thousand liveried Angels lacky her,
> Driving far off each thing of sin and guilt.
>   [ll. 453–56]

His hopes, however, prove unrealistic. The Lady does not succeed in subduing Comus with a glance or even by the force of argument, though she maintains her commitment to virtue. As the boys approach Comus's palace, the Elder Brother makes a significant advance when he admits the limitations of human powers and prays, "And som good angel bear a shield before us" (l. 658).

There is some justification in the masque for the Lady's and the Elder Brother's belief that virtue can summon heavenly defenses. Heaven does indeed lend them grace in the form of the Attendant Spirit. But the Spirit himself repeatedly emphasizes that his intercession is not miraculous, that divine help works through natural means. The audience, having been apprised that the Spirit descends from a heavenly realm to care for those favored by God, is fully conscious that a divine agent is at work in the world of *Comus*. But from a perspective within the fiction, expectations of a miraculous sortie of angels out of Heaven are not confirmed. Instead of miracles, the Spirit offers the children earthly antidotes to their plight: the shepherd, Thyrsis, haemony, and Sabrina.

The first of these to aid the children is the Attendant Spirit in his pastoral disguise. Thyrsis functions as a spiritual pastor, representing the divine help available to the virtuous in their spiritual teachers and guides. In "Elegy IV" Milton had described his teacher, the Scottish Presbyterian Thomas Young, as one of those men "qui laeta ferunt de caelo nuntia, quique / Quae via post cineres ducat ad astra, docent" ["who bring glad tidings from heaven and teach the way which leads beyond the grave to the stars"] (ll. 93–94). In effect, spiritual instructors mediate—as does the Attendant Spirit—between the realms of nature and grace.

Although Thyrsis does not and, in fact, cannot conquer evil, he teaches the children how to withstand it. His didactic speeches present some artistic problems, being too long and

gracelessly expository. There is also a problem with his veracity, for he describes in some detail how he came by knowledge
of haemony and Sabrina, suggesting in his explanations that
he has simply drawn on pastoral lore available to anyone who
cares to learn. Since he is not really Thyrsis, but a quasi-divine
guardian with other means of attaining such information, his
stories are presumably fabrications. They have a point, however, for in presenting the children with an account of his
discoveries he teaches them how they too may find defenses in
the world around them. Milton's educational plan in *Comus*,
like that set forth in his later prose tract on the subject, focuses
not on the acquisition of specific facts and skills, but on learning to learn.

The Spirit's lecture on haemony is representative of this plan:

> Amongst the rest a small unsightly root,
> But of divine effect, he cull'd me out;
> The leaf was darkish, and had prickles on it,
> But in another Countrey, as he said,
> Bore a bright golden flowre, but not in this soyl:
> Unknown, and like esteem'd, and the dull swayn
> Treads on it daily with his clouted shoon.
>   [ll. 629–35]

What other country possesses the favorable growing conditions that enable haemony to produce its blossoms is not clear.
Some critics have argued that Milton means Heaven; but he
may simply be contrasting seventeenth-century England with
other lands and other times more favorable to the pursuit of
virtue. "In another country" moral aids of the sort needed by
spiritual pilgrims like the two brothers are easily recognizable
and immediately accessible in a glorious and fully blossomed
form. In the world of the masque and in Milton's world, moral
assistance is more difficult to come by. The value of haemony
is not obvious from its "unsightly" appearance, and its special
powers are not widely known. Despite its unprepossessing appearance and the lack of information about its efficacy, the fact
that the ignorant "treads on it daily" suggests that haemony
and the moral support it represents are common enough. The
Attendant Spirit's discourse on haemony—his descriptions of

what it looks like and where it can be found—makes it possible for the children to find it for themselves should they need it in the future.

Haemony is introduced because the children's virtue alone is not enough to protect them from Comus. The brothers and Thyrsis determine that the Lady needs to be saved, and Thyrsis convinces the boys that their inherent abilities will not be adequate to defeat the enchanter's "hellish charms." He therefore gives them the haemony, claiming that it will enhance their understanding and their strength. Again he offers his experiences as exemplary, explaining that because of the herb "I knew the foul inchanter though disguis'd, / Enter'd the very lime-twigs of his spells, / And yet came off" (ll. 645–47). He claims that haemony will lend strength to the boys' youthful virtue: "if you have this about you / . . . you may / Boldly assault the necromancers hall" (ll. 647–49).

Although haemony endows its possessor with an increased ability to perceive and combat evil, what exactly the herb is meant to signify is not easy to determine.[41] Milton seems intentionally to evoke multiple interpretations and multiple frames of reference—the classical and the Christian, the symbolic and the etymological—without unequivocally endorsing a single one. Angus Fletcher argues that "Milton courts exegetical overrefinement in *Comus*. . . . By recollecting so many poets dead and gone, Milton revives their voices and their ghostly persons"; and by introducing "verbal and literary echoes" he achieves an "extension of the etymological domain."[42]

If Fletcher is right, and I think he is, the meaning of haemony lies in the very multiplicity of readings it evokes. Comprehending the classical wisdom that Renaissance allegorists like Sandys and Golding had found in Homer and Ovid, as well as Christian tenets, haemony with all its symbolic and etymological implications represents the weight of moral wisdom available in Milton's time. Unlike faith or virtue, two alternate readings given haemony, moral lore can be communicated by one individual to another, by the Shepherd Lad to Thyrsis, and by Thyrsis to the brothers. Understood as wisdom, haemony can offer protection, as the Attendant Spirit claims, allowing its possessor a means of recognizing evil and even countering it.

As a teacher, Thyrsis delivers haemony—that is, moral lore—to the two boys, indicating as he does so how to find it. That haemony is provided by the Attendant Spirit, himself a divine emissary, implies that it may be of heavenly origin, yet the Spirit makes clear that the wisdom it represents is available in the world around them, if only they recognize and use it properly. The Lady apparently has no need of haemony, perhaps because she is older and more knowledgeable than her brothers about the obstacles that confront a spiritual pilgrim. Even unaided by haemony she manages on her own to recognize the foul enchanter though disguised, to enter within range of his evil spells and yet resist them. While the brothers learn moral lore from their teacher, she acquires what knowledge she does not already have from her direct encounter with Comus.

Thyrsis implies that haemony alone is enough to thwart Comus's charms, that the brothers should be able to invade Comus's palace, spill his magical potion, seize his wand, reverse his spells, and eject him. But haemony—at least as it is wielded by the Egerton children—does not prove sufficient to free the Lady. It enables the Egerton boys to resist evil, but they are still too young and inexperienced to be completely successful at converting knowledge into practical action. Sabrina is needed to transform their virtue into an effective force.[43]

The Sabrina episode provides further development of two ideas introduced earlier in the masque: that chastity is not exclusively a human quality but instead infuses the entire natural world; and that chastity, though powerful, has its limits. Sabrina's past history is important, for she provides a cautionary example of the vulnerability of chastity:

> There is a gentle Nymph not farr from hence,
> That with moist curb sways the smooth Severn stream,
> *Sabrina* is her name, a Virgin pure. . . .
> She guiltless damsell flying the mad pursuit
> Of her enraged stepdam *Guendolen,*
> Commended her fair innocence to the flood
> That stay'd her flight with his cross-flying course,

The water Nymphs that in the bottom plaid,
Held up their pearled wrists and took her in,
Bearing her straight to aged *Nereus* Hall,
Who piteous of her woes, rear'd her lank head,
And gave her to his daughters to imbathe
In nectar'd lavers strew'd with Asphodil,
And through the porch and inlet of each sense
Dropt in Ambrosial Oils til she reviv'd,
And underwent a quick immortal change
Made Goddess of the River.   [ll. 824–26, 829–42]

Milton left out elements of the Sabrina myth that would have complicated his simple tale of chastity victimized: her illegitimacy, the just wrath of the true wife at having been replaced by a concubine, and the death of Sabrina either by suicide or as an inadvertent victim of her mother's suicide.[44] She appears in *Comus* as an unambiguously virtuous maiden, destroyed by overwhelming evil. She is not preserved by her recourse to elements in the natural world around her; the river to which she confides herself impedes her flight and drowns her. Her fate illustrates the possibility that the virtuous may suffer despite their moral and spiritual merits.

The meaning behind Sabrina's tale is not wholly pessimistic, however, for she is not in fact destroyed. Sabrina dies to her life as a chaste maiden to be transformed into a local spirit committed to preserving other virgins. Her chastity lives on as a force pervading the natural world. The catalogue of water gods and the poetic evocation of her watery qualities emphasize Sabrina's function as the presiding spirit of the river that encloses the lands ruled by the Earl of Bridgewater. Not a perfect place, Ludlow is vulnerable to the ills that plague the fallen world. Like the Genius of "Arcades," Sabrina does not banish evil but remedies its effects on nature. Still her association with Ludlow defines it as a virtuous place. By curing the disorder induced by "urchin blasts, and ill luck signes / That shrewd medling Elfe delights to make" (ll. 845–46), she does not simply obliterate the effects of evil but restores to the natural world the native order that bespeaks its inherent principle of chastity.

As chaste nymph and as curative force, Sabrina reveals the

essential chastity of nature, which the Lady had proclaimed in her rebuttal of Comus. Both disputants in that debate based their arguments on their conflicting visions of external nature. Comus's initial assumption, which even the severest Puritan would not have disputed, is that man praises and thanks God by taking delight in the good things provided him in the creation. But Comus also argues that nature was created as a servant to man's appetites:

> Wherefore did Nature poure her bounties forth,
> With such a full and unwithdrawing hand. . . .
> But all to please, and sate the curious taste?
> And set to work millions of spinning Worms,
> That in their green shops weave the smooth-hair'd silk
> To deck her Sons, and that no corner might
> Be vacant of her plenty.   [ll. 710–11, 714–18]

Further, that since nature tends to excess and disorganization, man's divinely ordained responsibility is to impose his own order through the process of consumption:

> . . . if all the world
> Should in a pet of temperance feed on Pulse,
> Drink the clear stream, and nothing wear but Frieze,
> Th'all-giver would be unthank't, would be unprais'd,
> Not half his riches known, and yet despis'd,
> And we should serve him as a grudging master,
> As a penurious niggard of his wealth,
> And live like Natures bastards, not her sons,
> Who would be quite surcharg'd with her own weight,
> And strangl'd with her waste fertility.
> [ll. 720–29]

There is just enough of traditional presumptions about the fallen world in Comus's argument to make it almost plausible. But when he applies his principles to man's use of his own body, his position becomes a barely disguised hedonism, which irreverently fuses the pagan carpe diem theme with the religious concept of divine gifts provided by a strategically unnamed creator:

> If you let slip time, like a neglected rose
> It [beauty] withers on the stalk with languish't head.

> Beauty is natures brag; and must be shown
> In courts, at feasts, and high solemnities
> Where most may wonder at the workmanship.
>
> [ll. 743–47]

Just as external nature serves man, so his body is made for delight alone; and as nature takes on ordered form through man's exploitation, so the human goods of physical beauty are meaningful only when used for the pleasure they yield. Comus appeals to divine intentions for creation, but he places human appetite at the center of the universe.

Without disputing Comus's basic premise that man worships God by his use of the world, the Lady repudiates his assumptions about the nature of nature, as well as his hedonistic ethics. Nature is not ruled by human appetites; she operates according to "sober laws" and a "holy dictate" that transcend human mastery. She is not excessively prolific or disorderly, but a "good cateress [who] / Means her provision onely to the good" (ll. 764–65). In the Lady's view, nature is not depraved, as Calvinists held. Rather Milton reflected much the same vision articulated by Sidney's Pamela in her debate with Cecropia and by Spenser's Guyon when he dismisses Mammon's claims. As Milton was to explain in the *Christian Doctrine*, "nature cannot mean anything except the wonderful power and efficacy of the divine voice which went forth in the beginning, and which all things have obeyed ever since as a perpetual command" (*CP*, 6:131). Nature is thus ruled by the same principle of chastity, the outward and active conformity to divine will, that ought to guide human life. Men make nature unchaste by misusing her.

As she concludes her refutation of Comus's position, the Lady reveals that she now understands more fully the implications of her argument. Earlier, when she had expressed her conviction that an angelic guardian would be sent to aid her, she had actually received divine help, not in the form of a miracle, but through natural means. "A sable cloud / Turn[s] forth her silver lining on the night" (ll. 223–24), and the Lady is granted some light in the darkness that surrounds her. So too, as she confutes Comus's hedonism, she envisions nature's own defense of chastity:

. . . the uncontrouled worth
Of this pure cause would kindle my rap't spirits
To such a flame of sacred vehemence,
That dumb things would be mov'd to sympathize,
And the brute Earth would lend her nerves, and shake,
Till all thy magick structures rear'd so high,
Were shatter'd into heaps o're thy false head.

[ll. 793–99]

The principle here is right, but the Lady's expectation of a complete and utter conquest of Comus is excessively optimistic. For Milton as for other Puritans, the individual freedom to be perverse ensures that there will always be those who choose to give themselves to evil. Comus will remain alive.

Milton did not view chastity as the magically potent force depicted in Caroline theatricals. It does not, he recognized, always enable virgins to defend themselves, provide the virtuous with the help they need against assailants, or inspire instant harmony. In *Comus*, the powers of chastity are qualified by its dependence on indirect means of support, by the individual freedom that allows men to reject it if they wish, and by the very fact that it does not inevitably, as in Sabrina's case, provide a practical defense against its opponents.

In his portrayal of the relative vulnerability of the virtuous, Milton spoke to a larger problem of his age: the anxieties provoked by religious and civil repression. *Comus* asserts that the world is neither wholly beneficent nor actively malevolent. It is not, as royalist masquers of the 1630s would have it, a paradisal garden where virtue can blossom without opposition. The world contains elements that try and occasionally succeed in destroying the chaste. Still, Milton asserted that the chaste will be preserved, if not in this life, then in the next; and that God provides everything good men need to sustain themselves in the world, if they only know how to find and use his aids. The fact that *Comus* introduces three different agents of release is important, for Milton meant to suggest that there are many supports and that men must continually learn of the gracious means available to them. He insisted on the strength of will and the intellectual resources the good must acquire to preserve their chaste love of God as a living force.

In *Comus* Milton repeated several times, in dramatic terms, that God helps those who help themselves and that his mysterious ways often involve the commonplace and immediate. With Sabrina he gave the forces that support chastity and chastity itself an added social importance. If the Lady's refusal to participate in Comus's revelry implies that chastity must often seem antisocial, that one must often choose not to join, the masque also gives hope for a chaste community that preserves and seeks to enhance the chastity of its individual members. Sabrina governs the lands along the Severn, restoring them to their proper order. In effect, she embodies the governing power of the earl, serving chastity by serving him. The implication is that the earl is a chaste man and an effective governor, though he is threatened, as are all postlapsarian men, by malignant forces in the world.

Through Sabrina, Milton suggested the moral strength of a virtuous community like Ludlow. Beyond the guidance of a teacher like Thyrsis and the traditional wisdom represented by haemony, a chaste community like the one Sabrina tends can help individual pilgrims on their way. Ludlow is in some sense self-sustaining. The Lady and her brothers are received into their parents' presence and absorbed into the life at Ludlow Castle:

> Noble Lord, and Lady bright,
> I have brought ye new delight,
> Here behold so goodly grown
> Three fair branches of your own,
> Heav'n hath timely tri'd their youth,
> Their faith, their patience, and their truth.
> And sent them here through hard assays
> With a crown of deathless praise,
> To triumph in victorious dance
> O're sensuall Folly, and Intemperance.
> [ll. 966–75]

The metaphor of a plant and its branches has something more than the obvious dynastic significance. Just as a healthy plant needs "goodly grown" limbs, so a virtuous community depends on the virtue of the individuals that compose it. Ludlow perpetuates itself as a physical entity and as a spiritual community by taking in new members who have proved themselves.

Although life at Ludlow is chaste, it is by no means ascetic. The festivities associated with Sabrina suggest that chastity is a rule of recreation, as well as the key to moral conduct. She inspires revelry that recalls the traditional rural recreations licensed by the *Declaration of the Book of Sports* but is in important regards different:

> . . . the Shepherds at their festivals
> Carrol her goodness lowd in rustick layes,
> Throw sweet garland wreaths into her stream
> Of pancies, pinks, and gaudy Daffadils.
>
> {ll. 848–51}

The context and the details Milton provided suggest one of the traditional shepherds' holidays, probably the traditional sheep-shearing festival usually held in June.[45] But he also created a distinct contrast between Sabrina's shepherds and the rustics "who thank the gods amiss," for whom Comus and his rowdy revelers had been mistaken. Sabrina's folk respond to their pastoral harvest, not with revels devoted to self-gratification and unruliness, but with prayerful thanks.

The brief description of the sports supervised by Sabrina foreshadows the moral sports that accompany the children's reception into their parents' immediate presence. The "Jiggs, and rural dance" and "mirth and chere" that greet the children's arrival demonstrate the inaccuracy of Comus's distorted belief that any kind of recreation different from his is "lean and sallow abstinence." Milton was careful to suggest that there is some regulation of the festive spirit at Ludlow. Comus's revels, like those of conventional masquers, may go on until dawn forces everyone home to bed, but the Attendant Spirit urges that the recreation at Ludlow not continue too late: "Come, let us haste, the stars grow high, / But night sits monarch yet in the mid sky" (ll. 956–57).

The dances that celebrate the children's arrival further define the kind and range of acceptable sport. First, rural folk, probably a local troop of dancers, perform a lively dance. They are abruptly dismissed, however, by the Attendant Spirit's song:

Back Shepherds, back, anough your play,
Till next Sun-shine holiday,
Here be without duck or nod
Other trippings to be trod
Of lighter toes, and such Court guise
As *Mercury* did first devise.

[ll. 958–63]

Next, the Egerton children enter and perform. This arrange-
ment may not initially appear satisfactory. Herford and Simpson, for example, have complained that the rural dance is
"gratuitous and unrelated to the plot" developed in the rest of
the masque.[46] One could also take issue with the snobbery that
seems to inform the presumed superiority of light-stepping
aristocrats to jigging peasants or with the curt, even rude,
tone of the Spirit's dismissal.

Close attention to the poetic detail, however, suggests that
Milton was making a crucial distinction between two kinds of
dancing, two kinds of sport—a distinction that hinges on his
allusion to Mercury as the children's choreographer. As Woodhouse observes, "There seems to be no classical sources for
Mercury as inventor of the dance."[47] But in other of his works,
Milton recognized Mercury's traditional roles as a patron of
learning and as a divine emissary. Earlier in the masque, he
cites Hermes as the source of knowledge about haemony. Milton associated the medicinal teaching with the lessons in dance
by giving a common teacher. Apparently Mercury is to be viewed
as a divine instructor. He choreographs the lighter trippings
of the Egertons which replace the rustic dance, because superior dancing symbolizes superior moral knowledge. The masque
systematically develops a metaphoric equation of a character's
moral state with the movements of his feet. As the children
perform, they express a victory over immorality which far
transcends the merely diverting dance of the country folk.

Through the two contrasting dances, Milton arranged a final test for his audience. Although Comus is no longer immediately present, the false revelry he represents remains as a
threat to moral life. The gratuitousness of the rustics' dance,
the abruptness of their dismissal, and the implied elitism are

intentional. The rustic dance is not presented as inherently immoral or evil. It celebrates the children's arrival and their successful completion of the early stages in their lifelong pilgrimage. The appearance of the rustics also helps to solidify our vision of Ludlow as a harmonious and well-governed realm. All members of the little society, from the earl down to the simple rural folk, have their contributions to make to communal gatherings and communal life. However, as the Attendant Spirit's dismissal makes clear, the lively country jig cannot be allowed to distract us from the serious business that pervades the masque as a whole. The Spirit sends the dancers away and redirects our attention to the more important matter of the children's escape from evil and the victory of virtue. As we move from country sport to the "triumph in victorious dance / O'er sensual Folly and Intemperance" (ll. 974–75), we are again reminded that recreation does not imply a release from moral responsibility.

Once there is an end to the children's performance (and to whatever social dancing may have taken place on that night in 1634), the Spirit, instead of sending us home, points the way for continued journeying. Further along in our pilgrimages are the earthly paradises, but beyond these lies the possibility for final consummation of our spiritual yearnings. Masques of the period habitually concluded with a vision of the wedded love of Charles and Henrietta Maria, understood broadly as a figure of personal, social, and cosmic harmony. *Comus*, too, closes with a vision of loving union. Milton offered us not one, but two couples:

> . . . young *Adonis* oft reposes,
> Waxing well of his deep wound
> In slumber soft, and on the ground
> Sadly sits th' *Assyrian* Queen;
> But far above in spangled sheen
> Celestial *Cupid* her fam'd Son advanc't,
> Holds his dear *Psyche* sweet entranc't
> After her wand'ring labors long,
> Till free consent the gods among
> Make her his eternal Bride,

> And from her fair unspotted side
> Two blissful twins are to be born,
> Youth and Joy; so *Jove* hath sworn.
>
> [ll. 999–1011]

However much the significance of this miniature allegory is debated, no one could possibly argue that Milton was drawing on the politicized love lore of the Caroline masque.[48] Instead, the passage is a logical development of that controlling figure of the amorous spirit smitten by love for God.

The first two lovers are not united. Venus, earlier invoked as the patroness of Comus's festivities, appears at this point as a beautiful Oriental goddess seated disconsolately beside her human lover, Adonis, who is wholly unconscious of her charms. Her lowly seat and her obvious inferiority to the "celestial *Cupid*," reigning far above, associate her with base love, not necessarily with wantonness but with all the things of the world that would claim our affection. Adonis, though not entirely healed of his wound, is mending, and his curative sleep renders him impervious to Venus's allure. He does not embody the assertive chastity that the Lady represents; but his lethargic posture suggests at least a withdrawal from the love of earthly things and a return to health.

The Attendant Spirit points to a final consummation of spiritual love in his description of the second couple. The tender embrace of the "celestial *Cupid*" and his beloved Psyche, who has completed her "wand'ring labors" in the world, is, as James Hanford suggests, a highly conventional symbol of the heavenly union of Christ and the human soul.[49] The embrace is to culminate in marriage and the production of offspring— not the human progeny of dynastic continuity expected in the Caroline love cult, but rather two aspects of eternal bliss, Youth and Joy. Milton significantly chose not to present here as the products of love those familiar Platonic twins, Knowledge and Virtue, for his meaning transcends a philosophically based ethics, ascending toward theological insight.[50] Neither does he intend the espousal metaphor to suggest a mystical ecstasy. Rather, the union of Christ with the individual soul or with the collectivity of souls represented by the church will occur once the moral trials of this life have ended and the Last Judgment ("free consent the gods among") has been concluded.

Joy is the feeling of supreme contentment that Milton and other theologians frequently associated with the heavenly life.[51] What Milton meant by "Youth" is less obvious. He may have had in mind the conquest of mortality, the attainment of eternal youth that Heaven represents. There is probably also an intended contrast between heavenly youth and the earthly variety, which, as the Lady and her brothers discover, can be a liability. When Comus urges the Lady to join his revelry, he reminds her of the strength of youthful appetites: "you are but young yet." The children's difficult journey illustrates that with youth goes moral inexperience and that a youngling virtue that has not been exercised by contact with its opposite is vulnerable. But in Heaven youth becomes a positive quality that contributes to the pleasures of the place. Knowing good by knowing evil and moral combat are no longer necessary, for one can know good directly through contemplation of God.

The looked-for consummation of the love between the divine Cupid and his human lover is only a future possibility as the Attendant Spirit's language makes clear ("Mortals that *would* follow me") because men are freed to love what they will. The masque as a whole indicates that Milton understood liberty, not in the Anglican sense of a freedom from restraints which permits morally indifferent acts, but as a freedom to do all that is necessary to one's calling. Comus claims to offer freedom from pain and anxiety, but the Lady recognizes that his diversions are imprisoning, not liberating, when she asks, "Wouldst thou seek again to trap me here?" Her recognition recalls the Spirit's description of men who "with low-thoughted care / Confin'd, and pester'd in this pin'fold here, / Strive to keep up a frail, and Feaverish being" (ll. 6–8). In their limiting obsession with satisfying the demands of physical existence, instead of with the pursuits of virtue, such men are like penned animals.

The Attendant Spirit's concluding instructions to the audience summarize the proceedings of the entire masque: "Love vertue, she alone is free." To choose vice is to limit the freedom to grow toward God, to become imprisoned by the passions, the appetites, or earthly objects. Milton assumed that true freedom has as its end conformity to the divine will and therefore is expressed through virtuous behavior in recreation as well as in all other activities. The same paradox that is the subject of the great epics and the tragedy Milton was later to produce informs the masque: true freedom is faithful service.

Strategies for Artistic Reform

AS A ROYALIST FORM, THE MASQUE BEFORE MILTON HAD been unavailable to those of Puritan leanings as a literary vehicle. Milton's achievement was to reform the masque, revising its conventions of form and thought, to make it answerable to Puritan concerns.

Puritan characters had occasionally appeared in court masques, but they were inevitably antimasque figures, stalking horses for royalist values, either malevolent villains to be exorcised or comic buffoons fit for ridicule. An example of the latter variety is Plutus, the comic villain in Jonson's *Love Restored*. Produced in 1612 on a limited budget, apparently because of Parliamentary intransigence, this masque depicts—naturally from a royalist perspective—the debate over sports which would erupt again in the 1630s. A representative of the king's Puritan opponents in Parliament, Plutus opposes masquing on moral and spiritual grounds:

> I tell thee, I will have no more masquing; I
> will not buy a false, and fleeting delight so
> deare: They merry madnesse of one hower
> shall not cost me the repentance of an age.

He offers alternatives to masquing:

> Let 'hem embrace more frugall pastimes
> . . . .
> Masking and Revelling? Were not these
> Ladies, and their gentlewomen more houswifely
> employ'd . . . i' their chambers, at home,
> and their old night-gownes . . . rather than
> to wake here, in their flaunting wyres and
> tyres . . . and other taken up braveries?[1]

Plutus damns himself. As his name implies, he is a materialist opposed to spending money, not to expense of the spirit. He is also satirized for his class envy. Hopelessly bourgeois in his tastes, he can only despise the masque's elegant and refined pleasures. Jonson finally has Plutus ejected and replaced by masquers cast as aristocratic virtues.

The difference between *Love Restored* and *Comus* reflects the distance between Royalist and Puritan perspectives on sports, the masque, and related religious and political matters. Comus at one point urges the Lady to join his revelry:

> Beauty is natures brag, and must be shown
> In courts, at feasts, and high solemnities
> Where most may wonder at the workmanship;
> It is for homely features to keep home,
> They had their name thence; coarse complexions
> And cheeks of sorry grain will serve to ply
> The sampler, and to teaze the housewife's wool.
> What need a vermeil-tinctur'd lip for that
> Love-darting eyes, or tresses like the Morn?
>
> [ll. 745-53]

Milton's villain offers the same simple either-or choice between courtly revelry and dreary pastimes at home that the villain in Jonson's royalist masque had outlined. Comus simply argues from the opposite side. Milton's Lady, however, while she rejects Comus's offer of courtly revelry, does not advocate staying at home in an old nightgown. Instead, through the Lady and through other characters, Milton's masque as a whole presents his alternative as pleasant and, in its own way, sophisticated. He gave the Puritan view sympathetically, developing a complexity of moral vision that far transcends Jonson's caricature of the Puritan as an envious, narrow-minded materialist.

What Milton articulated in his masque is no specific set of religious and political doctrines identified with a Puritan sect or sects, but a vision of life that reflects the concerns and values of Puritans during the period preceding the civil war. M. M. Knappen and William Haller have shown that the Puritan movement began as a program for living in the world, though it eventually culminated in the recognition that there is no set of guidelines external to the self.[2] *Comus* embodies Milton's early optimistic view that a pattern for virtuous living could be discovered, that a total reformation of society was possible, and that men could do more than simply cultivate their interior gardens. He assumed in the masque that individual faith can be readily translated into moral conduct, and that a community of the faithful can sustain and enhance the spiritual well-being of its members.

His vision of reformation as an individual and social necessity could not be contained within the forms of the conventional masque without radical revision. The masque tradition as Milton received it was shaped by royalist assumptions of a static rather than a dynamic world order and of a fixed hierarchy of powers that ruled out the need for individual moral judgments. Repudiating these assumptions, Milton reformed the masque. To reflect his sense that the spiritual life of an individual or of a community ought properly to be a process, not a state of being, he made critical changes in the conventions affecting plot, character, and audience response. He attempted to create a revised rhetoric, one that avoided the falsity of Caroline productions and integrated the masquing arts in an effective collaboration. In his treatment of chastity as an ideal of conduct, his concern was not with human love, sexual ethics, or the rituals of courtship, but with the Christian believer's love for God and the effect of that love on his moral life.

The differences between Milton's work and other masques are the key to its meaning. Critics like D. C. Allen, Enid Welsford, Jonson's Oxford editors, and Jean Martin, who have pointed out the work's significant deviations from the generic tradition, have in effect isolated the elements of the masque that Milton chose to reform. To gloss over such differences is to miss Milton's serious meanings. If we assume that a masque is merely intended to compliment noble patrons and guests by placing them in some flattering symbolic scheme, then we may argue that Milton's differs from other examples of the genre by being "more of a masque" because it manages to speak to occasional needs without sacrificing literary quality. If we read it as a conventional masque conforming to the standard patterns established in royalist masques, though without the usual royalist themes, we may well conclude that Milton offers us "a sublime empty-headedness."[3] But if we focus on

his violations of convention, we can take into account his characteristic handling of genre, the political and religious wran-
gling that provided the historical context for the work, and
his likely response to that context; at the same time his masque
emerges as a profound and sophisticated statement worthy of
a young poet completing his literary apprenticeship.

The large question of how Milton managed to get away with
his remaking of the masque remains. The fact that his work
was presented at a private home and not at court allowed the
masque-maker some freedom in his handling of convention.
As Paul Reyher has noted, the usual strictures regarding per-
sonation were often relaxed in private presentations, where high-
born performers could take speaking roles like those played by
the Egertons.[4] Other conventions regarding action, thematic
message, and rhetoric could also be altered. William Browne's
Inner-Temple Masque, privately presented by gentlemen of the
legal profession, lacks the morally edifying climax normally
expected. Jonson chose to experiment with the *stylo recitativo*
in *Lovers Made Men*, which was performed at the home of Lord
Hay. *Lovers Made Men* also lacks the political message normally
at the heart of a masque. And Jonson's *Gypsies Metamorphos'd*
was a ribald, rambling piece that deviated from accepted masquing patterns in almost all important regards. Even so, James
I liked it best of all Johnson's masques and had it performed
three times, each time at a private home.

Despite the relative looseness of literary decorums in private
masques, the conventional patterns established in court productions were not entirely dismissed. The court masque was
assumed as the standard against which deviations were to be
judged and in the light of which such deviations derived their
significance. Consider, for example, Jonson's handling of the
transformation motif in *Gypsies*. The ranking dignitary in attendance at a masque—at court masques generally the king—
conventionally possessed the power of inspiring the shift from
antimasque to main masque and thus of transforming disorder
to order. As Dale Randall explains, Jonson particularly calls
attention to this convention with his title and within the text
itself, then fails to fulfill the expectations he has raised (there
is no metamorphosis), and thereby focuses critical attention on

the king's power to transform (in real life terms, his governing powers) as a central theme.[5] Milton made more numerous and more far-reaching changes in conventional patterns. But as in *Gypsies*, his deviations challenge us to consider his masque in the light of the conventions established in court masques and to see precisely how he has reworked the form's political, religious, and moral assumptions.

Milton's deviations from convention apparently did not offend his audience at Ludlow Castle; the Puritan perspectives that shape *Comus* apparently did not either. Parker has suggested that the Egertons' favorable reception of *Comus* may be attributable to the Puritan leanings of some members of the family.[6] John Egerton, who played the Elder Brother, grew up to be a Cavalier. He married a daughter of the Duke of Newcastle and is said to have written in his copy of Milton's *First Defense* that the book deserved to be burnt. His father, however, though a loyal servant of the crown in various government capacities, appears to have shared the religious scruples of contemporary Puritans. His daughter Frances was to remember him with gratitude "for seasoning her against *Arminian principles*, and once *suspending her from the Sacrament* upon his *re-examination of her*, after that his *Chaplain* had passed an hasty approbation of her." His unwillingness to trust to the mystical efficacy of the sacrament alone, insisting instead on a thorough comprehension of communion, as well as his opposition to the Arminian doctrine of merit, places him in the Puritan, rather than the royalist, wing of the church. Furthermore, he provided for his daughters a Huguenot governess, whom Frances credited with teaching her "to be a *Calvinist* in point of *Doctrine*, and a *Presbyterian* as to Discipline."[7] Frances herself can obviously be termed a Puritan, at least in religious matters. Two other sisters, Elizabeth and Katherine, as well as Frances, looked to the distinguished Restoration Puritan divine, John Collinges, for spiritual guidance.

Some of the Egertons were apparently in sympathy with the more extreme Puritan position on courtly sports. Years after the Ludlow masque, Frances, regretting her youthful revels, engaged in "frequent *sad reflexions* upon her self, for mispending part of many *Lords dayes*, in masks, and other *Court pas-*

times, according to the fashion of others in her circumstances. This she would often *mention with bitterness*, and *honourably mention* and prefer before her self one of her *Noble Sisters*, who had in her youth had a just sense of that errour, and courage enough to resist the temptations to it."[8]

More important than Frances's regret for masquing long after the event is the unnamed sister's disapproval of court revelry during roughly the period when the Ludlow masque was performed. Existing records show that all of the Egerton daughters but Arabella (b. 1605) and Magdalen (b. 1615) participated in masques.[9] In view of their mother's love for the court and the authoritarian severity Frances attributed to her, the sister who refused to masque was unusually courageous for a girl of the time. It is likely either that she received support for her position from her father, or that her family was sympathetic enough to her views to tolerate them. In either case, at least some of the Egertons were in favor of the moral principles that lay behind Milton's antipathy to existing masquing patterns and his effort to reform the masque.

Whatever the special circumstances that made possible Milton's daring reform, the fact is that, when commissioned to write a masque, he did not and could not according to his principles have penned frothy lines of idle compliment. If chastity is understood as an unswerving love of God expressed in all life's actions, then Milton's masque is an example of chaste recreation. It encourages the pursuit of virtue; and, for those who have participated in it either directly or vicariously, an experience of the Ludlow masque *is* the pursuit of virtue. A recent critic has suggested half-jokingly that associating Puritan thought with the delicate weave of a masque "is rather like stamping on a butterfly."[10] But Milton would probably have seen it as giving the butterfly back his soul.

Milton's Successors: Flecknoe, Shirley, & the Reform of Occasional Theatricals

ALTHOUGH THE INTEREST IN PROMOTING A DRAMA THAT RE-spected Puritan scruples did not inspire many actual composi-tions, those few that were produced appeared during the Common-wealth as unemployed but enterprising playwrights struggled to circumvent the Parliamentary ordinance closing the public theaters. Parliament did not absolutely ban dramatic presentations but ended their performance in public places. Private theatrical entertainments for Commonwealth dignitaries and their families were presented from time to time, just as masques and plays had been presented for roy-alist audiences before the civil war. Pastoral entertainments were staged when Cromwell's daughters were married, and a masque was given by the Lord Commissioners of the Great Seal to celebrate Cromwell's assumption of the Protectorate.[1] Two examples of occasional produc-tions designed with the political realities of the Commonwealth in mind are Richard Flecknoe's *Love's Dominion* and James Shirley's *Cupid and Death*, both of which make some effort to respond to the special needs of their Puritan audiences.

Flecknoe's *Love's Dominion* is not a masque, but a pastoral tragi-comedy of the sort that was popular in the court of Charles I. Its models were such works as the anonymous *Florimène* (performed at court in 1635), Walter Montagu's *Shepheard's Paradise*, and Fletcher's *Faithful Shepherdess*. Because it exists in two forms, one written for a Puritan, the other for a royalist audience, it provides us with one view of what Puritan theatrical entertainments might be and how they differed from the better known variety that flourished under the monarchy.

The first version of the piece, entitled *Love's Dominion*, was never performed, apparently because of its author's fears about "how the palat of the Time may relish such Things yet."[2] He published it in 1654 with an elaborate dedication to Cromwell's daughter, Lady Elizabeth Claypole, in which he claimed his work as a model for the reformed stage:

For my part I have endeavoured here the clearing of it [i.e., drama], and the restoring it to its former splendor, and first institution; (of teaching *Virtue*, reproving *Vice*, and amendment of *Manners*,) so as if the rest but imitate my example, those who shall be Enemies hereafter must declare themselves Enemies of *Virtue*, as formerly they did of *Vice*: Whence we may justly hope to see it restored again, with the qualification of an humble coadjustor of the Pulpit, to teach *Morality*, in order to the others *Divinity*, and the moulding and tempering mens minds for the better receiving the impression of Godliness.

Flecknoe described the theater, much as Milton had more generally viewed sports in the *Reason of Church Government*, as a vehicle for moral teaching that complements, without rivaling, the pulpit.

Unlike Milton's proposal for reform, Flecknoe's avowed interest in amending the stage probably arose from expediency. With the Restoration, he made slight revisions in the play and republished it in 1664 as *Love's Kingdom*. Still, the very fact that he would appeal for the creation of a reformed drama in an attempt to make his work acceptable during the Commonwealth suggests something of the currency of the idea.

When Flecknoe remade his Puritan play for the Restoration state, he altered little in his cast of characters beyond changing some names, and he retained the same general plot. He did make a few telling revisions that reveal something of his original sense of what constitutes a Puritan drama. Most obviously, he changed the title from *Love's Dominion* to *Love's Kingdom* to accord with shifting political circumstances. More important, he revised his treatment of love. In his preface to the Puritan version of the work, Flecknoe explained that his contribution to reforming the stage hinges on a properly virtuous handling of the amorous passion: "I thought it necessary there first to apply the Remedy, where the harm was most universal, *Love* being the general passion of every breast, and there to begin the Reformation of the Stage."

In both of its forms, Flecknoe's play traces the trials and tribulations of several pairs of pastoral lovers. In the earlier version, Flecknoe attempted to please his audience by playing to attitudes about love and marriage which recent scholars have described as characteristic of seventeenth-century Puritans.[3] He condemned the traditional poetic language of love that was standard in courtly literature as the "canting language of Enamourists, / Of *darts* and *flames*, and *dying* and *languishing*," and he dismissed the current Neoplatonic style of love with the comment that "the propagating [of] *Ideas* . . . has / So slippery a way to go" that it "most commonly falls fowl /

O' th' Body in its passage towards the Soul" (pp. 12–13). At one point a chorus of the Priests of Love presents the thematic underpinning of the work, describing true love as a charity toward our fellow men that is akin to divine love and as a rational ordering of the self that makes social organization possible (pp. 12–15). The plot emphasizes marriage as the ultimate expression of true love. The central pair of lovers is married by the end of the fourth act, and their wedding provides a standard against which the couplings of other characters in the final act are measured.

In *Love's Kingdom*, the revised version designed for a cavalier audience, the conceptual perspective is firmly Neoplatonic.[4] The sensory appreciation of beauty is not restrained but encouraged as a necessary preliminary step in the process of moving toward the higher love of the soul. Quite shamelessly, Flecknoe uses the conventional love language that he had ridiculed earlier. Marriage is not given the emphasis it had received in the earlier version. None of the couples speak of wedding until the final scene, in which marriage serves simply as a ready means of providing the obligatory happy ending.

A much more serious and comprehensive effort at forging a distinctively Puritan entertainment was James Shirley's *Cupid and Death*, performed as an officially sanctioned, private entertainment for the ambassador of Portugal. Its two publications, in 1653 and again in 1659, probably indicate some degree of acceptance by the Commonwealth public.[5]

As the author of the Caroline extravaganza, the *Triumph of Peace*, Shirley was certainly well versed in the conventional patterns of the masque. In a prefatory statement, *Cupid and Death* is specifically called a "masque," but it is one in which the form has been transmuted to meet the demands of a Puritan audience and patrons. The work contains some conventional features. There is a general distinction between early scenes of disorder and later scenes in which a new order is attained, a distinction that recalls the expected contrast between antimasque and main masque. In addition, the vision of order depends largely on the appearance of a group of gentlemen masquers who express themselves in dance. There are, however, obvious differences. Most important, Shirley revised the assumptions of the genre. Royalist principles become the bugaboos of his antimasque; the main masque celebrates Puritan ideals. In *Cupid and Death*, the final resolution of conflict is achieved, not by the intervention of the god-man who is king, as in conventional masques of the prewar period, but by the direct involvement in human affairs of divine powers who aid and support earthly governors. This crucial change in plot signally rejects the theories of divine right and monarchical absolutism that had justified the Caroline autocracy and substitutes a Commonwealth myth that treated the Lord Protector as a human ruler upheld by the powers of Providence.

Cupid and Death is based on one of Aesop's fables, drawn probably from John Ogilby's version for which Shirley had provided commendatory verses (p. xiii). According to the fable, the gods of Love and Death spend a night at the same inn, where their arrows happen to be exchanged. As a result, Cupid kills young lovers and Death inspires elderly ones quite inappropriately to fall in love. The masque has three scenes. The first, an inn surrounded by dense forest, recalls some of the antimasque sets designed by Inigo Jones for Stuart masques but also draws on the familiar topos of the spiritual wilderness.[6] As the central contrast of the work makes clear, this forest scene represents unredeemed Nature, disordered not so much by a failure of human art as by a resistance to divine will. The second scene is Nature's bower, which we first see disrupted by an intrusion of disorderly forces from the forest and later rendered calm and harmonious by the intervention of the divine. The final set presents a paradisal bower with glorious thrones, which we are invited to understand as a heavenly realm where the blessed dead live out their afterlives.

The exchange of arrows occurs in the first scene, but even before the actual mix-up it becomes clear that love and death have been perverted from their natural functions, each tainted by the other. Properly a vitalizing force, love when corrupted by death becomes a killing tyrant, in its perverted form provoking the sufferings of unrequited loves and the passionate excesses that lead men to die to higher human responsibilities. The corrupted Cupid, in short, symbolizes the vanities that distract men from their spiritual callings, vanities that Shirley depicts in terms distinctly reminiscent of cavalier life. Cupid is attended by Folly and Madness, who represent respectively aristocratic liberality (regarded as waste) and the noble quest for honor (regarded as self-love) and are described as models of "What most of our nobility are come to" (pp. 15, 16). Just as Love is tainted by Death, so Death, normally the welcome rest with which life concludes, becomes a force that frustrates all ideals that make life worthwhile. War is impossible because gentle feelings render men unwilling to die for principle. Death no longer serves as the natural culmination of a fulfilled life; men struggle for untimely death through suicide or cling to life for the superficial pleasure it affords. The exchanging of Cupid's and Death's darts confirms in an emblem that blurring the two forces perverts the natural order.

The bower of the second scene is probably to be understood politically as the garden of the British nation and morally as the realm of
nature (in contrast to the realm of grace), conceived microcosmically
as human nature and macrocosmically as the natural world. We first
see perversions of the natural order caused by the tyranny of the
perverted Cupid and Death: young lovers die, the old cut grotesque
capers of courtship, a man falls passionately in love with apes, war-
riors embrace instead of fighting for their cause.

The proper order is restored to the bower when Mercury, acting at
the behest of the supreme gods, brings grace to the natural realm.
Cupid and Death regain their own darts, and, each cleansed of the
other, resume their normal functions in the world. Further, Mercury
places specific limitations on the power of each. He charges Love:

> Thou must be Confin'd to cottages,
> To poor and humble cells.
> Love must no more Appear
> In princes' courts, their heart
> Impenetrable by thy dart,
> And from softer influence free,
> By their own wills must guided be.

And Death is instructed:

> Presume not hence-forth to engage
> On persons in whose breast divine
> Marks of Art or honour shine;
> Upon these, if thy malice try,
> They may bleed, but never die.
> [pp. 63–66]

Good governors thus win immunity to the disorders of passion, and
God's chosen people, those who bear "divine Marks of Art or honour," win immortality.

In the final scene we are given a vision of a paradisal bower so like
heaven that "gods by their own wonder led mistake it" and "Old
Nature's sight grows feeble at the brightness of this glory" (pp. 71,
72). In this scene the masquers, cast as slain lovers, appear seated on
thrones like the redeemed in Revelation, descend to dance, and finally return to their seats as the masque concludes. The presence of
the masquers is explained in ways that clarify the extent of the order
that divine powers have restored. We are specifically told that the
dead lovers cannot be returned to life again—"They cannot be Re-
duc'd to live again with thee"—but an eternal resting place has been
provided for those who are the recipients of grace. The moral is clear:

only a relative order can be attained in this world. Yet, although men may suffer unfairly here, they will ultimately be rewarded in heaven.

Shirley's masque sets forth a political and a moral message, the two so closely intertwined they are nearly inseparable. Like the great masques of the Jacobean and Caroline periods, *Cupid and Death* is about government; but, unlike the earlier masques, the governing agent is not a king who rules by divine right, providing by his presence a bridge between the heavenly and earthly realms. Order is ordained and maintained by divine powers through their direct involvement in human affairs. In their provision of fit rulers, heavenly beings make possible the proper government of the body politic. They also furnish a pattern basic to the moral ordering of each individual—a pattern clarified by our progress through the masque from visions of nature unredeemed, to nature ordered by conformity to divine behest, and finally to a paradisal afterlife. The masque obviously traces the progress of the Christian pilgrim through the spiritual wilderness of the world, to the comfort and peace of the state of grace, and finally to his heavenly reward.

A basic similarity, arising out of a common purpose, unites Milton's *Comus* with Flecknoe's *Love's Dominion* and Shirley's *Cupid and Death*: all are in some degree dedicated to transforming a royalist form in accordance with Puritan moral and aesthetic principles. Milton made many of the same artistic choices that the later writers were also to make. Like Flecknoe, he attempted to purify the content of occasional entertainments, revising the Neoplatonic assumptions of Caroline court theatricals. And even more like Shirley in *Cupid and Death*, Milton retained such conventional elements as the masquers and the contrast between order and disorder, while he stretched his received materials to form an extended moral allegory of the life of the wayfaring, warfaring Christian.

APPENDIX B

Line References to Virtues and Vices in Comus

VIRTUES

Chastity: 146, 215, 420, 425, 442, 450, 453, 909, 919

Controlled Appetites: 705

Goodness: 277, 307, 489, 497, 512, 594, 609, 658, 665, 703–4, 740, 764–65, 849

Honesty (Truth): 10, 385, 437, 791, 971

Moderation: 773, 776

Proper Worship: 774–76

Purity: 16, 213, 427, 826, 912

Sobriety: 263, 766

Temperance: 32, 721, 767

Virginity: 148, 350, 427, 437, 448, 507, 582, 689, 738, 787, 826, 856, 860, 905, 922

Virtue: 9, 165, 373, 589, 761, 1019, 1022

VICES

Blasphemy, False Worship: 136, 176–77, 535, 719, 720–24, 776–79

Evil: 432, 593

Excess: 771

Gluttony: 776–78

Incontinence: 397

Intemperance: 67, 170–75, 975

Lust: 445, 463

Luxury: 770

Sensuality: 77, 474, 538, 975

Sin: 17, 126, 456, 465

Unchastity: 464

Uncontrolled Appetites: 358, 524

Wantonness: 176, 464

Notes

INTRODUCTION
Milton's Masque: Meaning, Form, and Context

1. For useful commentary on distinctions between Puritans and Anglicans, see Christopher Hill, *Society and Puritanism in Pre-Revolutionary England* (London: Secker and Warburg, 1964), chap. 1; and John F. H. New, *Anglican and Puritan: The Basis of Their Opposition, 1558–1640* (Stanford: Stanford University Press, 1964). My own distinctions depend primarily on the issues emerging from the recreation debate.

2. The translation is from *Virgil*, trans. and ed. H. Rushton Fairclough (Cambridge: Harvard University Press, 1957), p. 15.

3. Major statements on the generic deviations of *Comus* include C. H. Herford and Percy Simpson, *Ben Jonson* (Oxford: Clarendon Press, 1925), 2:274, 307–9; Enid Welsford, *The Court Masque* (London: Cambridge University Press, 1927), pp. 316, 320; D. C. Allen, *The Harmonious Vision: Studies in Milton's Poetry* (Baltimore: Johns Hopkins University Press, 1954), pp. 29–32; Rosemond Tuve, *Images and Themes in Five Poems by Milton* (Cambridge: Harvard University Press, 1962), pp. 120–21; and Stephen Orgel, *The Jonsonian Masque* (Cambridge: Harvard University Press, 1967), pp. 102–3. The following argue that Milton's masque is so different from others that it should be viewed as something other than a masque: Walter W. Greg, *Pastoral Poetry and Pastoral Drama* (1906; reprint, New York: Russell and Russell, 1959), p. 396; Mario Praz, *The Flaming Heart* (Gloucester, Mass.: Peter Smith, 1966), pp. 30–31; Gretchen Finney, "*Comus*, Drama per Musica," *Studies in Philology* 37 (1940): 482–500; John Arthos, *On "A Mask Presented at Ludlow Castle"* (Ann Arbor: University of Michigan Press, 1954), pp. 32–33. However, John Demaray, *Milton and the Masque Tradition* (Cambridge: Harvard University Press, 1968), p. 143, counters that *Comus* differs from other masques not in kind, but in superior quality. Angus Fletcher,

Transcendental Masque: An Essay on Milton's "Comus" (Ithaca: Cornell University Press, 1971), p. 118, claims that the difference lies in the expanded scope and content, which cause an enlargement in the "containing shape" of the genre. An inclusionist approach to the masque is also taken by Eugene Haun, "An Inquiry into the Genre of *Comus*," in *Essays in Honor of Walter Clyde Curry* (Nashville: Vanderbilt University Press, 1954), pp. 221–39; and C. L. Barber, "*A Masque Presented at Ludlow Castle*: The Masque as Masque," in *The Lyric and Dramatic Milton*, ed. Joseph H. Summers (New York: Columbia University Press, 1965), pp. 35–63.

4. I do not attempt here a complete bibliography on inquiries into the intellectual content of Milton's masque. Some representative studies of the masque's debt to Platonic and Neoplatonic thought are: J. S. Harrison, *Platonism in English Poetry of the Sixteenth and Seventeenth Centuries* (New York: Columbia University Press, 1903), pp. 48–50; George Sensabaugh, "The Milieu of *Comus*," *Studies in Philology* 41 (1944): 238–49; Irene Samuel, *Plato and Milton* (Ithaca: Cornell University Press, 1947), pp. 10–11; John Arthos, "Milton, Ficino, and the *Charminides*," *Studies in the Renaissance* 5 (1959): 261–74; and Sears Jayne, "The Subject of Milton's Ludlow Mask," *Publications of the Modern Language Association of America* 74 (1954): 533–43. As A. S. P. Woodhouse notes, "The Christian strain in *Comus* admits of no such precise documentation of sources as even the Platonic does" (*A Variorum Commentary on the Poems of John Milton*, ed. Merritt Y. Hughes [New York: Columbia University Press, 1972], vol. 2, pt. 3, p. 782). Some examinations of the masque's debt to Christian thought are R. L. Ramsay, "Morality Themes in Milton's Poetry," *Studies in Philology* 15 (1918): 147–48; Maynard Mack, *Milton* (New York: Prentice-Hall, 1950), pp. 7–8; G. Rans, "Mr. Wilkinson on *Comus*," *Essays in Criticism* 10 (1960): 364–69; Alice-Lyle Scoufos, "The Mysteries in Milton's *Masque*," *Milton Studies* 6 (1975): 113–42. A. S. P. Woodhouse has been an influential spokesman for the pervasive view that *Comus* is a humanist blend of Christian and classical elements. See his developing interpretation in "The Argument of Milton's *Comus*," *University of Toronto Quarterly* 19 (1950): 218–23; *Variorum Commentary*, vol. 2, pt. 3, pp. 802–4, 854–55; and *The Heavenly Muse* (Toronto: University of Toronto Press, 1972), pp. 56–83.

5. The effect on *Comus* of the Castlehaven scandal is studied by Barbara Brested, "*Comus* and the Castlehaven Scandal," *Milton Studies* 3 (1971): 201–4. See also Rosemary K. Mundhenk, "Dark Scandal and the Sin-Clad Power of Chastity: The Historical Milieu of Mil-

ton's *Comus,*" *Studies in English Literature* 15 (1975): 141–52. The impact of Michaelmas observances are the subject of James Taaffe, "Michaelmas, the 'Lawless Hour,' and the Occasion of Milton's *Comus,*" *English Language Notes* 6 (1968–69): 257–62; and William B. Hunter, "The Liturgical Context of *Comus,*" *English Language Notes* 10 (1972): 11–15. How other circumstances of performance might have shaped the masque are considered by William Riley Parker, *Milton: A Biography* (Oxford: Clarendon Press, 1960), pp. 128–29; and Demaray, *Milton and the Masque Tradition*, pp. 83–121.

6. See Mary Ann Radzinowicz, *Toward "Samson Agonistes"* (Princeton: Princeton University Press, 1978) and Joseph A. Wittreich, *Visionary Poetics: Milton's Tradition and His Legacy* (San Marino, Calif.: Huntington Library, 1979). In *Process of Speech: Puritan Religious Writing and "Paradise Lost"* (Baltimore: Johns Hopkins Press, 1976), Boyd M. Berry also examines historical context, though with less attention to authorial context.

7. Five versions of the masque, some substantially different from others, were produced during Milton's lifetime: the versions in the Bridgewater and Trinity Manuscripts, the anonymous 1637 edition, and the authorized editions of 1645 and 1673. Philip Gaskell offers a textual history of Milton's masque in *From Writer to Reader: Studies in Editorial Method* (Oxford: Clarendon Press, 1978), pp. 29–61. John S. Diekhoff presents what has been the standard view on the multiple texts in "The Text of *Comus,* 1634 to 1645," in *"A Maske at Ludlow": Essays on Milton's "Comus,"* ed. John S. Diekhoff (Cleveland: Case Western Reserve University Press, 1968), pp. 251–75. Diekhoff's position that the masque as we know it was composed for the most part before the 1634 performance is disputed by John Shawcross, who argues that essential revisions took place from 1637 to 1638. Shawcross's complex evidence can be found in scattered articles: "Certain Relationships of the Manuscripts of *Comus,*" *Publication of the Bibliographical Society of America* 54 (1960): 38–54, 293–94; "Speculations of the Dating of the Trinity MS of Milton's Poems," *Modern Language Notes* 75 (1960): 11–17; "Henry Lawes' Settings of Songs for Milton's *Comus,*" *Journal of the Rutgers University Library* 28 (1964): 22–28. In *"A Maske": The Earlier Versions* (Toronto: University of Toronto Press, 1973), pp. 3–33, S. E. Sprott takes issue with Shawcross's conclusions and offers a chronology of revisions that posits an early date for composition of the essential text. Because of the uncertainties regarding the dates of revisions, because the 1645 version is the first Milton allowed to appear in public under his own name, and because he sanctioned it as definitive by reproducing the

1645 text with only minor changes in 1673, I have taken the 1645 text as the basis for my study. Citations of *Comus* and of Milton's early English poetry are drawn from *Poems of Mr. John Milton* (1645; reprint, Menston, Eng.: Scolar Press, 1970). For the Latin poems, I use the Merritt Y. Hughes edition with its fine translations (*John Milton: Complete Poems and Major Prose* [New York: Odyssey, 1957]). Quotations from Hughes's volume are cited in the text by the abbreviation *CPP*. My references to the later poetry are also based on Hughes's volume.

8. Recent studies of the involvement of Jacobean and Caroline masques in contemporary politics include: Stephen Orgel and Roy Strong, *Inigo Jones: The Theater of Majesty* (Berkeley: University of California Press, 1973), 1:63–66; Dale B. J. Randall, *Jonson's Gypsies Unmasked: Background and Theme of the "Gypsies Metamorphos'd"* (Durham: Duke University Press, 1975); Leah Sinangolou Marcus, "The Occasion of Ben Jonson's *Pleasure Reconciled to Virtue*," *Studies in English Literature* 19 (1979): 271–93; Marcus, "'Present Occasions' and the Shaping of Ben Jonson's Masques," *English Literary History* 45 (1978): 201–25; Stephen Orgel, *Illusions of Power* (Berkeley: University of California Press, 1975), pp. 70–87.

9. Orgel, *Illusions of Power*, p. 37.

10. *The Reason of Church Government*, in *Complete Prose Works of John Milton*, ed. Don M. Wolfe, 4 vols. (New Haven: Yale University Press, 1966): 1:822–23. Quotations from *Complete Prose Works* are cited in the text by the abbreviation *CP*. As Harris Fletcher notes in *The Intellectual Development of John Milton* (Urbana: University of Illinois Press, 1961), 2:537, the period during which Milton composed the masque is one of the "more obscure" in his life. For further discussion of his Puritan leanings in the decades before the war, consider Don M. Wolfe, *Milton in the Puritan Revolution* (New York: Nelson, 1941), pp. 2–5; Christopher Hill, *Milton and the English Revolution* (New York: Viking Press, 1977), pp. 22–29.

11. *Variorum Commentary*, vol. 2, pt. 1, pp. 43, 50–51; vol. 2, pt. 2, pp. 567–69, 575, 583, 672–74.

12. See the annotations for Psalm 114, *Geneva Bible*, ed. Lloyd E. Berry (facsimile, 1560 ed.; Madison: University of Wisconsin Press, 1969).

13. Rosalie Colie, *Resources of Kind: Genre-Theory in the Renaissance*, ed. Barbara K. Lewalski (Berkeley: University of California Press, 1973), p. 29.

14. Fletcher, *Transcendental Masque*, p. 18.

15. William Haller, *The Rise of Puritanism* (New York: Columbia

University Press, 1965), pp. 141–42; Hill, *Milton and the English Revolution*, p. 47; Radzinowicz, *Toward "Samson Agonistes,"* pp. 126–27; Georgia Christopher, "The Virginity of Faith: *Comus* as a Reformation Conceit," *English Literary History* 43 (1976): 479–99.

16. Stanley Fish, "Problem Solving in *Comus*," in *Illustrious Evidence: Approaches to English Literature of the Earlier Seventeenth Century*, ed. Earl Miner (Berkeley: University of California Press, 1975), pp. 115–31.

17. David Masson, *The Life of John Milton* (London: Macmillan, 1971), 1:833.

CHAPTER ONE

Reforming the Masque: Milton and the Recreation Controversy

1. The *OED* includes as Renaissance definitions of "sport": any pleasant pastime, entertainment, or amusement; amorous dalliance; hunting, fishing; games, athletic exercises; jokes and other matters for mirth; diversionary occupations, such as theatrical performances. The listing under "recreation" includes references to eating, refreshment of senses or body, consolation of mind, and pleasant employments.

2. For information regarding Puritan and Anglican views on sports, I am much indebted to Christopher Hill, *Society and Puritanism in Pre-Revolutionary England* (London: Secker and Warburg, 1964), pp. 170–76, 183–94, as well as to the more recent works of Dennis Brailsford, *Sport and Society: Elizabeth to Anne* (Toronto: University of Toronto Press, 1969), pp. 124–33, and Winston Solberg, *Redeem the Time: The Puritan Sabbath in Early America* (Cambridge: Harvard University Press, 1977), pp. 40–80.

3. The literature about the Sabbath is voluminous, but I have found most useful Robert Cox, *The Literature of the Sabbath Question* (Edinburgh: Maclachlan and Steward, 1865), 2 vols.; A. H. Lewis, *A Critical History of Sunday Legislation from 321 to 1888 A.D.* (New York: Appleton, 1888); and W. B. Whitaker, *Sunday in Tudor and Stuart Times* (London: Houghton, 1933). In *History of England* (London: Longmans, Green, 1884), 7:319, S. R. Gardiner discusses immorality and popular sports; in *Les Masques anglais* (Paris: Hachette, 1909), pp. 39–43, Paul Reyher comments on court masques as the occasions for sexual misconduct.

4. *The Political Works of James I*, ed. Charles H. McIlwain (Cambridge: Harvard University Press, 1918), p. 27.

5. Roy Strong, *Van Dyck: Charles I on Horseback* (New York: Viking, 1972), pp. 46–47.

6. Stephen Orgel, *Illusions of Power* (Berkeley: University of California Press, 1975), p. 83.

7. Stephen Orgel and Roy Strong, *Inigo Jones: The Theater of Majesty* (Berkeley: University of California Press, 1973), 2:572.

8. Ibid., 2:576, 577, 573.

9. Lucy Hutchinson, *Memories of the Life of Colonel Hutchinson*, ed. James Sutherland (London: Oxford University Press, 1973), p. 42.

10. G. E. Bentley, *The Jacobean and Caroline Stage* (Oxford: Clarendon Press, 1956), 4:535–36. Laurens Mills's argument to the contrary, in *Peter Hausted: Playwright, Poet, Preacher* (Bloomington: Indiana University Press, 1947), pp. 17–37, is unconvincing.

11. A member of Corpus Christi in residence at Cambridge during the royal visit reported: "The killing blow was a dislike of that comedy [i.e., Hausted's *Rival Friends*] and a check of the Chancellor, who is said to have told him [i.e., Dr. Butts] that the King himself had more confidence in his discretion than they found cause, in that he thought such a comedy fitting, &c." David Masson, *The Life of John Milton* (London: Macmillan, 1971), 1:256.

12. Peter Hausted, "The Preface to the Reader," in *Rival Friends*, ed. Laurens J. Mills (Bloomington: Indiana University Press, 1951), p. 6.

13. Ibid., pp. 24–26, 35–39, 105–7.

14. Ibid., p. 5.

15. C. H. Herford and Percy Simpson, *Ben Jonson* (Oxford: Clarendon Press, 1925), 7:811–12. For a study of the more traditional Anteros, see Robert Valentine Merrill, *Platonism in French Renaissance Poetry* (New York: New York University Press, 1957), chap. 9.

16. Hausted, "The Preface to the Reader," p. 15, 6.

17. Ibid., p. 7.

18. Henry Burton, *For God and King* (London, 1636), pp. 48–49.

19. Harris Fletcher, *The Intellectual Development of John Milton* (Urbana: University of Illinois Press, 1961), 2:531.

20. William Lamont, *Marginal Prynne, 1600–1669* (Toronto: University of Toronto Press, 1963), pp. 13–16.

21. S. R. Gardiner, ed., *Documents Relating to the Proceedings against William Prynne* (Westminster: Camden Society, 1877), p. 2.

22. See William Haller, *Rise of Puritanism* (New York: Columbia University Press, 1965), pp. 393, 219; W. K. Jordan, *The Development of Religious Toleration in England* (Cambridge: Harvard Univer-

sity Press, 1938), 3:277; Alfred Harbage, *Cavalier Drama* (New York: Modern Language Association, 1936), pp. 14–15.

23. William Prynne, *Histrio-mastix: The Players Scourge* (1633), "Epistle Dedicatory." The information on the place and publisher of this book is not available because the printer feared reprisal. Prynne's work was secretly printed, and it was not paginated.

24. *Proceedings against William Prynne*, p. 16.

25. Ibid., p. 24.

26. William Laud, *A Speech Delivered in the Star-Chamber* (London, 1637), a7.

27. Prynne, *Histrio-mastix*, "Epistle Dedicatory."

28. In a funeral sermon, *The Pilgrims' Profession* (London, 1622) Thomas Taylor argued that duty to king and civil law is less important than duty to God and divine law.

29. *Proceedings against William Prynne*, pp. 2–3.

30. Solberg, *Redeem the Time*, p. 73.

31. *The King's Maiesties Declaration to His Subjects Concerning Lawful Sports to Be Used (1618)*, in *Reprints, 1618–1751* (London: Smeeton, 1817), pp. 8–9.

32. The contemporary historian, Sir Richard Baker, marveled in his *Chronicle of the Kings of England* (London, 1674), p. 474, at the political ineptitude that moved Charles to republish it: "The truth is, the ill reception it had among the people, in the former Publication of it, in the time of the King's Father, might have deterred the like at this time, for that the first observation of the Lord's Day was much increased since that time."

33. *The Kings Maiesties Declaration to His Subjects Concerning Lawfull Sports to Be Used* (London, 1633), p. 11. See also Thomas G. Barnes, "Country Politics and a Puritan Cause Célèbre: Somerset Church Ales, 1633," *Transactions of the Royal Historical Society* 9 (1959): 103–22.

34. Solberg, *Redeem the Time*, pp. 73, 77; Nellis M. Crouse, "Causes of the Great Migration, 1630–40," *New England Quarterly* 5 (1932): 3–36; William Prynne, *Canterburies Doome* (London, 1646), p. 151; Gardiner, *History of England*, 7:32.

35. See, for example, Nicholas Byfield [William Prynne ?], *The Lord's Day, the Sabbath Day* (1636), pp. 25–27.

36. Christopher Dow, *Innovations Unjustly Charged upon the Present Church and State* (London, 1637), p. 78; Francis White, *An Examination and Confutation of a Lawlesse Pamphlet* (London, 1637), p. 126.

37. Robert Sanderson, *A Sovereign Antidote against Sabbatarian*

Errours (London, 1636), p. 24; Dow, *Innovations Unjustly Charged*, p. 86.

38. Dow, *Innovations Unjustly Charged*, p. 79; Prynne, *Canterburies Doome*, pp. 131–32; Peter Heylyn, *Aerius Redivivus; or, The History of the Presbyterians* (Oxford, 1670), pp. 389–90; *Political Works of James I*, p. 27.

39. Dow, *Innovations Unjustly Charged*, p. 80; Sanderson, *A Sovereign Antidote*, pp. 26–27.

40. Thomas Taylor, *The Progresse of Saints to Full Holiness* (1631), pp. 89, 30, 82.

41. J. Sears McGee, *The Godly Man in Stuart England* (New Haven: Yale University Press, 1976), pp. 68–113.

42. See, for example, Peter Heylyn, *The History of the Sabbath* (London, 1636), p. 270.

43. William Haller, *Liberty and Reformation in the Puritan Revolution* (New York: Columbia University Press, 1955), xii–xiii; Hill, *Society and Puritanism*, chap. 5.

44. See, for example, William Prynne, *A Divine Tragedie Lately Acted* (1636).

45. Richard Baxter, *Reliquiae Baxterianae* (London, 1696), p. 2; William Prynne, *News from Ipswich* (1636), a2.

46. John S. Coolidge, *The Pauline Renaissance in England* (Oxford: Clarendon Press, 1970), p. 40.

47. McGee, *The Godly Man in Stuart England*, pp. 195–97; Richard Baxter, *Practical Works* (London: James Duncan, 1830), 13:458–63.

48. *Variorum Commentary*, vol. 2, pt. 1, pp. 224–27.

49. D. C. Allen, *The Harmonious Vision: Studies in Milton's Poetry* (Baltimore: John Hopkins University Press, 1954), p. 17. Consider also Blake's interpretation of the progression traced by the paired poems, as explained by Stephen C. Behrendt: "Blake treats *L'Allegro* as a general portrait of the . . . poet engaged in mundane experiences, whose slight though attractive productions please for perhaps a generation or so among 'polite society' and then disappear forever. Blake reads *Il Penseroso* as a portrait of . . . the true poet who progresses in imaginative insight in turning to the larger concerns of the epic and tragic modes and thereby creating poetry that outlasts its competitors" (in "Bright Pilgrimage: William Blake's Designs for 'L'Allegro' and 'Il Penseroso,'" *Milton Studies* 7 (1975): 126.

50. Michael Fixler, "The Orphic Technique of 'L'Allegro' and 'Il Penseroso,'" *English Literary Renaissance* 1 (1971): 174–75.

51. Rosemond Tuve suggests that "sweet Liberty" is the delight-

ful absence of all responsibility and more particularly the innocence produced by the lack of moral responsibility (*Images and Themes in Five Poems by Milton* [Cambridge: Harvard University Press, 1962], pp. 18–19).

52. William Riley Parker, *Milton: A Biography* (Oxford: Clarendon Press, 1960), pp. 125–28.

53. *Variorum Commentary*, vol. 2, pt. 1, pp. 224–27.

54. *CP*, 1:489–90; see also Ruth Mohl, *John Milton and His "Commonplace Book"* (New York: Frederick Ungar, 1969), pp. 313–34, 322.

55. Prynne, *Histrio-mastix*, pp. 6–7; Baxter, *Christian Directory* (London, 1673), pp. 811–18. For more on Puritan theater see Leslie Hotson, *The Commonwealth and Restoration Stage* (Cambridge: Harvard University Press, 1928). Most studies treat Puritans as unilaterally opposed to theater and Milton as something of a freak—more humanist than Puritan. However, Hotson mentions some instances of Puritan interest in reforming the stage. Also helpful is Lawrence A. Sasek, *The Literary Temper of the English Puritans* (Baton Rouge: Louisiana State University Press, 1961), pp. 97–98.

56. See appendix A.

57. The original occasion for "Arcades" is considered in *Variorum Commentary*, vol. 2, pt. 2, pp. 519–23. For an expanded version of my reading of Milton's entertainment, see "Milton's *Arcades* and the Entertainment Tradition," *Studies in Philology* 75 (1978): 451–70. Consider also John Wallace's excellent study, "Milton's *Arcades*," in *Milton: Modern Essays in Criticism*, ed. Arthur E. Barker (New York: Norton, 1965), pp. 77–87; and John Demaray, "*Arcades* as Literary Entertainment," *Papers in Language and Literature* 7 (1972): 15–25.

58. The Countess Dowager is described as "divine" and is compared to several classical goddesses; she also serves as a living beacon, providing by her presence a bright example for others and bringing illumination to seekers of truth. See Wallace's comments on her central place in the entertainment ("Milton's *Arcades*," pp. 80–82).

59. Sir Walter Raleigh, *Milton* (New York: Putnam, 1900), p. 28, equates Comus with cavalier ideals of love and beauty, which he feels Milton with his narrow Puritan perspective could only perceive as immoral. Douglas Bush admits his own sympathy for Milton's villain—"One would rather live with Comus than the Lady" (*The Renaissance and English Humanism* [1933; reprint, Toronto: University of Toronto Press, 1968], p. 108)—and describes Comus's allure: "Comus is, in fact, a cultured gentleman, a cavalier poet" (*English Literature in the Earlier Seventeenth Century* [1945; reprint, Oxford:

Clarendon Press, 1946], p. 356). *Variorum Commentary*, vol. 2, pt. 3, p. 752, surveys critical studies of the difference between Milton's elegant libertine and more conventional antimasque figures, particularly the belly-god in Jonson's *Pleasure Reconciled*. In "Transformations of Genre in Milton's *Comus*," *Genre* 10 (1977): 205–9, Jean Martin notes that Milton endows his villain with powers usually assigned to heroes of the main masque.

60. For more on the masque's pastoralism, consider Orgel, *Illusions of Power*, pp. 51–52; and Strong, *Van Dyck*, pp. 77–81. Comus's praise of the Lady (ll. 265–70) suggests her ability to control the weather as did masquers in *Chloridia*. His praise of the Brothers recalls the celestial motif used in *Tempe Restored* and *Coelum Britannicum*.

61. Orgel and Strong, *Inigo Jones*, 2:578.

62. Consider Jonson's *Vision of Delight*, which concludes: "They yeild to Time, and so must all. / As Night to sport, Day doth to action call" (Herford and Simpson, *Ben Jonson*, 7:471).

63. John Steadman, *Milton's Epic Characters: Image and Idol* (Chapel Hill: University of North Carolina Press, 1968), p. 391.

64. The parody of main masque conventions in an antimasque is not a Miltonic innovation. Orgel suggests that the satyr's song in *Oberon* is a "parody of two central masque conventions, the masquer's invitation to his lady and the final dance" (*The Jonsonian Masque* [Cambridge: Harvard University Press, 1967], p. 86). There are some differences, however. Not only is Milton's parody in *Comus* more extended than Jonson's, but in addition, while Jonson uses the device to establish the contrast between antimasque and main masque, Milton aims for moral satire.

65. Allardyce Nicoll, *Stuart Masques and the Renaissance Stage* (New York: Harcourt, Brace, 1938), p. 213; Reyher, *Les Masques anglais*, pp. 387–89, 409–10.

66. James Taaffe, "Michaelmas, the 'Lawless Hour,' and the Occasion of Milton's *Comus*," *English Language Notes* 6 (1968–69): 260–62.

67. A. R. Wright, *British Calendar Customs*, ed. T. E. Lones (London: William Glaisher, 1936), 1:186.

68. Christina Hole, *English Sports and Pastimes* (Freeport, N.Y.: Freeport Press, 1968), p. 99; John Brand, *Observations on the Popular Antiquities of Great Britain* (1849; reprint, Detroit: Singing Tree Press, 1969), 2:27, 16, 23. For more on misconduct during harvest festivities, see R. Chambers, *The Book of Days* (Edinburgh: Chambers, 1864), 2:380.

69. Brand, *Observations on the Popular Antiquities of Great Britain*, 1:253; Enid Welsford, *The Court Masque* (London: Cambridge University Press, 1927), p. 26.

70. *CP*, 1:588–89; 2:358–59; 3:235, 276, 281, 339; 6:707–8.

71. Boyd M. Berry, *Process of Speech: Puritan Religious Writing and "Paradise Lost,"* (Baltimore: Johns Hopkins Press, 1976), p. 96.

72. *CP*, 2:370, 376–77, 383, 386–87, 389, 392, 394.

73. Ibid., 2:381–82 n. 65; 409 n. 15; 411 n. 26.

74. Irene Samuel, *Plato and Milton*, (Ithaca: Cornell University Press, 1947), pp. 103–5.

75. Berry, *Process of Speech*, pp. 100–101, suggests a link between this interest in reforming recreation and the daring literary ambitions Milton expressed in the subsequent passages of the *Reason of Church Government*.

76. John G. Demaray, *Milton's Theatrical Epic: The Invention and Design of Paradise Lost* (Cambridge: Harvard University Press, 1980), p. 65.

77. *CP*, 3:343. Consider also Milton's assertion that "a king must be adored like a demigod, with . . . vast expense and luxury, masks and revels" (in *A Readie and Easie Way: The Works of Milton*, ed. Patterson et al. [New York: Columbia University Press, 1932], 6:120).

78. Demaray, *Milton's Theatrical Epic*, pp. 57–101.

79. Welsford, *The Court Masque*, p. 309.

80. *Paradise Lost*, 7:594–603; 3:370–71.

81. Demaray, *Milton's Theatrical Epic*, p. 80 ff.

82. *Paradise Regained*, 4:288–92; Burton Jasper Weber, *Wedges and Wings: The Patterning of "Paradise Regained"* (Carbondale: Southern Illinois University Press, 1975), pp. 28–29.

83. William Kerrigan, *The Prophetic Milton* (Charlottesville: University of Virginia Press, 1974), p. 208 ff.; *Samson Agonistes*, ll. 529, 532–34.

84. Mary Ann Radzinowicz, *Toward "Samson Agonistes"* (Princeton: Princeton University Press, 1978), pp. 100–101, 107.

CHAPTER TWO

The Journey: Transformations in Character and Plot

1. See, for example, the response to female actors appearing in *Artenice* (Stephen Orgel and Roy Strong, *Inigo Jones: the Theater of Majesty* [Berkeley: University of California Press, 1973], 1:383–84).

2. William Empson, *Milton's God* (Norfolk, Conn.: New Directions, 1961), pp. 2–10.

3. Balachandra Rajan explains the central problem in "*Comus*: The Inglorious Likeness," *University of Toronto Quarterly* 37 (1947): 113–35.

4. In *The Shadow of Heaven: Matter and Stance in Milton's Poetry* (Ithaca: Cornell University Press, 1968), pp. 64–65, Jon Lawry considers the Egerton children as characters whose positions on important issues change during the course of the masque. He does not, however, suggest how their development as quasi-dramatic characters relates to the masque tradition. In "Problem Solving in *Comus*," in *Illustrious Evidence: Approaches to English Literature of the Earlier Seventeenth Century*, ed. Earl Miner (Berkeley: University of California Press, 1975), Stanley Fish does not maintain a consistent position on the children's development. He claims that "these perspectives [of the children] are present and distinguished from the opening lines, and the events of the plot serve only to confirm the previously chosen allegiances of the characters. Just as there is no progression in the action, so there is no advance in the level of insight displayed by the villain and heroine who merely reaffirm and redefine the positions from which they speak" (p. 128). Yet he also comments on the Brothers' developing perspective in their long dialogue (pp. 123–24).

5. Rosamond Tuve, *Images and Themes in Five Poems by Milton* (Cambridge: Harvard University Press, 1962), p. 115.

6. See J. C. Maxwell, "The Pseudo-Problem of *Comus*," *Classical Journal* 1 (1948): 376–80.

7. A. S. P. Woodhouse divides *Comus* into scenes in *Heavenly Muse* (Toronto: University of Toronto Press: 1972), p. 60 ff.

8. Patricia A. Parker, *Inescapable Romance: Studies in the Poetics of a Mode* (Princeton: Princeton University Press, 1979), pp. 128–31.

9. Samuel Johnson, *The Lives of the English Poets*, ed. George Hill (Oxford: Clarendon Press, 1905), pp. 167–69. I use the terms *representational* and *presentational* as they were developed by Alexander Bakshy, *The Theatre Unbound* (London: Cecil Palmer, 1923), p. 92.

10. C. L. Barber, "*A Masque Presented at Ludlow Castle*: The Masque as Masque," in *The Lyric and Dramatic Milton*, ed. Joseph H. Summers (New York: Columbia University Press, 1965), pp. 36–39.

11. Barbara K. Lewalski, "Innocence and Experience in Milton's Eden," in *New Essays on Paradise Lost*, ed. Thomas Kranidas (Berkeley: University of California Press, 1969), p. 88.

12. Arnold Stein, *The Art of Presence: The Poet and "Paradise Lost"* (Berkeley: University of California Press, 1977), pp. 20, 179 n. 7;

Ann D. Ferry, *Milton's Epic Voice: The Narrator in "Paradise Lost"* (Cambridge: Harvard University Press, 1963); Stanley Fish, *Surprised by Sin: The Reader in "Paradise Lost"* (New York: St. Martin, 1967), pp. 38–54; Mother Mary C. Pecheux, "Sin in *Paradise Regained*: The Biblical Background," in *Calm of Mind*, ed. Joseph A. Wittreich (Cleveland: Press of Case Western Reserve University, 1971), pp. 40–50. Joseph A. Wittreich also comments on the dramatic quality of the later poetry in *Visionary Poetics: Milton's Tradition and His Legacy* (San Marino, Calif.: Huntington Library, 1979), pp. 54–55, 69–72.

13. John Huntley, "Images of the Poet and Poetry in Milton's *The Reason of Church Government*," in *Achievements of the Left Hand*, ed. Michael Lieb and John T. Shawcross (Amherst: University of Massachusetts Press, 1974), p. 87.

14. Joseph A. Wittreich, *Angel of the Apocalypse: Blake's Idea of Milton* (Madison: University of Wisconsin Press, 1975), p. 83.

15. Fish, "Problem Solving in *Comus*," p. 115 ff.

16. Parker, *Inescapable Romance*, pp. 4, 6.

17. Maynard Mack, *Milton* (New York: Prentice-Hall, 1950), pp. 7–9.

18. Donald R. Howard, *Writers and Pilgrims: Medieval Pilgrimage Narratives and Their Posterity* (Berkeley: University of California Press, 1980), p. 7.

19. John S. Coolidge, *The Pauline Renaissance in England* (Oxford: Clarendon Press, 1970), pp. 105–6; William Haller, *The Rise of Puritanism* (New York: Columbia University Press, 1965), pp. 128–72; Barbara K. Lewalski, *Protestant Poetics and the Seventeenth-Century Lyric* (Princeton: Princeton University Press, 1979), pp. 93–94.

20. See Enid Welsford, *The Court Masque* (London: Cambridge University Press, 1927), chaps. 1–2 passim.

21. D. J. Gordon, "The Imagery of Jonson's Masques of *Blackness* and *Beauty*," in *The Renaissance Imagination*, ed. Stephen Orgel (Berkeley: University of California Press, 1975), pp. 134–56.

22. Orgel and Strong, *Inigo Jones*, 1:89.

23. C. H. Herford and Percy Simpson, *Ben Jonson* (Oxford: Clarendon Press, 1925), 7:207.

24. Stephen Orgel, *The Jonsonian Masque* (Cambridge: Harvard University Press, 1967), chap. 7.

25. Ibid., pp. 151–52.

26. Herford and Simpson, *Ben Jonson*, 7:486.

27. Cf. *Hymenaei* in which actors serve as surrogates for the newly married couple whom the masque honors.

28. Orgel and Strong, *Inigo Jones*, 1:287.

29. *Pleasure Reconciled* would not have been available until the publication of Jonson's *Works* in 1641.

30. See Jones's explanation in Orgel and Strong, *Inigo Jones*, 2:454.

31. Ibid., 2:579.

32. Ibid.

33. J. N. Figgis, *The Divine Right of Kings* (Cambridge: Cambridge University Press, 1934); Ernst H. Kantorowicz, *The King's Two Bodies* (Princeton: Princeton University Press, 1957).

34. Sears Jayne, "The Subject of Milton's Ludlow Mask," *Publications of the Modern Language Association of America* 74 (1954): pp. 534–35.

35. B. A. Wright, Letters in *Times Literary Supplement*, 1 Aug., 27 Oct. 1945, pp. 367, 511; Irene Samuel, *Plato and Milton* (Ithaca: Cornell University Press, 1947), pp. 10–11, 162.

36. See also Phil. 3.14, 1 Cor. 9.24–29.

37. Woodhouse, *Heavenly Muse*, pp. 63–65.

38. Pecheux, "Sin in *Paradise Regained*," pp. 50–52.

39. Merritt Y. Hughes, "Spenser's Acrasia and the Circe of the Renaissance," *Journal of the History of Ideas* 4 (1943): 381–99.

40. Leonora Leet Brodwin, "Milton and the Renaissance Circe," *Milton Studies* 6 (1974): 21–83.

41. Georgia Christopher, "The Virginity of Faith: *Comus* as a Reformation Conceit," *English Literary History* 43 (1976): 480–82.

42. Brodwin, "Milton and the Renaissance Circe," p. 50.

43. *CP*, 3:488; also *CP*, vol. 4, pt. 1, p. 518.

44. Tuve, *Images and Themes*, p. 144.

45. John Preston, *Sermons Preached before His Majestie* (London, 1634), sermon 4, unpaginated.

46. R. Blenner-Hasset, "Geoffrey of Monmouth and Milton's *Comus*," *Modern Language Notes* 64 (1949): 315–18; Jack Oruch, "The Sabrina Myths of Drayton and Milton," *Anglia* 90 (1972): 60–70.

47. See Denis Danielson, "Milton's Arminianism and *Paradise Lost*," *Milton Studies* 12 (1978): 47–73; Mary Ann Radzinowicz, *Toward "Samson Agonistes"* (Princeton: Princeton University Press, 1978), pp. 66, 339–47.

48. *CP*, 6:80; "At a Solemn Music," ll. 17–18, 26.

49. Christopher, "The Virginity of Faith," p. 486.

50. Jean Martin, "Transformations of Genre in Milton's *Comus*," *Genre* 10 (1977): 205.

51. Arnold Van Gennep, *The Rites of Passage*, trans. Monika B. Vizedon (Chicago: University of Chicago Press, 1960).

52. See U. Milo Kaufmann, *The Pilgrim's Progress and Traditions*

in Puritan Meditation (New Haven: Yale University Press, 1966), pp. 80–81, for a discussion of the Puritan rhetorical devices of "person-as-example" and "event-as-example."

53. Fish, *Surprised by Sin*, p. 12 ff.

54. Stephen Orgel, *Illusions of Power* (Berkeley: University of California Press, 1975), pp. 75–76.

55. Orgel and Strong, *Inigo Jones*, 1:365, 368.

CHAPTER THREE
Poetry and the Other Masquing Arts: Toward an Integrated Rhetoric

1. Jean Hagstrum, *The Sister Arts: The Tradition of Literary Pictorialism and English Poetry from Dryden to Gray* (Chicago: University of Chicago Press, 1958), pp. 89–90. See also H. James Jensen, *The Muses' Concord: Literature, Music, and the Visual Arts in the Baroque Age* (Bloomington: Indiana University Press, 1976).

2. Angus Fletcher, *Transcendental Masque: An Essay on Milton's "Comus"* (Ithaca: Cornell University Press, 1971), p. 11.

3. Samuel Daniel, *The Complete Works in Verse and Prose*, ed. Alexander B. Grosart (London: Hazell, Watson, and Viney, 1885–96), 3:196.

4. Daniel, *Complete Works*, 3:193–94.

5. D. J. Gordon, "Poet and Architect," in *The Renaissance Imagination*, ed. Stephen Orgel (Berkeley: University of California Press, 1975), pp. 77–101.

6. Stephen Orgel and Roy Strong, *Inigo Jones: The Theater of Majesty* (Berkeley: University of California Press, 1973), 1:4–6; Stephen Orgel, "The Poetics of Spectacle," *New Literary History* 2 (1971): 372.

7. C. H. Herford and Percy Simpson, *Ben Jonson* (Oxford: Clarendon Press, 1925), 7:209–10.

8. Gordon, "Poet and Architect," pp. 79–80.

9. Herford and Simpson, *Ben Jonson*, 8:609–10, 628.

10. Ibid., 7:91.

11. Ibid., 7:403–5.

12. See Stephen Orgel, *The Jonsonian Masque* (Cambridge: Harvard University Press, 1967), pp. 116–201; Orgel and Strong, *Inigo Jones*, 1:39; Andrew J. Sabol, ed., *Four Hundred Songs and Dances from the Stuart Masque* (Providence: Brown University Press, 1978),

pp. 8–12; and John C. Meagher, *Method and Meaning in Jonson's Masques* (Notre Dame, Ind.: University of Notre Dame Press, 1966), pp. 67–69, 87–91, 116–24.

13. Orgel, *Jonsonian Masque*, p. 113 ff.

14. Orgel and Strong, *Inigo Jones*, 2:408.

15. Ibid., 2:454.

16. Ibid., 2:455.

17. See, for example, Michael Murrin, *The Veil of Allegory* (Chicago: University of Chicago Press, 1969), p. 168.

18. Orgel and Strong, *Inigo Jones*, 2:456.

19. Ibid., 2:482.

20. Ibid., 2:578.

21. In *Illusions of Power* (Berkeley: University of California Press, 1975), pp. 77–83, Stephen Orgel discusses the original audience's misunderstanding of the *Triumph of Peace*. Jones's difficulties in *Tempe Restored* may have been produced by his effort to make a complex statement about the relation of physical and moral beauty, a statement that demanded some revision of conventional assumptions. He explains Henrietta Maria's appearance as Divine Beauty in proper Neoplatonic terms: "Corporeal beauty, consisting in symmetry, colour and certain unexpressable graces, shining in the Queen's majesty, may draw us to the contemplation of the beauty of the soul, unto which it hath analogy." But the queen's villainous opposite in the masque, Circe, is also beautiful, her voice pleasant, her costume rich and graceful, her physical realm the same lovely Vale of Tempe, which is to become the queen's own. Jones explains that in making Circe beautiful he is simply acknowledging the allure of evil (Orgel and Strong, *Inigo Jones*, 2:483). Although his appended statement clarifies the difference between mere bodily beauty and the ideal variety, the distinction was probably not at all obvious to spectators, who expected antimasque figures to provide a clear contrast to the beautiful masquers.

22. See John Demaray, *Milton and the Masque Tradition* (Cambridge: Harvard University Press, 1968), pp. 122–43.

23. Ibid., pp. 97–121. Demaray offers an excellent description of the playing space.

24. *The Political Works of James I*, ed. Charles H. McIlwain (Cambridge: Harvard University Press, 1918), p. 43.

25. Orgel, *Illusions of Power*, pp. 59–87.

26. *The Political Works of James I*, p. 12.

27. See Roy Strong, *Van Dyck: Charles I on Horseback* (New York: Viking, 1972), pp. 99 nn. 2–3.

28. *The Letters, Speeches, and Proclamations of King Charles I*, ed. Sir Charles Petrie (London: Cassell, 1935), p. 63. Italics mine.

29. Richard Hooker, *Ecclesiastical Polity*, in *Complete Works of Richard Hooker*, ed. John Keble (Oxford: Oxford University Press, 1974), vol. 4, chap. 1, sec. 3.

30. See, as an example, Robert Shelford, *Five Pious and Learned Discourses* (Cambridge, 1635).

31. John Philips, *The Reformation of Images* (Berkeley: University of California Press, 1973).

32. Consider Paul Seaver, *The Puritan Lectureships* (Stanford: Stanford University Press, 1970), p. 42; Christopher Hill, *Society and Puritanism in Pre-Revolutionary England* (London: Secker and Warburg, 1964), pp. 64–65; and U. Milo Kaufmann, *The Pilgrim's Progress and Traditions in Puritan Meditation* (New Haven: Yale University Press, 1966), pp. 55–60, on revelation as *logos*.

33. Barbara K. Lewalski, *Protestant Poetics and the Seventeenth-Century Lyric* (Princeton: Princeton University Press, 1979), pp. 188–96.

34. Roland Mushat Frye, *Milton's Imagery and the Visual Arts: Iconographic Tradition in the Epic Poems* (Princeton: Princeton University Press, 1978), pp. 3–6, 20–23.

35. See *CP*, 3:342–43, 345, 347, 361, 364, 365, 374, 376.

36. *CP*, 1:829. Consider also *CP*, 1:520.

37. *A Variorum Commentary on the Poems of John Milton*, ed. Merritt Y. Hughes (New York: Columbia University Press, 1972), vol. 2, pt. 2, pp. 672–86.

38. Sabol, *Four Hundred Songs and Dances*, p. 27. See also Manfred Bukhofzer, *Music in the Baroque Era* (New York: Norton, 1947), p. 185.

39. The philosophic assumptions informing Renaissance music are discussed at length by Gretchen Ludke Finney, *Musical Backgrounds for English Literature* (New Brunswick, N.J.: Rutgers University Press, 1962); Wilfred Mellors, *Harmonious Meeting* (London: Dobson, 1965); Kathe Maier-Bauer, *Music of the Spheres and the Dance of Death* (Princeton: Princeton University Press, 1970).

40. Louis Martz, "Music in *Comus*," in *Illustrious Evidence: Approaches to English Literature of the Earlier Seventeenth Century*, ed. Earl Miner (Berkeley: University of California Press, 1975), p. 108.

41. Herford and Simpson, *Ben Jonson*, 2:308.

42. Orgel, *Illusions of Power*, pp. 51–52; Orgel and Strong, *Inigo Jones*, 1:40.

43. Sabol, *Four Hundred Songs and Dances*, p. 29.

44. See Fletcher's excellent analysis of Milton's "principle of echo"

and of his use of strategic repetition in *Transcendental Masque*, pp. 198–209.

45. See, for example, A. E. Dyson, "The Interpretation of *Comus*," in *A Maske at Ludlow*, ed. John Dickhoff (Cleveland: Press of Case Western Reserve University, 1968), p. 115.

46. S. E. Sprott, *"A Masque": The Earlier Versions* (Toronto: University of Toronto Press, 1973), p. 64.

47. Fletcher, *Transcendental Masque*, pp. 166–75, speaks of the Lady's "triumph of song."

48. William Perkins, *The Works of Mr. William Perkins* (London, 1635), 2:670; Philip Stubbes, *The Second Part of the Anatomie of Abuses* (London, 1583), p. 76.

49. See Martz's comment on the inconclusiveness of the brothers' dialogue, "Music in *Comus*," pp. 102–4.

CHAPTER FOUR
Merriment Well Managed: Chastity as a Rule of Life

1. Significant comments on chastity in *Comus* include A. S. P. Woodhouse, *Heavenly Muse* (Toronto: University of Toronto Press, 1972), pp. 63–65, 68–71; William Madsen, *The Idea of Nature in Milton's Poetry*, in *Three Studies in the Renaissance* (New Haven: Yale University Press, 1958), pp. 185–212; Angus Fletcher, *Transcendental Masque: An Essay on Milton's "Comus"* (Ithaca: Cornell University Press, 1971), pp. 118–19, 149–50, 219–20; John Demaray, *Milton and the Masque Tradition* (Cambridge: Harvard University Press, 1968), p. 93; Robert M. Adams, *Ikon: John Milton and the Modern Critics* (Ithaca: Cornell University Press, 1955), pp. 83–84; Georgia Christopher, "The Virginity of Faith: *Comus* as a Reformation Conceit," *English Literary History* 43 (1976): 486 ff.

2. George Sensabaugh, "Love Ethics in Platonic Court Drama," *Huntington Library Quarterly* I (1938): 277–304; Sensabaugh, "Platonic Love and the Puritan Rebellion," *Studies in Philology* 37 (1940): 457–81.

3. Alfred Harbage, *Cavalier Drama* (New York: Modern Language Association, 1936), p. 36. For more on D'Urfe, see Jacques Ehrmann, *Un Paradis désespéré: L'amour et l'illusion dans L'Astrée* (New Haven: Yale University Press, 1963) and Bernard Germa, *L'Astrée de Honore D'Urfé, sa composition, son influence* (Paris: Picard, 1904). The cult's importation to England is examined in Louis Carlane, *L'Influence Française en Angleterre au XVIIe siècle* (Paris: Société Française,

1904), pp. 274–78, and Kathleen M. Lynch, *The Social Mode of Restoration Comedy* (New York: Octagon).

4. Other plays by Beaumont and Fletcher revived or republished during Charles's reign include: *A King and No King*, *Philaster*, *The Maid's Tragedy*, *Rollo*, *The Scornful Lady*, *Cupid's Revenge*, *The Loyal Subject*, and *The Lover's Progress*. For the influence of Sidney's *Arcadia* on Caroline drama, see G. E. Bentley, *The Jacobean and Caroline Stage* (Oxford: Clarendon Press, 1956), 3:440; 4:480, 921, 933; 5:1035, 1074–75, 1367.

5. James Howell, *Familiar Letters*, ed. J. Jacobs (London: Nutt, 1892), 1:317. Shackerley Marmion's comment appears in *The Poems of William Habington*, ed. Kenneth Allot (London: Hodder and Stroughton, 1948), xxiii.

6. Ehrmann, *Un Paradis désespéré*, pp. 11–12.

7. Walter Montagu, *The Shepheard's Paradise* (London, 1629 [actually 1659]), pp. 22–23.

8. Francis Beaumont and John Fletcher, *Faithful Shepherdess*, in *Beaumont and Fletcher*, ed. J. Strachey (London: T. F. Unwin, n.d.), vol. 2. See act 2, scene 2.

9. Nancy Cotton Pearce, *John Fletcher's Chastity Plays: Mirrors of Modesty* (Lewisburg: Bucknell University Press, 1973), p. 68. For a typical example of the lady errant, see Lodowick Carliell, *The Deserving Favorite*, ed. Charles H. Gray (Chicago: University of Chicago Press, 1905), pp. 96–97, 105, 112, 141.

10. For a classic explanation, see Montagu, *The Shepheard's Paradise*, pp. 51, 141.

11. See Sensabaugh, "Platonic Love," pp. 458–63, 480–81, on supposed violations of this rule.

12. Mark Rose, *Heroic Love: Studies in Sidney and Spenser* (Cambridge: Harvard University Press, 1968).

13. Montagu, *The Shepheard's Paradise*, p. 51.

14. Stephen Orgel and Roy Strong, *Inigo Jones: The Theater of Majesty* (Berkeley: University of California Press, 1973), 1:53–55.

15. Ibid., 2:422, 458, 553, 580; see also 1:407; 2:604, 667, 709.

16. Ibid., 2:597.

17. See Milton's references to *Astraea*, the *Arcadia*, and other popular romances in *CP*, 3:363–64, 366–67.

18. Sensabaugh, "Platonic Love," p. 462 ff.

19. Demaray, *Theatrical Epic*, pp. 42–43.

20. *The Works of Milton*, ed. Frank Allen Patterson et al. (New York: Columbia University Press, 1931–38), 17:233–34.

21. Walter W. Greg, *Pastoral Poetry and Pastoral Drama* (1906; reprint, New York: Russell and Russell, 1959), pp. 399–401; D. C. Allen, *The Harmonious Vision: Studies in Milton's Poetry* (Baltimore: Johns Hopkins University Press, 1954), pp. 33–34; Mario Praz, *The Flaming Heart* (Gloucester, Mass.: Peter Smith, 1966), p. 30.

22. E. M. W. Tillyard, *Studies in Milton* (London: Chatto and Windus, 1951), pp. 93–99.

23. M. M. Ross, *Poetry and Dogma* (New Brunswick, N.J.: Rutgers University Press, 1954), p. 196.

24. St. Thomas Aquinas, *Summa Theologiae* (New York: McGraw-Hill, 1964), 1a2ae.23,1; 2a2ae.28–33; 2a2ae.37–39. Richard Hooker, *Laws of the Ecclesiastical Politie* (1594), I, ix, 6; VI, v, 6; V, xiii, 1; IV, xiv, 6. For more on orthodox concepts of celibacy see Dietrich Von Hildebrand, *In Defense of Purity: An Analysis of the Catholic Ideals of Purity and Virginity* (Baltimore: Helicon, 1962), pp. 7–18; J. M. Ford, *A Trilogy on Wisdom and Celibacy* (Notre Dame, Ind.: University of Notre Dame Press, 1967), pp. 165–215; John Bugge, *Virginitas: An Essay on the History of a Medieval Ideal* (The Hague: Martinus Nijhoff, 1975), pp. 75–99.

25. Luther's distinction in his 1535 commentary on Galatians is telling: "But here stands Paul in supreme freedom and says in clear and explicit words: 'That which makes a Christian is faith working through love.' He does not say: 'That which makes a Christian is a cowl or fasting or vestments or ceremonies.' But it is a true faith toward God, which loves and helps one's neighbor—regardless of whether the neighbor is a servant, a master, a king, a pope, a man, a woman, one who wears purple, one who wears rags, one who eats meat, or one who eats fish. Not one of these things, not one, makes a man a Christian; only faith and love do so" (*Luther's Works*, ed. Jaroslav Pelikan [St. Louis: Concordia, 1964], 27:31).

26. Luther, *Luther's Works*, 27:378; John Calvin, *Institutes of the Christian Religion*, ed. John T. McNeil (Philadelphia: Westminster, 1960), 3.14.15.

27. John S. Coolidge, *The Pauline Renaissance in England* (Oxford: Clarendon Press, 1970), p. 46; Robert Sanderson, *A Sovereign Antidote against Sabbatarian Errours* (London, 1636), pp. 26–27; Robert Shelford, *Five Pious and Learned Discoveries* (London, 1635), p. 118.

28. Richard Sibbes, *The Saints Cordialls* (London, 1629), p. 189 ff.

29. The importance of the Canticles in the Renaissance is demonstrated by Lily Bess Campbell, *Divine Poetry and Drama in Sixteenth-Century England* (Los Angeles: University of California Press, 1959), pp. 141–60; George Scheper examines Puritan treatments of the

Song of Songs in "Reformation Attitudes toward the Song of Songs," *Publications of the Modern Language Association of America* 89 (1974): 552–59.

30. John Preston, *The Breast-Plate of Faith and Love* (London, 1630), p. 20. Preston also uses the nuptial metaphor, pp. 15–16, 19, 54. Consider Sears McGee, *The Godly Man in Stuart England* (New Haven: Yale University Press, 1976), pp. 27–28, on the Puritan association of idolatry with sexual relations.

31. See Calvin, *Institutes of the Christian Religion*, 2.8.42–44; 3.10.5; William Perkins, *The Works of Mr. Perkins* (London, 1635), 2:547.

32. Calvin bears primary responsibility for the amplification of this Protestant doctrine (*Institutes of the Christian Religion*, 1.14.20–22).

33. Preston, *Breast-Plate*, p. 107.

34. *CP*, 6:642. The nuptial metaphor appears elsewhere in Milton's theology: 6:378, 477, 532, 529, 633.

35. Jason P. Rosenblatt, "Audacious Neighborhood: Idolatry in *Paradise Lost*," *Philological Quarterly* 54 (1975): 553–68.

36. C. S. Lewis, "A Note on *Comus*," *Review of English Studies* 8 (1932): 175.

37. Harbage, *Cavalier Drama*, p. 37 ff.

38. *A Variorum Commentary on the Poems of John Milton*, ed. Merritt Y. Hughes (New York: Columbia University Press, 1972), vol. 2, pt. 3, pp. 774–75.

39. Thomas Randolph, *Poetical and Dramatic Works* (London: Reeves and Turner, 1875), 3:129.

40. *Variorum Commentary*, vol. 2, pt. 3, p. 879.

41. John Arthos, *On "A Maske Presented at Ludlow Castle"* (Ann Arbor: University of Michigan Press, 1954), pp. 44–45, sees haemony as merely a magical herb. For an example of an ethical reading of haemony see J. Maxwell, "The Pseudo-Problem of *Comus*," *Classical Journal* 1 (1948): 376–90. Representative religious interpretations of the herb are offered by Edward Le Comte, "New Light on the Haemony Passage in *Comus*," *Philological Quarterly* 21 (1942): 283–98; Rosemond Tuve, *Images and Themes in Five Poems by Milton* (Cambridge: Harvard University Press, 1962), p. 143; Jon Lawry, *The Shadow of Heaven: Matter and Stance in Milton's Poetry* (Ithaca: Cornell University Press, 1968), p. 86; Sacvan Bercovitch, "Milton's 'Haemony': Knowledge and Belief," *Huntington Library Quarterly* 33 (1969): 351–59.

42. Fletcher, *Transcendental Masque*, p. 203.

43. I am much indebted here to Douglas Bush's comments in *Variorum Commentary*, vol. 2, pt. 3, pp. 937–38.

44. Cf. Geoffrey of Monmouth, *Historia Regum Britanniae*, trans. R. E. Jones (Oxford: Longman, Green, 1920), 2:1–5; Edmund Spenser, *Faerie Queene*, II, x, 19; Thomas Lodge, "The Complaint of Elstred," *Complete Works* (New York: Russell and Russell, 1963), pp. 59–84.

45. John Brand, *Observations on the Popular Antiquities of Great Britain* (1849; reprint, Detroit: Singing Tree Press, 1969), 2:34–37. See C. A. Patrides, *Milton and the Christian Tradition* (Oxford: Clarendon Press, 1966), p. 53 ff.

46. C. H. Herford and Percy Simpson, *Ben Jonson* (Oxford: Clarendon Press, 1925), 2:308.

47. *Variorum Commentary*, vol. 2, pt. 2, p. 974.

48. Ibid., vol. 2, pt. 2, pp. 984–87.

49. James Holly Hanford, "The Youth of Milton," in *John Milton, Englishman* (New York: Crown, 1949), p. 152.

50. Milton does retain the traditional pair in the *Apology* (*CP*, 1:892).

51. See, for example, *Paradise Lost*, bk. 10, ll. 23–24.

AFTERWORD
Strategies for Artistic Reform

1. C. H. Herford and Percy Simpson, *Ben Jonson* (Oxford: Clarendon Press, 1925), 7:378, 381.

2. M. M. Knappen, *Tudor Puritanism* (Chicago: University of Chicago Press, 1930); William Haller, *Rise of Puritanism* (New York: Columbia University Press, 1965).

3. John Demaray, *Milton and the Masque Tradition* (Cambridge: Harvard University Press, 1968), p. 143; Angus Fletcher, *Transcendental Masque: An Essay on Milton's "Comus"* (Ithaca: Cornell University Press, 1971), p. 243.

4. Paul Reyher, *Les Masques anglais* (Paris: Hachette, 1909), pp. 86–88, 213–14.

5. Dale B. J. Randall, *Jonson's Gypsies Unmasked: Background and Theme of the "Gypsies Metamorphos'd"* (Durham: Duke University Press, 1975), pp. 144–75.

6. William Riley Parker, *Milton: A Biography* (Oxford: Clarendon Press, 1960), p. 792.

7. John Collinges, *The Excellent Woman* (London, 1669), p. 4.

8. Ibid., p. 6.

9. The two Egerton boys appeared in *Coelum Britannicum* as torch-bearers. Lady Alice, along with her two older sisters, Katherine (b. 1611) and Elizabeth (b. 1606), danced in *Tempe Restored*. Penelope (b. 1610) performed in *Chloridia*, Mary (b. 1609) in the *Temple of Love*, and Elizabeth in *Luminalia*.

10. Georgia Christopher, "The Virginity of Faith: *Comus* as a Reformation Conceit," *English Literary History* 43 (1976): 479.

APPENDIX A
Milton's Successors: Flecknoe, Shirley, and the Reform of Occasional Theatricals

1. Percy Scholes, *The Puritans and Music* (London: Oxford University Press, 1934), pp. 191, 193.

2. Richard Flecknoe, *Love's Dominion, A Dramatique Piece, Full of Excellent Moralitie* (London, 1654), "To the Lady Elizabeth Claypole."

3. Puritan views on love, sex, and marriage are discussed in William and Mandeville Haller, "The Puritan Art of Love," *Huntington Library Quarterly* 5 (1942): 235–72; Roland M. Frye, "The Teachings of Classical Puritanism on Conjugal Love," *Studies in the Renaissance* 2 (1955): 148–59; and John Halkett, *Milton and the Idea of Matrimony* (New Haven: Yale University Press, 1970).

4. Richard Flecknoe, *Love's Kingdom: A Pastoral-Tragi-Comedy* (New York: Garland, 1973).

5. James Shirley, *Cupid and Death*, ed. Edward J. Dent (London: Lowe and Brydone, 1965), xii.

6. E.g., the wild vistas in Stephen Orgel and Roy Strong, *Inigo Jones: The Theater of Majesty* (Berkeley: University of California Press, 1973), 1:210, 324.

Index